Biking ARIZONA TRAIL

THE COMPLETE GUIDE TO DAY-RIDING AND THRU-BIKING

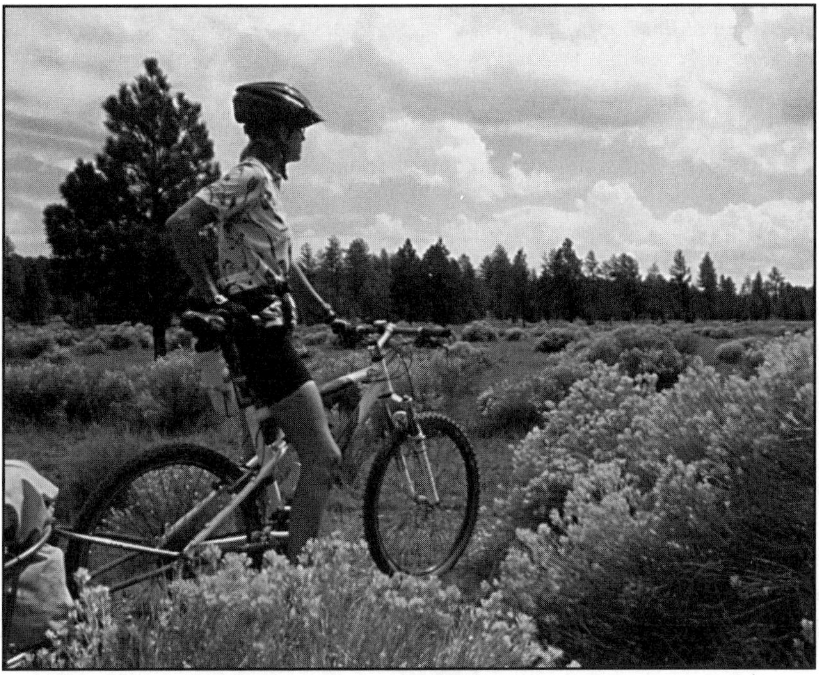

TEXT AND PHOTOGRAPHY BY
ANDREA LANKFORD

www.westcliffepublishers.com

International Standard Book Number: 1-56579-437-0
Text and photography copyright: Andrea Lankford, 2002. All rights reserved.
Editor: Elizabeth Train
Design: Carol Pando and Craig Keyzer
Production Manager: Craig Keyzer
Published by:
Westcliffe Publishers, Inc.
P.O. Box 1261
Englewood, CO 80150
www.westcliffepublishers.com
Printed in the USA by: Versa Press, Inc.

No portion of this book, either text or photography, may be reproduced in any form, including electronically, without the express written permission of the publisher.

Library of Congress Cataloging-in-Publication Data:
Lankford, Andrea.
    Biking the Arizona Trail : the complete guide to day-riding and thru-biking / by Andrea Lankford.
       p. cm.
    Includes bibliographical references and index.
    ISBN 1-56579-437-0
      1. Bicycle touring—Arizona—Arizona Trail—Guidebooks. 2. Arizona Trail (Ariz.)—Guidebooks. I. Title.
GV1045.5.A62 L36 2002
796.6'4'09791—dc21
                                                                  2002028886

For more information about other fine books and calendars from Westcliffe Publishers, please contact your local bookstore, call us at 1-800-523-3692, write for our free color catalog, or visit us on the Web at www.westcliffepublishers.com.

Please Note: Risk is always a factor in backcountry and high-mountain travel. Many of the activities described in this book can be dangerous, especially when weather is adverse or unpredictable, and when unforeseen events or conditions create a hazardous situation. The author has done her best to provide the reader with accurate information about backcountry travel, as well as to point out some of its potential hazards. It is the responsibility of the users of this guide to learn the necessary skills for safe backcountry travel, and to exercise caution in potentially hazardous areas, especially in places prone to floods and avalanches. The author and publisher disclaim any liability for injury or other damage caused by backcountry traveling or performing any other activity described in this book.

Front Cover: *Riders weave through saguaro below the Superstition Mountains.*
Previous Page: *Rabbitbrush bloom under the Arizona sky near Moqui Stage Stop.*

Acknowledgments

To the public employees and volunteers who continue to work so hard on the Arizona Trail for so little reward, keep it up. The Arizona Trail will be a long-term legacy you can be proud to have played a part in building. A special thanks to the following people for route advice and description review: Vic Brown, Catie Fenn, and Tom Folks at the Bureau of Land Management; Kurt Speers and Bryan Wisher at the National Park Service; Trish Callahan and Brian Poturaski at the U.S. Forest Service; Chuck Horner, Cynthia Lovely, John Neeling, Steve Sayway, Larry Snead, Walt Thole, and Steve Wood at the Arizona Trail Association; and Rosemary Shearer at Superstition Area Land Trust.

And thanks to all the people I met on the trail who shared their water, food, and advice. To the Shielamonster male support crew—John Benson for giving us the idea, Nick Kraft of Indigo8.com for the awesome web page design, and Dan Overton for the bicycle maintenance expertise and for the Thai food when we needed it most.

To Dad, for accepting that his little southern girl turned out to be more like Davy Crockett than Scarlett O'Hara. To my brother, for never doubting I could do it. To Mom, sorry you had to worry; despite the chapter on hazards, the trip was completely safe—honest. To Beth Overton, for being my guinea pig, for your sense of humor, and for joining me on my maniacal Captain Ahab schemes. What are we doing next?

To Kent Delbon for being the supportive husband, for letting me trash your truck, and for thinking tomboys are sexy. This one is for you.

Tonto National Forest.

Contents

Arizona Trail Map 6
Foreword 8
Preface 10
Introduction 12
   The Arizona Trail 12
   Biking the Trail 13
   Planning Your Trip 22
How to Use This Guide 29
Segment 1: Utah State Line to US 89A 34
Segment 2: US 89A to East Rim View 39
Segment 3A/B: East Rim View to North Kaibab Trailhead .. 46
Segment 4: North Rim to South Rim (Trekking) ... 53
Segment 5: Tusayan to Grandview Lookout 59
Segment 6: Grandview Lookout to Moqui Stage Stop 63
Segment 7: Moqui Stage Stop to Forest Road 523 .. 68
Segment 8: Forest Road 523 to Buffalo Park 73
Segment 9: Buffalo Park to Flagstaff Urban Trail 81
Segment 10: Flagstaff Urban Trail to Mormon Lake 85
Segment 11: Mormon Lake to Blue Ridge Ranger Station ... 93
Segment 12: Blue Ridge Ranger Station to
   General Springs Cabin 100
Segment 13: General Springs Cabin to Payson ... 107
Segment 14: Payson to Jake's Corner 113
Segment 15: Jake's Corner to Roosevelt Lake Dam 118
Segment 16: Roosevelt Lake Dam to
   Lost Dutchman State Park 123
Segment 17: Lost Dutchman State Park to US 60 .. 128
Segment 18: US 60 to Gila River 132
Segment 19: Gila River to Oracle 138

Segment 20: Oracle to Molino Basin Campground 144
Segment 21: Molino Basin Campground to Colossal Cave .. 150
Segment 22: Colossal Cave to Oak Tree Canyon 155
Segment 23: Oak Tree Canyon to Patagonia 159
Segment 24: Patagonia to Parker Canyon Lake 167
Segment 25: Parker Canyon Lake to Mexico Border 172
Appendix A: 28 Day Rides on the Arizona Trail 176
Appendix B: Resupply and Lodging 179
Appendix C: Agencies and Organizations 182
Appendix D: Bike Shops, Guide Services, and Outfitters .. 184
Appendix E: Equipment Checklists 186
Appendix F: References and Suggested Reading 187
Index 189

A biker stops to chat with a hunter on the Kaibab Plateau.

6 Biking the Arizona Trail

Arizona Trail Map

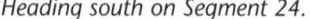
Heading south on Segment 24.

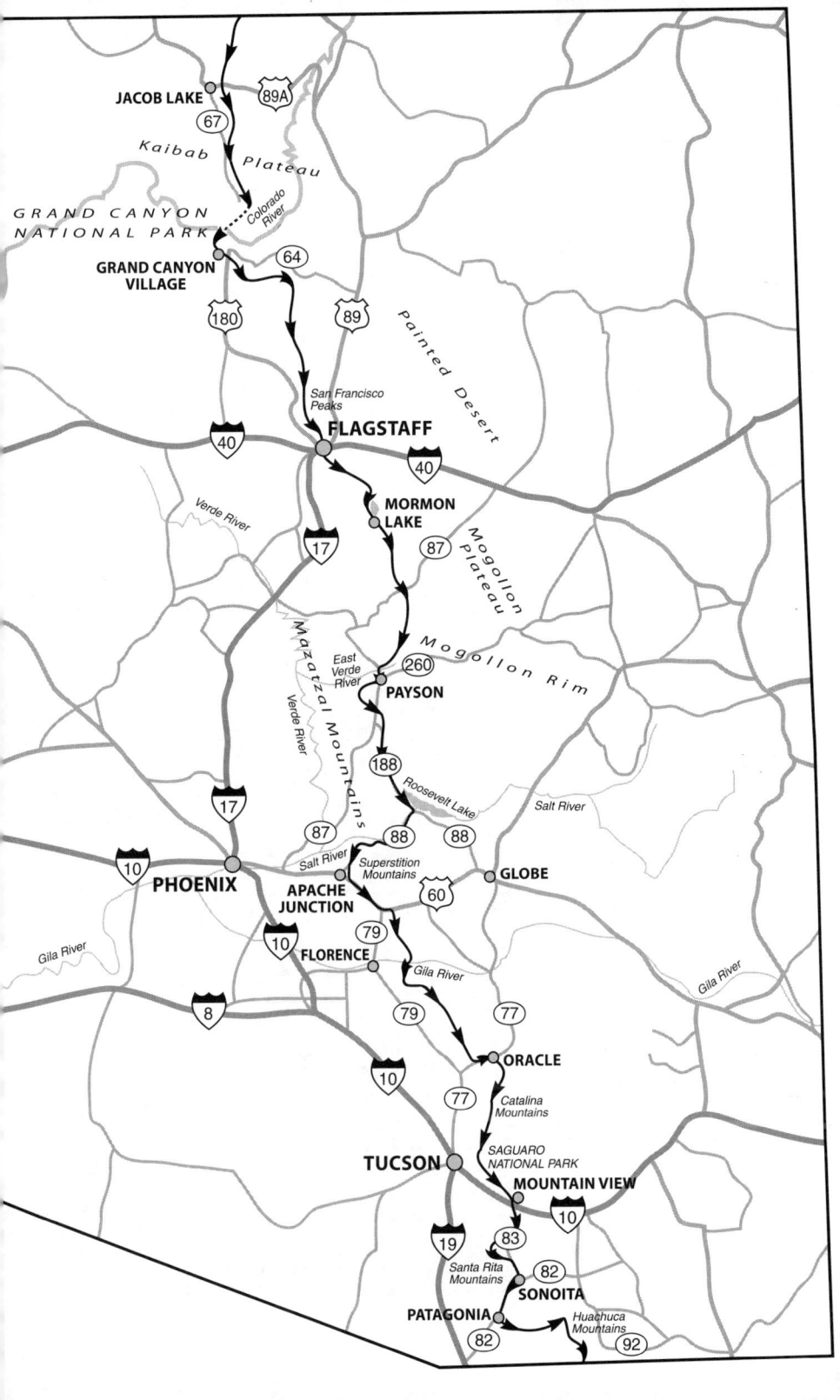

Foreword

When Andrea asked me to join her on the Arizona Trail, at first I thought she was kidding. We had thrown the idea around for several months, fantasized about how we'd be the first to bike the whole thing, and compared ourselves to the likes of Lewis and Clark. I secretly hoped that one of us would come to our senses or suffer a non-life-threatening injury—just debilitating enough to give us an excuse to call off the trip. You could say I had my reservations.

What I didn't know then is that when Andy sets her mind to doing something, she does it. No ifs, ands, or buts. I am not sure why I thought a woman who hiked the Appalachian Trail the year before would shy away from pioneering a bike route along the Arizona Trail. Like her bulldog Shiloh, she grabbed on and didn't let go until we were finished.

So, on a windy, cold, and rainy September day, we set off from the Buckskin Trailhead on the Utah state line and headed south toward the Mexico border. "Follow the Yellow Brick Road" rang in my ears as we began our journey. I smiled bravely to the volunteers who had assembled for the National Trail Days celebration, kissed my husband good-bye, and pedaled off. As the trailhead and well-wishers became smaller, my realization of the isolation and exposure I was facing became larger until all I could see was an incredible blue sky filled with

Beth Overton heads out on the Trail near Oracle Ridge.

threatening storm clouds that billowed above the red-walled canyon. And so our journey began.

Every day offered up its own challenges and rewards. In the north, we hauled our gear over hundreds of tree blowdowns and were rewarded with spectacular fall foliage colors. Through central Arizona, we had rain (the wettest October in years) and tire-sucking mud, while we were rewarded with majestic views of the Mazatzal and Superstition mountain ranges. And finally, in the south, I had flats—lots of them—until I discovered Slime. Then we reveled in the rolling, savanna-like hills near the town of Sonoita and Canelo Pass.

Throughout our journey we tried to ride, hike, push, pull, and throw our bikes and gear over as much of the Arizona Trail as possible. We were pioneers. We owed it to ourselves and to those who would follow to explore the AZT on two wheels. There were truly spectacular biking stretches and incredibly difficult hike-a-bike sections, especially when hauling gear. For the tough parts, Andrea has included alternate routes that are just as scenic, mostly on dirt, and perfect for thru-bikers.

You have in your hands the finished product—a book starring what is arguably one of the best long-distance mountain bike routes to be designed. Should you decide to thru-ride, day ride, or section ride any portion of this route, the plants, animals, scenery, and adventure you'll find will utterly amaze you. I hope you do, so that you, too, can experience the wonders of Arizona. **Happy trails!**

—Beth Overton

Preface

Long-distance hiking takes its toll on a body. I learned this the hard way during my 1999 thru-hike of the Appalachian Trail. Around mile 1,500, my feet and knees began to protest, and I began to fantasize about other methods of travel. In New England, I met a hiker who had completed a cross-country bike tour the previous year. "Why don't you try bike touring?" he asked, in response to my whining. "It is much easier on your body."

Bike touring, multi-day traveling by bicycle, continues to be a popular form of long-distance travel. Most bikers associate the term "bike touring" with cycling on pavement. Using road bikes loaded with panniers, thousands of cyclists pedal across the United States, Europe, and other countries or continents each year. The more I read about bike touring, the more traveling long-distance by bike intrigued me, but the thought of miles and miles of pedaling alongside busy highways was unappealing.

"Bikepacking," riding off-pavement routes with loaded mountain bikes, has just recently begun to attract its own contingent of bike enthusiasts who, like I did, desire a more rugged and remote experience. The "thru-hiker" tradition of walking a continuous route from point A to point B in one season or year began with Earl Shaffer's famous traverse of the Appalachian Trail in 1948. Today, the term "thru-biker" is now heard in reference to hardy mountain bikers taking on challenging routes such as the Great Divide, between Canada and Mexico, and the Dalton Highway in Alaska.

In the winter of 2000, while driving through a snowstorm on I-17, a friend suggested that I bike the Arizona Trail. "I don't think anybody has done that yet," he said. That settled it. I couldn't let the chance to be the first at something slip away. When mountain biker Beth Overton agreed to go with me, the plan was set in motion. In Beth, I had found a kindred spirit—another woman with the strange need to punish her body under the guise of outdoor recreation and fitness. We would be the first to thru-bike the Arizona Trail. Combining Beth's mountain bike experience and my long-distance hiking skills, we figured we would make a good team. Others weren't so sure. One bike-shop mechanic declared, "It can't be done."

In a way, he is right. The Arizona Trail remains incomplete as of January 2003 and several sections of the trail travel through Wilderness Areas that are off-limits to mountain bikers. In order to make a continuous route, I had to find a way to fill in the gaps. I spent hours studying maps and talking to trail stewards on the phone. Eventually, I pieced together a route that avoided pavement for most of the way and stayed on or near the Arizona Trail. We learned the hard way which portions of the Arizona Trail were best for mountain biking. Being the first at something definitely has its downsides.

With mock seriousness, Beth and I referred to our trip as the "expedition." After 23 days and 800 miles, we touched our bike tires to the barbed-wire fence at the Mexico border and proved the naysayers wrong. It can be done. A continuous backcountry route from Utah to Mexico for mountain bikers exists.

I envisioned a route where bikers could get away from the roar of traffic on the highways, where bikepackers could pedal up to remote campsites, and where the diverse scenery of Arizona could be appreciated from the seat of a mountain bike—a route that takes advantage of the best bikable sections of the Arizona Trail. *Biking the Arizona Trail* guides you over such a route. Whether you are interested in day rides or a thru-bike of the entire trail, *Biking the Arizona Trail* sets the foundation for you to plan your own Arizona adventure. And you don't have to figure out the best route the hard way! So tune 'er up, load 'er down, click 'em in, and pedal on. The Arizona Trail is waiting.

—Andrea Lankford

Author Andrea Lankford and friend Beth Overton ride southbound on Segment 25.

Introduction

THE ARIZONA TRAIL

If it hadn't been for the inspiration of a Flagstaff schoolteacher, there might not be an Arizona Trail (AZT). In 1985, Dale Shewalter linked a potential hiking corridor as he backpacked from Mexico to Utah. After his hike, he took his vision to state and federal agencies, eventually gaining their support. Today, Shewalter and hundreds of other dedicated volunteers continue the crusade to establish a border-to-border multiuse trail across Arizona. "Trails not only connect places. Trails connect people," says Shewalter. Anyone who has experienced a long-distance trail already understands that self-propelled travel is a social experience as much as it is a wilderness adventure. Thanks to the stamina of visionaries like Shewalter, soon a continuous route across Arizona's inspiring landscapes will be a reality.

Though 20% of the official AZT remains incomplete as of January 2003, it still covers a lot of territory. Traveling from Utah to Mexico, the trail crosses the seventh natural wonder of the world (the Grand Canyon), skirts the base of Arizona's tallest mountain (Humphreys Peak), and ventures into habitats of animals found nowhere else in the United States. You will ride past abandoned mining settlements, through bustling university towns, and over historic stagecoach routes. You will see more than seven mountain ranges, cross four rivers, pass five lakes, and visit three National Parks and four National Forests. You will experience three types of desert, 12 life zones, and elevations ranging from 1,700 feet at the Gila River to 9,000 feet at the base of the San Francisco Peaks. You might not find a mountain biking trail anywhere that offers more diversity.

Geographic Highlights of the Arizona Trail

Seven Mountain Ranges: San Francisco Peaks, Mazatzal Mountains, Superstition Mountains, Catalina Mountains, Rincon Mountains, Santa Rita Mountains, and Huachuca Mountains
Four River Crossings: Colorado River, East Verde River, Salt River, and Gila River
Five Lakes: Marshall Lake, Mormon Lake, Blue Ridge Reservoir, Roosevelt Lake, and Parker Canyon Lake
Three National Parks: Grand Canyon, Saguaro, and Coronado
Four National Forests: Kaibab, Coconino, Tonto, and Coronado

BIKING THE TRAIL

Because 20% of the AZT remains undesignated, and because Wilderness Areas are closed to mountain biking, connecting a backcountry bike route across the state required a little creativity. The first obstacle was the 277-mile barrier to transportation known as the Grand Canyon. Because the canyon is closed to bikes, you would have to take a 200-mile detour on busy state highways. If you biked around the canyon, you would miss a chance to hike through one of the most spectacular places in the world. The Grand Canyon is the only segment in this book where I could not find an acceptable bicycle detour. I suggest you hike it. Segment 4 provides information on how to hike across the canyon while your bikes are shuttled to the other side.

Cacti and rocks will accompany bikers along many segments of the Arizona Trail.

The second obstacle was the six Wilderness Areas (off-limits to bikers) that are traversed by the Arizona Trail. This guide gives scenic alternatives for biking around these areas.

Finally, there are the few sections of the AZT that are open to mountain bikers but are unpleasant or impractical if you are on a thru-bike. Any segment of the official AZT omitted from the thru-route was excluded for a reason. I wanted the thru-route to be challenging but not to the point of misery. Although I sifted out many of the worst areas, you should still expect to portage your bike through some sections. This is, after all, still a backcountry route.

Of the thru-bike routes recommended in this book, 40% follow the official AZT route, 22% cross areas of incomplete AZT, and 38% involve detours around Wilderness Areas and sections that are difficult for bikers. As for the road and trail surfaces you'll encounter along these recommended thru-bike routes, 72% are single-track trails or dirt roads, and 28% follow paved roads.

Day riders aren't bound by the limitations of trying to get from point A to point B in a continuous journey. Sections of the AZT that are open to mountain bikers but not on the thru-route are also described in this book. Appendix A lists the best day rides along the route, and many of the segments include loops and spurs that are particularly fun for day riders.

Many sections of the AZT are not signed consistently and will require map-reading and route-finding skills. The AZT is not as well signed as the Appalachian Trail. I've tried my best to alert you to confusing sections. However, weather and time change the way the route appears, and you might find that signs have been damaged or removed. Be prepared to rely on your abilities and common sense in combination with this guide.

Ways to Bike the Trail

Day Ride (Section by Section)
Just you and your bike. Maybe a hydration pack with some tools, a lunch, and a rain jacket. Unburdened by weight, you can ride the entire trail one section at a time and still return to the comforts of your home or your hotel room every evening. Take a month or a lifetime to complete the whole trail or just ride your favorite sections. Several loop opportunities for day riders are given throughout this guidebook, and you can tailor your own out-and-back rides to suit your group's skill and fitness level.

Combination Hike and Bike
Biking the Arizona Trail includes alternative routes around Wilderness Areas and other sections that are impractical for mountain bikers. However, you might want to hike through areas like the Superstition Wilderness. Pick up *Guide to Arizona's Wilderness Areas* or *The Arizona Trail: The Complete Guide* (available soon), both hiking/backpacking guidebooks by Westcliffe Publishers, and travel the AZT by a combination of methods. If you are truly multitalented, consider traveling some sections by horseback.

Vehicle Supported Ride (SAG Wagon or Guided Trip)
Whether you prefer the term "Support And Gear" or "Support And Grub," a SAG Wagon is a good way to go. For a month, a week, or a weekend, bike all or part of the route while friends or a guide service supports you with a vehicle. (Take a high-clearance vehicle for better maneuverability on Forest Service roads.) Unencumbered by the weight of your camping gear, you can bike all day and meet the support

vehicle at night. Coolers with cold drinks, camp chairs with armrests, and car trips into town are among the luxuries of traveling with a support vehicle. Try not to feel too guilty. Try not to have too much fun. Biking with a support vehicle is the best way to do this route.

Thru-Bike (Self-Contained Bike Tour)
With panniers or a trailer, load up your bike and begin the journey of a lifetime across the state. As a thru-biker, you will fully immerse yourself in the landscapes and the cultures of Arizona. You will also experience the best and the worst that nature has to offer, so plan thoroughly. Water will become a precious and rare commodity. Flexibility, physical endurance, mental strength, and self-reliance are the qualities of a thru-biker. If you don't have those qualities before the trip, trust me, you will afterward. Having remote campsites all to yourself, ample opportunities to view wildlife, and time for reflection are just some of the rewards of thru-biking. In towns, people will be friendly and curious. Friends and family will get a vicarious thrill through your adventure. You'll feel special. You'll feel charmed. You'll be hungry.

Hazards
During my 12-year career as a Search and Rescue Ranger and Wilderness EMT for the National Park Service, I witnessed firsthand how improper planning, poor decision-making, unpreparedness, foolish behavior, or rotten luck can turn an outdoor adventure into a horrifying tragedy. Please pay attention to all the warnings mentioned in this book and posted on trailhead signs. Do your homework. Appendix F has a selection of reference reading on how to prevent and treat backcountry medical conditions. If you have an appreciation for the morbid, read *Over the Edge: Death in Grand Canyon* by Michael Ghiglieri and Thomas Meyers for examples of how good trips went bad and insight on how you can avoid turning your own trips into nightmares.

Prepare yourself mentally. A proper attitude can go a long way. The first priority of the trip should be for everyone to come home uninjured. Discuss safety concerns with your group before and during the trip. View your trip as an expedition with safety being one of the primary goals.

This book gives only a limited discussion of a few of the most obvious hazards you might encounter on the Arizona Trail. Many other hazards exist. Use common sense. Have a plan in case something goes wrong. Designing an emergency plan for your group will greatly enhance your chances of survival if faced with hazardous situations, and might allow you to avoid them in the first place.

Dry gullies and washes can fill quickly with water during desert rainstorms.

Flash Floods

Many areas along the Arizona Trail are prone to flash flooding. If you are on the move and run into a flooded area across the trail, you should wait until water levels subside before crossing.

Avoid camping in dry washes or close to streams during stormy weather. Even if the skies are clear, if you are camping in an area with signs of flood activity, discuss with your group what you plan to do in case of a flash flood. For example: "Hey, see the debris wrapped around that tree? Looks like it floods here sometimes. The sky looks clear right now, but just in case, let's plan on running up that slope to high ground if we sense a flood coming, okay?" If you smell, see, or hear a flash flood, run to the nearest high ground. Running down-canyon or behind a barrier such as a tree won't cut it.

Hypothermia

With elevation changes from 1,700 to 9,000 feet, Arizona's extreme terrain mandates that you prepare for weather extremes. Always have dry clothes and your sleeping bag packed in plastic bags. Carry a few hand warmers and spare plastic bags. If you or someone in your group gets wet and cold and/or begins to shiver uncontrollably, and you cannot get to shelter, remove his or her wet clothes and use plastic bags as vapor barriers to hold in warmth. Get the person into a tent and a dry sleeping bag. Have him or her eat high-calorie foods and drink warm liquids.

High-Altitude Sickness
This route frequently travels above 7,000 feet and gets near 9,000 feet in a couple of places. If you live at a low elevation, know that you will have to "acclimate" to the lower oxygen levels at higher elevations. Some people experience symptoms of high-altitude sickness at elevations as low as 6,000 feet. Headache, dizziness, nausea, and difficulty breathing are some of the more common symptoms. If you think you or a member of your group is suffering from high-altitude sickness, descend to lower elevations as soon as possible.

Heat Illnesses
Diagnosing dehydration, heat exhaustion, and heat stroke can be difficult. Symptoms such as nausea, altered mental status, fatigue, and hot/dry or cool/moist skin can be seen in all three conditions.

When biking the AZT, plan on consuming at least a gallon of water per day. Rescue rangers at the Grand Canyon recommend that you monitor your urine output to keep track of your hydration level. Dark yellow or brown urine might mean you are dehydrated. Clear urine usually indicates you are well hydrated. Maintaining your urine at a pale yellow color is optimum. Eating salty and high-carbohydrate foods can help balance electrolyte levels. Cramping muscles often result from low electrolyte (salt) levels in the muscles. If you take medications for high blood pressure or related conditions, contact your doctor for advice before exposing yourself to the risk of heat-related illnesses.

Avoiding exertion during the hottest parts of the day can prevent heat exhaustion and heat stroke. Ride during early morning and late evening hours. If heat levels are high, get in the shade *before* you start feeling uncomfortable. If water is plentiful, wet down shirts, hats, and bandannas to enhance your body's evaporative-cooling abilities.

Heat stroke is a life-threatening condition caused by extremely high body temperatures. If a member of your group begins to act strangely or becomes unconscious, and you suspect heat stroke as the cause, move them out of the sun, wet them down, or submerge them in cool water to bring down their body temperature.

Stay hydrated but not too hydrated. Drinking excessive amounts of water, sweating out too much salt, and not replacing lost electrolytes by eating adequately can lead to a condition called hyponatremia—low brain and blood sodium. As rangers at the Grand Canyon have witnessed, hyponatremia can send someone to the intensive care unit as fast as you can say, "Pass me the canteen." Confusion, blurred vision, nausea, projectile vomiting, headaches, and strange behaviors are some of the symptoms of this odd condition.

Lightning

Especially during the summer monsoon season, plan on avoiding high elevations, ridgelines, and other prominent exposed areas during the afternoons. If you are caught in a lightning storm, stay away from lone trees or rocks and avoid shallow caves or alcoves. Small overhangs and cave entrances might attract arcs of electricity. If you find yourself caught in the open and at immediate risk of a strike, put a foam pad, clothing, or some other form of insulation between yourself and the ground, then squat or sit in a balled-up position (hugging your knees to your chest).

Wildlife

Rattlesnakes might be found on many portions of the route, but bicyclists have little to worry about. Snakes are most active at night, and the majority of people who have been bitten by snakes were asking for it. Avoid hiking in desert areas on warm nights and always watch where you step.

Scorpions are prevalent throughout most of the state. Check your shoes and shake your clothing before you dress. Although the small centroides scorpion can have a deadly sting in rare cases, most people have relatively minor reactions when stung. Children and the elderly are at highest risk.

The Arizona Trail travels through the habitats of both black bears and mountain lions. The chance of being attacked by these two mammals is extremely remote. If you encounter a bear or a mountain lion, stay calm, back away slowly, and be sure you give it plenty of room to escape. Most bears and lions are very frightened of humans and will do everything they can to avoid confrontation.

However, if you do come in contact with an animal that seems aggressive, stand your ground, make yourself look big by picking up your bike, speak firmly, and otherwise give the impression that "I'm a predator just like you, so back off." If attacked by a mountain lion or a bear, do *not* run—fight back! Throw things and make lots of noise in order to frighten the animal away.

It is also important to be cautious when approaching unfamiliar people on the trail. I have traveled solo for nearly 5,000 miles without experiencing any significant threats from people. In fact, my long-distance journeys have reassured my faith that most people are good-hearted and more than willing to help a person in need (once they get over their own fears that *you* might be someone dangerous). Still, staying alert at all times, avoiding camping within sight of roads, and having a plan of action in case of assault are safe habits to form. Trust your instincts.

Cactus and Thorns

Cat-claw acacia, thorny locust, prickly pear, jumping cholla, and agave are among the many plants along the trail just waiting to scratch your calves and puncture your tubes.

Treat your bike tires with a sealant such as Slime. Consider carrying long pants or gaiters, or you can count a few scratches and a little bloodshed as part of the trip. Carry betadine or alcohol swabs, anti-bacterial ointment, gauze pads, athletic tape, and Band-Aids.

The infamous jumping chollas of the Sonoran Desert can be a serious hazard. If a member of your group crashes into one, things could get ugly. A small plastic comb from your toiletry kit can be used to comb out the tenacious balls of spines if they get deeply embedded.

Agave plants are one of the many reasons to carry spare inner tubes while biking the AZT.

Stay on the trail to protect the desert vegetation from unnecessary damage. Or suffer the consequences. Be nice to the cactus and hopefully the cactus will be nice to you. In February 1982, a man suffered from "cactus karma" after he plugged a Saguaro with two shells from his shotgun. A 23-foot section of the cactus collapsed and killed him.

Getting Lost

Even with maps and a guidebook, you can get lost on this trail. At this printing, the Arizona Trail is not consistently signed or maintained. Many sections of the route follow unsigned dirt roads in remote areas. Be alert and have at least one group member who is comfortable interpreting maps. Day riders should carry a jacket, food and water, a flashlight, and other gear to get them through an emergency overnight stay in the backcountry. When traveling in a group, make a rule that the lead cyclist will always wait at any fork or turn that has even a remote possibility of being confusing. This way, your group won't get separated.

Aches and Pains

In my experience, traveling by bike is much easier on your body than backpacking. Blisters are usually not an issue. Soreness is rare and less severe. Recovery is quicker. However, knee strain and chafing are common biker ailments that can spoil a trip. Refer to Appendix F for a list of books that give detailed information on injuries and strains common to bicycling and backcountry travel.

Hints: Bring a tube of chamois butter to prevent and soothe chafing. Make sure your bike seat is adjusted properly to prevent knee strain. Don't overdo it as this is a tough route; be sure to increase your levels of skill and fitness gradually.

Crashes

If the terrain is above your skill level, dismount and walk your bike. Riding through intimidating sections just to say you did it is not worth having to end your trip because of an injury. Wear your helmet at all times while on the bike. Wear gloves to protect your hands in case you fall. Wear protective eyewear or sunglasses while riding.

Hunting Season

Travelers will encounter hunters along the entire length of the AZT from late August into November. Wear bright clothing and stay alert.

Traveling on Highways

Always ride with the direction of traffic and obey all traffic laws while biking on highways and other roads open to motor vehicles. Wear bright clothing and avoid riding during times of low light.

Mind Your Manners

As I made the transition from park ranger to long-distance hiker to bikepacker, I began to experience firsthand the negative opinion that many nature enthusiasts have of mountain bikers. This view is unjustified but understandable considering how mainstream biking magazines promote the image of mountain bikers as a bunch of slacker downhill maniacs who have no appreciation for the scenery, wildlife, or history of the areas they ride. This portrayal might sell magazines and guidebooks but has not encouraged public-lands managers to include mountain biking as a legitimate and appropriate use of backcountry areas. So, it behooves mountain bike enthusiasts to promote an image of mountain bikers as polite, environmentally conscious, law-abiding, low-impact users of the backcountry. Our access to public and private lands depends on it.

Minimize Your Impact on the Environment
- Stay on established trails and roads.
- Stay off of trails and other areas that are closed to bicycles. Do not take your bicycle into designated Wilderness Areas.
- Camp in designated or already impacted campsites whenever possible. Camp at least 200 feet from natural water sources.
- Bury human waste in a "cathole" at least 4 inches deep. Go a good distance (at least 200 feet) from campsites and trails to do your business. Go at least 100 yards away from water sources.
- Rarely build campfires. Use preexisting fire rings and always put out your fire with water until the coals are cold to the touch. Use a stove for cooking.
- Pack out all trash. This includes pieces of wrappers from sports bars and gels, cigarette butts, fruit peels, toilet paper, and feminine-hygiene products.

Minimize Your Impact on Other Users
- Give hikers the right-of-way. Slow down or stop and be sociable. Smile and say hello. Thank them if they step aside to let you pass. Share some of the experiences you've had or the sights you've seen.
- Give equestrians the right-of-way. The sight of a mountain bike might spook some horses. Stop a good distance from horses. Say hello to riders and ask them what they would like you to do. When in doubt, get off and let horses pass safely.
- Respect the wishes of private landowners. Follow the directions of any posted signs. Ask permission before camping or using water sources on private property.
- Leave gates in the position you found them.
- Obey the rules and regulations of the areas you travel through.
- Stay alert. Report suspicious activity to the appropriate authorities.
- Respect historic and archaeological sites. Avoid camping near archaeological sites and leave them as you found them.
- Save taxpayers some money. Don't put search and rescue workers at risk by getting hurt, lost, or requesting help when it is not necessary. Use good judgment. Bike smart. Make avoiding injury more important than finishing your trip or logging miles. Be prepared for emergencies. If someone in your group is injured or ill, attempt to self-rescue when possible and when it won't aggravate the situation. Use common sense.
- Volunteer. Join a trail association in your area. Take part in a trail-maintenance project.

PLANNING YOUR TRIP
When to Ride
Arizona Climate
While biking across the state of Arizona, you will experience frequent changes in elevation. Gains and losses of more than 4,000 feet can be seen in one day. The benefit to dramatic elevation changes is dramatic weather differences. During winter, when the areas above 7,000 feet might get snow, the temperatures in the low elevations are pleasant. Summer brings extremes as well. The forests of the high elevations offer cool riding, while the areas below 5,000 feet are scorching ovens. These dramatic differences make mountain biking a year-round activity in Arizona. The trick is to avoid the summer low-elevation heat and the winter high-elevation snow.

The Kaibab Plateau between the North Rim of the Grand Canyon and the Utah border can be snowed-in from mid-October to June. The deserts between Payson and Patagonia can be unbearably hot from May through September. The monsoon season during July and August will bring frequent rain showers, thunderstorms, lightning, flash floods, and muddy conditions. The section of the trail between the Utah border and Payson is often wet and muddy due to snowmelt in the early spring. Day riders can ride each section during the season recommended in the route description. Thru-bikers need to pick one month to complete the entire route. So when should you attempt a thru-bike? Well, it depends on which direction you are going.

North to South ("Southbounders")
If going north to south, "southbounders" need to be off the Kaibab Plateau before the first significant snow (you might see flurries during any month of the year). You can start at the Utah border anytime between the last week of August and first week of October. By starting in the last half of September, you get warm days, chilly evenings, and golden aspen as you make your way to the Mogollon Rim. When you descend into the Sonoran Desert, the days might still be quite warm and sunny at low elevations. Starting after snowmelt in June, you might run into muddy trails, and you will hit the desert portions during the hottest part of the year. That's why fall travel is logistically the easiest and the most enjoyable for north to south thru-biking.

South to North ("Northbounders")
If you start at the Mexican border, you must reach the Kaibab Plateau after snowmelt (usually in late May or early June) or before snowfall

(mid-October to mid-November). If you believe you can make it to Utah before snowfall, start at southern end in early September. Be prepared for extreme heat while in southern Arizona. In the spring, you must leave the Mexico border by early April to avoid the desert heat, but if you arrive at the high elevations too soon after snowmelt, the route will be too muddy for pleasant biking.

Flip-Flop or Leap Frog

Get creative. Because you must trek the Grand Canyon section, consider using the location to break up your tour into parts. Thru-hikers call this a flip-flop or leap frog. Bike either direction between the North Rim and the Utah border from the last part of June through the first week of October. Bike either direction between Mexico and Payson from the end of September through the end of April. The section between Payson and the South Rim of the Grand Canyon can be biked anytime except during or immediately after significant snowstorms.

Mileage Per Day

Expert riders traveling with a support vehicle can possibly ride 60 miles a day and finish the route in 12 days. I've also seen experienced bikepackers make that kind of mileage on off-pavement routes. Yuck. Why rush it? There is too much to see along this route. I enjoy 40-mile days (on average) when I am bikepacking. This pace strikes a good balance between making miles and enjoying myself at camp and during breaks. With a 40-mile average, you can do the trip in about 20 days. Plan a few days off (zero days—where you log no miles) for recovery, resupply, bike repairs, and sightseeing. The more time you have the more fun you will have.

Beginners should plan on 20- to 30-mile days at the most, maybe even less. You will probably be up to 40-mile days by the last half of your trip, but there is no shame in starting out with low-mileage days as you build up your fitness level. Better yet, try to talk a friend into providing vehicle support for the first few days of your trip. Having a support vehicle for the first few days will ease your fears, build your confidence, and allow you to escape if weather gets bad or the trip turns out to be more than you bargained for. Beginners should be in good shape, have practiced pedaling a loaded-down bike, and have planned their food and gear supplies according to their estimated daily mileage.

Water

It's a dry heat all right. One of the major challenges along the Arizona Trail is finding water sources. The importance of good planning to ensure that you are always carrying enough water cannot be overemphasized. You will use a least a gallon of water per day per person. That doesn't mean you are always carrying one gallon. Some days you might need to carry two gallons; some days you can get by with carrying two liters between water sources. Although you should lean toward carrying too much water, good planning can minimize the amount of weight you carry. Caching water at road crossings is another option worth considering. Reliable water sources are listed in each segment description.

The good news is that bikers actually have it easier than hikers on the Arizona Trail. Because you will cover more miles per day than hikers, you will encounter more water sources per day. Going a mile or so off the trail to get water is less of an ordeal for you than for someone traveling on foot. Also, carrying water weight on a bicycle is a little easier on your body than carrying it on your back.

Hint: *Plan on dry camping a lot. Camping next to lakes or gurgling streams is overrated anyway. No bugs, better views, and fewer neighbors are some of the benefits to camping where there is no water nearby. I often load up on water at the last known water source I will pass for the day. With enough water for dinner, breakfast, and drinking (usually a gallon per person), I then bike to a dry campsite where I intend to stop for the night. The following day, I fill up my water bottles at the next water source.*

Some of the water sources on this route are beautiful clear streams. Some are cow-trodden scummy ponds. Whenever you see the words "stock tank," expect a less-than-desirable water source. Purify all water from natural sources with a filter or iodine tablets. If the water has lots of silt or debris in it, use a bandanna as a coarse pre-filter before using your purification filter or treatment.

A typical stock tank water source found along the AZT.

Resupply Points

Appendix B lists convenient resupply points along the route, as well as places where riders can find facilities for camping and lodging. Depending on your pace, you should be able to hit a store or town every three to four days. Many of the towns are small, and grocery stores might have little besides processed pasta meals and snack foods. So choosy eaters might want to mail food ahead. Post offices are at most of the resupply points if you plan to use mail drops. Another option is to have friends meet you with food and water at predetermined locations.

Choosing a Bike

This route can be done on a rigid (no suspension) mountain bike, but you will have more fun and your arms will be happier if you get a bike with at least a suspension fork. I traveled from Utah to Flagstaff on a 10-year-old rigid and had no problems. So, it is possible to do the route on a $150 bike. However, when I switched to a front-suspension bike in Flagstaff, I traveled faster and had more fun. My biking partner Beth rode a full-suspension bike with an attached trailer. A full-suspension bike will give you more cushioning as you bounce over rocky roads, but will limit you to carrying a trailer. Full-suspension bikes are usually more expensive as well.

There are bike shops in Flagstaff, Payson, Phoenix, and Tucson (see Appendix D), but most of the route will be hundreds of miles from the nearest bike mechanic. Investing in a sturdy bike with reliable components is highly recommended, especially if you are planning a thru-bike. Buy a new bike or upgrade your current bike in order to have a gear for grinding up rocky hills while carrying weight. There are publications listed in Appendix F that you should read for more detailed information on the ins and outs of bikepacking.

Trailer vs. Panniers

There are two types of bikepackers, those who prefer trailers and those who prefer a rack and panniers. Each system has its trade-offs. Personal preference and bike compatibility will have to be your guide when choosing a packing system.

Hint: Cyclosource, *a catalog published by the Adventure Cycling Association, has most of the items you need for a mountain bike tour in one catalog. Cyclosource or www.adventurecycling.org (see Appendix D for more information) is a good place to start, but many other companies sell clothing and equipment that's specifically designed for bikepacking.*

Some bikepackers prefer a trailer and full-suspension bike.

Rack and Panniers

By attaching a good quality rear rack and panniers to your mountain bike, you can carry camping gear and food with you. Be sure the bike has rear eyelets for attaching the panniers. Some front-suspension and most full-suspension bikes do not have eyelets, making the trailer (described on next page) your only option. A bike with a rack and panniers is easier to portage than a bike with a trailer. Also, getting in and out of vehicles and hotels is easier with a pannier system. A good-quality rack and pannier system costs about the same as a trailer system.

   Hint: When shopping for panniers, look for simple designs that can be repaired in the field. I've seen parts come off of fancy attachment systems that cannot be replaced in remote locations. My Canadian-designed Arkel panniers have done well for more than 1,200 miles of rough travel.

   Waterproof fabrics and rain covers are useful features. The panniers should be able to carry roughly 2,000 cubic inches of gear. You will also need bungee cords or straps to cinch down large items like tents to the top of your rack. Balance the weight high and forward in line with your center of gravity. Although often used for road touring, front panniers will be cumbersome on the technical terrain and narrow trails along this route. Good packers can get everything they need in rear panniers and on top of a rack. I've never used one, but a handlebar bag might be a nice accessory.

Trailer

A trailer system will allow you to use a full-suspension bike and carries more weight than panniers. I can vouch for the BOB (back-of-bike) trailer's usability on technical terrain. Trailers are low to the ground, making them more aerodynamic than panniers. Less wind drag means faster, easier biking. Many trailers also come with waterproof storage bags and more cubic inches of space than panniers. The major downsides to the trailer system are transportation and portaging. Pushing a bike with a trailer is difficult. Getting over obstacles like downed trees might require unhooking the trailer if you are traveling alone. The trailer system is also more cumbersome when staying in hotels and getting in and out of vehicles.

Hint: *Heavier cyclists might be better off with a trailer system. At 135 pounds with up to 60 pounds of gear, I've never had an issue with wheel spokes collapsing due to extra weight. However, larger cyclists might overtax the strength of wheel spokes when they add gear weight to a bike. Men seem to have more problems with wheel spokes breaking, probably because of their larger size.*

Bike Equipment
Tires
Your bike should be equipped with knobby mountain bike tires and inner tubes that have been treated with a puncture-resistant sealant such as Slime. Cactus will be in and around the trail during your entire trip. Get your tubes treated for about $2 each at a local bike shop and maybe, if you're like me, you won't get any flats. My friend Beth got five. So be prepared to change a tire. Carry a spare folding tire for the group and at least one spare tube, pump, and patch kit per person.

Cactus thorns make flat tires a likely occurrence.

Gloves
Padded full-finger gloves will give you the best protection. Waterproof gloves are nice in cold weather.

Helmet
Don't ride without it. Make sure it fits snugly.

Odometer (Cyclocomputer)
Highly recommended as an aid to route finding.

Tools
The compact multi-tool kits on the market will have most but not all of the tools you need for an extended bike trip. See Appendix E for a detailed list of bike tools you should carry with you.

Hints: Get in the habit of checking your seat, rack, water bottle cage, cleats, and various bolts on your bike each morning before you start. Make sure they're all tight. Bolts have a tendency to come loose over time, especially on rough terrain. Losing a bolt while in a remote area can be frustrating. Lubricate your chain daily for smooth pedaling and effective gearing.

Camping Gear and Clothing
Go light! Perfecting the art of carrying enough gear to be prepared for varying weather conditions, emergencies, and mechanical breakdowns while still maintaining a light load comes with experience. The book *Beyond Backpacking: Ray Jardine's Guide to Lightweight Hiking* (AdventureLore Press) is the authority on how to efficiently pack for extended trips. Although carrying weight on a bicycle is easier than carrying it on your back, you will still feel it, especially on ascents. Beginners should do an overnight practice trip to determine which items are unnecessary. Appendix E has a checklist of essential gear and clothing.

Repair and Maintenance
Bike shops are located in Flagstaff, Payson, Phoenix, and Tucson (see Appendix D). Shops in Flagstaff and Payson are practically right on the trail, but getting to Phoenix or Tucson will require biking a significant distance off the trail or getting a ride. Having enough gear and knowledge to make emergency repairs is essential. Bring the tools recommended in Appendix E. Educate yourself on how to make bike repairs in the field. Several books on the subject are recommended in Appendix F.

Be ready to make emergency bike repairs.

How To Use This Guide

This guide divides the Arizona Trail into 25 segments. The segments range from 3 to 50 miles—lengths that were largely determined by the location of convenient trailhead access points. The segments are presented from north to south, and are named after their starting and ending points. You should plan your rides based on your own skills, schedule, and fitness.

Each segment includes a map, elevation profile, difficulty rating, route information, and any opportunities for day and loop rides. In order to keep this book lightweight and packable, descriptions of natural history and scenery have been kept to a minimum. Appendix F lists reading sources for more detailed information on area history and natural features. The segments are organized as follows:

 Author's Favorites: I have indicated noteworthy characteristics of certain segments with this symbol.

Distance

Most of the distances listed were taken from bicycle odometer readings. My odometer readings were sometimes slightly different from the mileage given on trail signs. Because of calibration differences, expect a margin of error between my cyclometer and yours. The track you take and changes in the trail due to trail maintenance and weather events might also cause your odometer readings to differ from the mileages given in the book. With all of these factors in mind, you should plan for roughly a 0.2-mile margin of error.

Difficulty

Ratings used to show the difficulty of each segment are **Easy, Moderate,** and **Strenuous**. However, one person's easy is another person's nightmare. Difficulty is inherently relative to experience, physical conditioning, weather, attitude, and equipment. Difficulty ratings indicate the level of exertion required for each segment in terms of the uphill grade (for southbound riders), the estimated mileage per hour, and how frequently beginners and thru-bikers might need to dismount and portage over difficult areas. Expect most of the route to be a challenging workout. Easy doesn't mean you won't get your heart rate up.

Technical Rating

This rating system indicates the amount of technical mountain biking skill required on the segment. As mentioned earlier in this chapter, segments that demand what I consider expert technical skills are not included in this guide. However, there are several short, technical sections throughout this guide where beginners should dismount and walk their bikes.

Beginner indicates that the surface is relatively smooth single track or dirt road with few obstacles and few rocky climbs or descents. If you have never ridden a bike off pavement before, you are going to find even the Beginner sections in this guide challenging. Those who are brand-new to mountain biking should first attempt short out-and-back rides on the sections rated Easy.

Intermediate indicates that the surface is rocky with some obstacles to climb, hop, or maneuver around. An Intermediate rating also indicates that the segment includes steep rocky descents or climbs where beginners or thru-bikers might need to dismount and walk their bikes. Most riders will have to portage their bikes for short distances on the Intermediate segments.

Advanced is used to describe short sections where most riders will have to dismount or "dab" their feet on the ground to maintain balance. The Advanced rating is also used to describe some of the day rides on sections of AZT that are open to bikes but tough to ride.

If you have never ridden a bicycle off pavement before, consider yourself a step below a Beginner, and if you have never ridden a bike loaded down with camping gear, consider yourself a step lower in skill than you normally would be. For example, if you are an Intermediate day rider, you should consider yourself a Beginner the first time you try bikepacking.

Trail Status

The recommended thru-route is defined as official AZT, proposed AZT, or a bike detour.

Season

Many segments of the Arizona Trail are ridable all year except during extreme weather conditions. However, I have indicated in the Introduction the best seasons to ride each segment as well as the times of year that might provide weather complications. Some segments have elevation gains/losses of 4,000 feet or more. Be prepared for weather ranging from sunny and hot to cold and wet on segments with extreme elevation changes, regardless of the season.

Maps

The maps in this guide are designed to give you a general idea of each segment. Supplemental maps should be carried along with this guidebook on all but the most well-signed segments. The United States Forest Service (USFS), Bureau of Land Management (BLM), National Geographic *Trails Illustrated* National Park and Forest maps, or other recreational maps listed will suffice for most sections. United States Geological Survey (USGS) 7.5-minute quadrangles are listed for some segments as well, particularly when the area is signed poorly. You might find that the AZT is not shown on many of these maps. You will have to use the trail names and road numbers listed in the route descriptions to locate the route on most maps. Thru-bikers should also carry an Arizona state highway map to use for getting off the trail to resupply.

Signage

Ratings of **Good, Fair,** or **Poor** accompany a description of what level of signing to expect on the trail. Most AZT signs are either white decals mounted on flexible fiberglass (Carsonite) posts or a brand burned into a wood plaque or post. On segments that are rated as Poor, the signage is inconsistent and often nonexistent. Remember, the sections that bypass the official AZT will be marked with their own corresponding road/trail signs.

Water Sources

Year-round, reliable water sources—or lack thereof—are indicated for each segment. Assume that water treatment is required for all natural water sources. See Planning Your Trip, p. 24, for more information on water.

Trail Access

Directions for road access to trailheads are given from the nearest town or major paved road. Segments are designed so that you can reach their trailheads by normal passenger vehicles. However, high-clearance vehicles are usually better for traveling on Forest Service roads, especially during bad weather. Other vehicle-access options are sometimes mentioned here and in the route description.

Water sources as good as this one are rare on the AZT.

Permits and Fees

Information on required permits, entrance fees, and reservations is provided if applicable.

Trail Overview and Elevation Profiles

A general description is given of the surface, scenery, highlights, and hazards found in the segment. Elevation profiles like the one shown below indicate the amount of overall elevation gain and loss on each segment. They are best used as guides to help you decide which direction of travel is most desirable. The profile line represents the average change in elevation between regularly spaced intervals, *not the actual contours of the trail.* Don't let what looks like a flat section in a profile fool you. Most of the routes contain short climbs and steep descents that do not show up on the profile, and a series of steep climbs can be more tiring than one long, grinding ascent. Always consult the Route Description for detailed information about the topography of the trail. Information for the elevation profiles was obtained from the USGS 7.5-minute quadrangles listed in the Maps section of each segment.

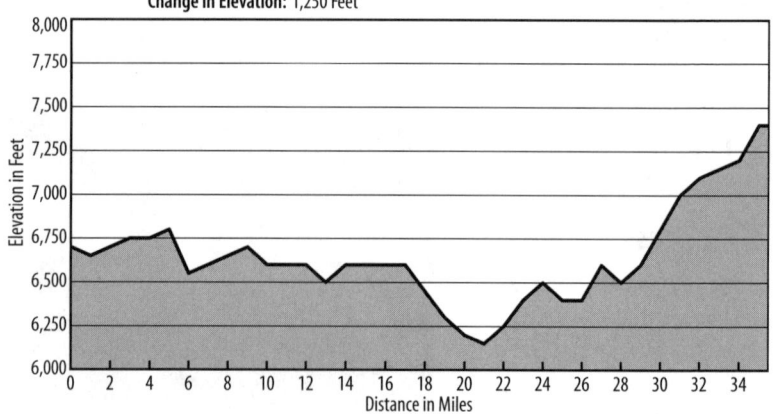

Segment Maps

Each segment has a map showing the route in a southbound direction. The following symbols are used in the segment maps:

- Biking Route
- Day Ride or Loop
- Actual AZT Route
- Detour
- Segment Start/End Point
- National Forest
- Wilderness Area
- Mountain or Butte
- Campground
- Water Source
- Interstate Highway
- U.S. Highway
- State Highway
- City or Town
- Point of Interest

Route Descriptions

The route for each segment is described in detail. Mileages might differ slightly from those of official sources, such as signs on the trail, because of the variances between a bicycle odometer reading and other methods of estimating distance. You should plan for at least a 0.2-mile margin of error due to minor route variations and calibration differences.

Directions given such as "west" or "northeast" are not absolute compass bearings, but approximate direction guides. Cattle guards and power lines are often mentioned in the route descriptions because they are permanent landmarks that are important for route finding. Route directions, scenic highlights, resupply access, potential campsites and water sources, loop options and side trips, and interesting local facts are also given.

In order to save space, the thru-route is described in a southbound direction. Northbound bikers need to change right/left orientation as needed. For sections that are extremely confusing, a "Northbounders" notice might appear next to this symbol: N. Either direction of travel is acceptable, but traveling north to south is slightly more convenient for thru-bikers because of weather considerations (see When to Ride, p. 22).

Development of the AZT is still in progress. You might find changes to the route described in this book. Hopefully, any realignments of the AZT will be well signed.

Day Rides

This section, which concludes each applicable segment, is designed specifically for day riders and thru-riders who just can't get enough of the Arizona Trail. I have done most of these rides and used information from the Arizona Trail Association (ATA), trail stewards, maps, and guidebooks to describe the rest. I have included some AZT passages that are open to bicycles but might be too technical for bikepackers burdened by gear. If the difficulty rating is listed as Strenuous, be prepared for a challenge. See Appendix A for a list of the featured day rides.

Scenic biking at the base of the Superstition Mountains, Tonto National Forest.

Segment 1 UTAH STATE LINE to US 89A

Total Distance: 20.9 miles
Distance from Utah: 0.0 miles
Distance to Mexico: 703.9 miles
Difficulty: Moderate
Technical Rating: Beginner
Trail Status: Official AZT and bike detour around a tough climb.

Season
Except during or after winter snowstorms or prolonged rain, you can ride this segment all year. The track might be too muddy after rainstorms. The low elevations near the state line can be extremely hot during summer.

The trailhead at the Utah border.

Maps
BLM: Arizona Strip Field Office Visitor Map
USFS: North Kaibab Ranger District
USGS: Pine Hollow Canyon, Coyote Buttes, Cooper Ridge, Jacob Lake

Signage
Good: AZT stickers and Forest Service road numbers on Carsonite posts.

Water Sources
No reliable sources. Fill up at Jacob Lake or cache water along the way.

Trail Access
SOUTHBOUND: Stateline Trailhead
From Jacob Lake, go east on US 89A to BLM 1065 (House Rock Valley Road). There are some rustic buildings at the signed intersection where the dirt road heads north up Coyote Valley. Go north on BLM 1065 for about 20 miles to Stateline Trailhead, where there is camping but no water.

NORTHBOUND: Orderville Trailhead
From Jacob Lake, take US 89A east for 2 miles. Orderville Trailhead is on the right (south) side of the highway. There is parking and a restroom but no water.

Trail Overview

With the help of volunteers and the Arizona Trail Association (ATA), the Bureau of Land Management (BLM) has built a wonderful trailhead for the northern terminus of the Arizona Trail. At the Utah/Arizona state line, you will find a campground/picnic area with shade shelters, restrooms, a trail register, interpretive signs, and a well-groomed trail leading to benches facing inspiring views of the Paria Canyon–Vermilion Cliffs Wilderness Area. The "well-groomed" designation only applies to the first 0.25 mile. Soon after leaving the trailhead, the AZT becomes more rugged as it ascends 26 switchbacks and climbs nearly 1,000 feet in 2 miles. Southbound bicyclists should take the detour to where the AZT crosses BLM 1025 (Winter Road) as given in the route description. Northbounders can take the AZT down from the intersection at BLM 1025 if they don't mind descending switchbacks that might be intimidating for beginners. Thru-bikers wanting to ride more than push should definitely take the detour given here. Both routes give you views of the surreal colors of Coyote Valley as you climb Buckskin Mountain. The red cliffs to the southeast are where California condors are released into the wild. You have a good chance of spotting these rare birds by the time you reach the South Rim of the Grand Canyon at the end of Segment 4.

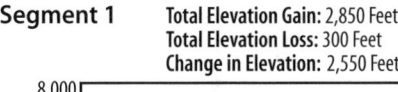

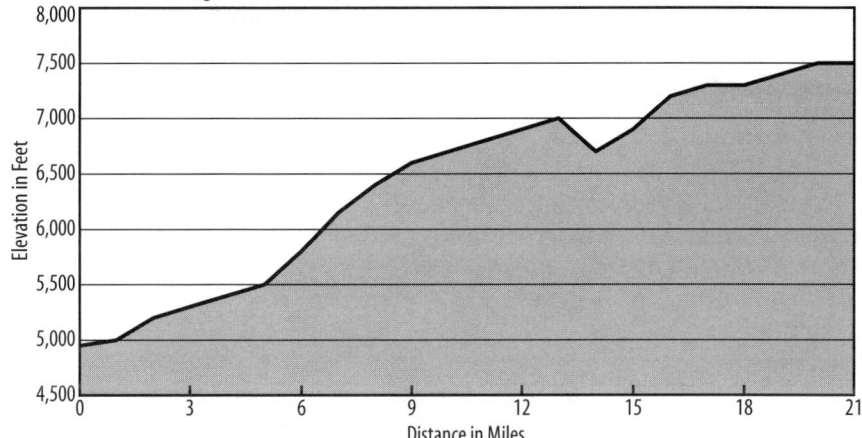

36 Biking the Arizona Trail

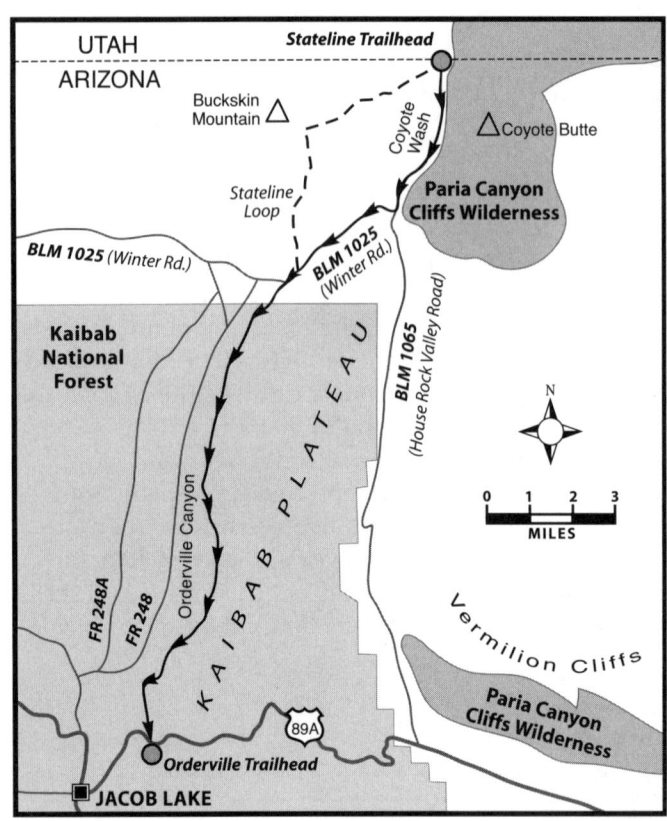

Route Description

Southbound | | Northbound
Southbound		Northbound
0.0	From the Stateline Trailhead, take the groomed path for a short distance to check out the view from the bench. The trail gets much tougher from this point south. Go back down to the parking lot to BLM 1065 (House Rock Valley Road).	20.9
0.1	Turn right (south) onto BLM 1065.	20.8
2.3	Climb above Coyote Wash. Look east for views of the palette of mauve, beige, and gray striped hills that make up the Chinle Formation.	18.6
5.0	Turn right (west) onto BLM 1025 (Winter Road) and begin a steady climb up Buckskin Mountain.	15.9
7.0	The road gives you a break from climbing as it skirts the edge of Long Canyon. Don't forget to look back to see the Vermilion Cliffs and Navajo Mountain.	13.9

Southbound			Northbound
9.0	Slow down and stay alert for the brown Carsonite posts that mark where the AZT crosses the road from the north. Southbounders, continue west for a short distance to find the AZT. Turn left (south) onto the single-track trail between the signs. This rarely used portion of the trail might be faint and soft in spots. Roll over cattle-trodden track that winds through piñon-juniper forest.		11.9
	Northbounders: You can take the AZT for 11 miles back to the trailhead, but be prepared for a steep descent.	N	
10.5	Kaibab National Forest Boundary. The AZT now follows the Kaibab Plateau Trail #100, marked with an AZT sticker that has a Kaibab squirrel in the center. Kaibab squirrels have black bodies and bright white tails. You might see them foraging in the pine forests of the plateau.		10.4
12.0	The first ponderosa pine you see is cause for celebration. You have climbed above 6,000 feet. Only 2,000 more to go!		8.9
13.8	After you cross the Navajo Trail #19, a sign points out Joe's Tank 0.5 mile to the west. This tank was dry when I went through. Views to the north reveal the cliffs of the Grand Staircase. The trail continues to improve as you head south.		7.1
17.0	The trail should be well marked as you cross FR 249. Go through another gate in 0.3 mile.		3.9

Down the Grand Staircase

As you climb up the Kaibab Plateau, you are, in a geologic sense, going "downstairs." The Grand Staircase is a series of four cliffs that drop down from Bryce Canyon to the North Rim of the Grand Canyon. From the north, the Pink Cliffs of Bryce Canyon rise above the White Cliffs that make up Zion National Park. The White Cliffs lead to the Gray Cliffs, then to the Vermilion Cliffs that can be seen at the Stateline Trailhead.

The Kaibab Plateau is the bottom of the staircase. When you step off the North Rim to hike to the Colorado River, you leave the 200-million-year-old Grand Staircase formations behind and descend toward the 2-billion-year-old rocks found at the bottom of the Grand Canyon. Keep looking northeast to catch views of these cliffs. On clear days, you will be able to see them rising above the Colorado Plateau like a set of gigantic stairs suitable for the likes of Paul Bunyan.

Southbound			Northbound
17.9	A sinkhole next to the trail is one of the largest in the area. After the sinkhole, you will cross FR 257.		3.0
20.9	Descend along a fence just before you cross AZ 89A. Take the faint single track for a short distance to the Orderville Trailhead and the start of Segment 2. Two miles west on US 89A is Jacob Lake, where you will find a lodge, a USFS visitor center, water, and a restaurant/store that sells great homemade cookies.		0.0

Day Rides

Stateline Loop
Total Distance: 20 miles
Difficulty: Moderate
Technical Rating: Intermediate

For a great loop ride, take BLM 1065, then BLM 1025 south from the Stateline Trailhead. To get there, see Trail Access: Southbound. After nine miles the AZT crosses the road; take the trail north back to the state line.

A big push!

Segment 2 — US 89A to EAST RIM VIEW

Best Wildlife Viewing and Best Fall Colors

Total Distance: 30.2 miles
Distance from Utah: 20.9 miles
Distance to Mexico: 683.0 miles
Difficulty: Easy to Moderate
Technical Rating: Beginner
Trail Status: Official AZT

Season
Spring to fall. The Kaibab Plateau receives up to 30 inches of precipitation a year. Most of that arrives in the form of snow, in amounts that shut down the roads during winter.

Maps
USFS: North Kaibab Ranger District
USGS: Jacob Lake, Telephone Hill, DeMotte Park

Golden alleys of aspen line the single track on the Kaibab Plateau.

Signage
Good: AZT stickers on Carsonite posts and Kaibab Trail #101 brand on wooden signs.

Water Sources
Jacob Lake (2 miles west of the trail), Ridge Tank, Crane Lake, Dog Lake

Trail Access
SOUTHBOUND: Orderville Trailhead
From Jacob Lake, take US 89A east for 2 miles to Orderville Trailhead, which is on the right (south) side of the highway. There is parking and a restroom but no water.

NORTHBOUND: East Rim View
From Jacob Lake, drive 23 miles south on AZ 67 to FR 611. Turn left (east) onto FR 611 and go 4 miles to East Rim View, where there is parking and a restroom but no water.

Trail Overview

Segment 2 ranks as one of the most scenic and biker-friendly sections of the Arizona Trail. If you only ride a few sections of the AZT, be sure to do this one. The views will take your breath away, especially when the fall colors are at their peak. In summer, wildflowers bloom in the open parklike areas under large ponderosa pines. Deer, Kaibab squirrels, wild turkeys, foxes, and grouse are among the wildlife frequently seen in alpine forests and grassy meadows. Also known as "mountain grassland parks," the meadows of the Kaibab Plateau remain enigmas to scientists. Perhaps forest fires or the wet conditions from snowmelt are responsible for keeping the meadows safe from encroaching trees. Southbound riders will gain 1,000 feet in elevation as they make the long and steady ascent from the Orderville Trailhead to Telephone Ridge. After you top out on Telephone Ridge, the grade evens out a bit as the trail follows along an old roadbed. You will make several descents and climbs in and out of drainages and across ridges on your way to East Rim View. Crane Lake and Dog Lake provide water sources for bikepackers. You will find plenty of primitive campsites located in ideal spots.

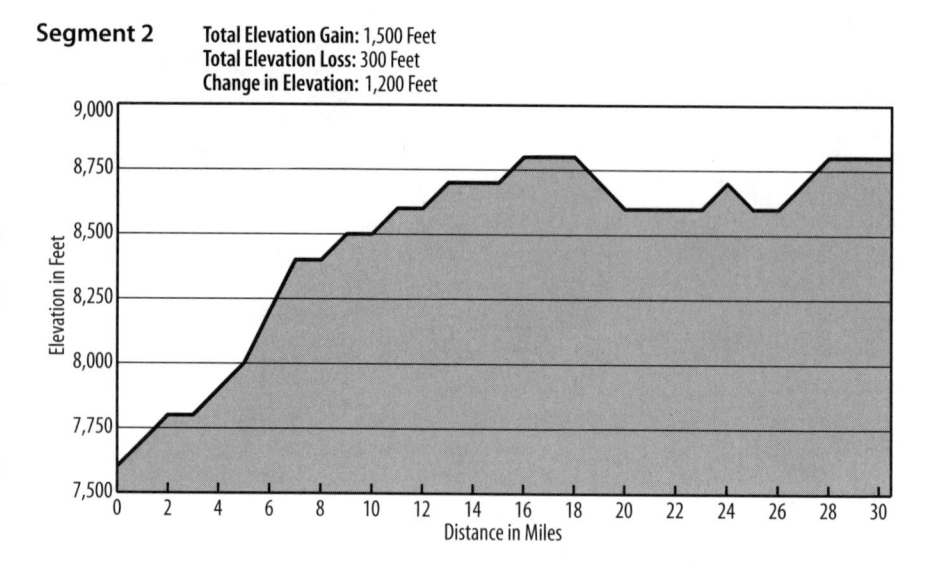

Segment 2
Total Elevation Gain: 1,500 Feet
Total Elevation Loss: 300 Feet
Change in Elevation: 1,200 Feet

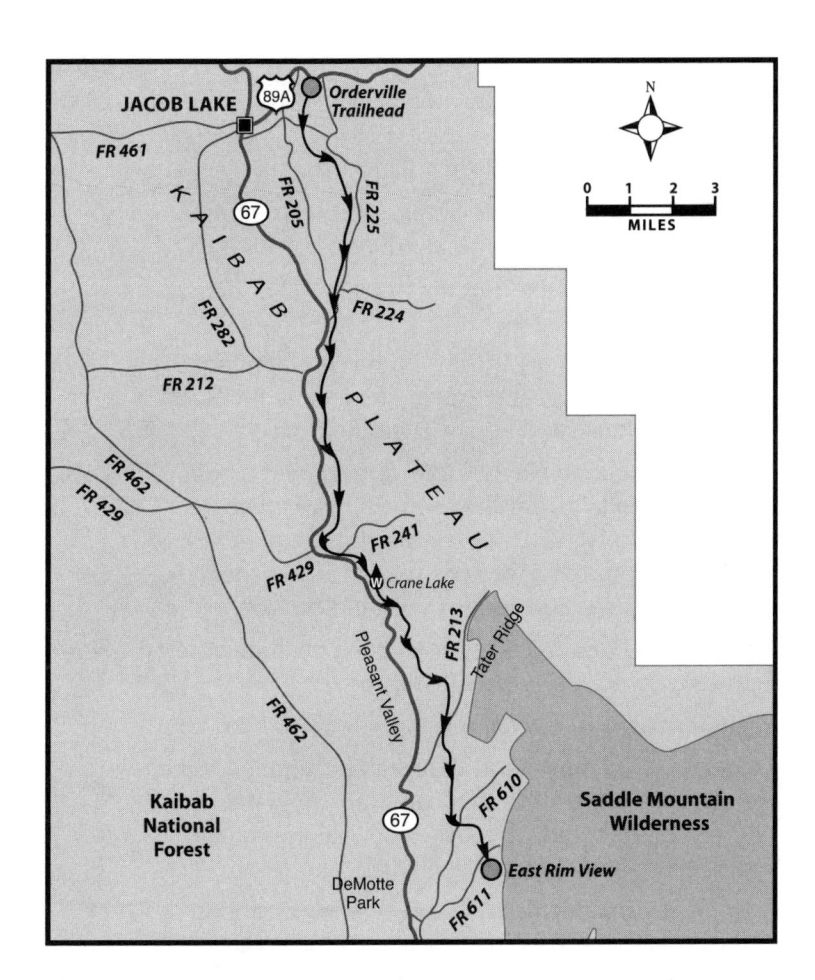

Route Description

Southbound *Northbound*

0.0	The AZT heads south from the east side of the Orderville Trailhead parking lot.	30.2
0.4	At the bottom of a rocky descent, you drop onto a dirt road and turn left (south).	29.8
0.5	Turn right up the road to the west.	29.7
0.8	A sign directs you to take the right (west) fork.	29.4
1.6	Maneuver down a short technical section into a drainage that leads to FR 258 and a corral. A sign indicates that FR 205 is 7 miles from here.	28.6

Southbound **Northbound**

2.2	A big chock stone attempts to stop vehicle traffic from going beyond the point where the trail begins a long, steady climb to the top of the Kaibab Plateau.	28.0
2.6	Stay right at the fork in the trail. Keep climbing. Purple lupine are abundant here during the summer.	27.6
3.3	Pass a metal stock tank that might have water. Keep climbing.	26.9
4.5	Continue climbing up through a narrow drainage lined with evergreens and aspen. The look of the forest will change significantly as you near 8,000 feet.	25.7
5.5	Celebrate! The long climb is almost over, and Ridge Tank will provide a scummy source of water if you are desperate. You will cross two more dirt roads and pass by several campsites. After you ascend above the tank, the trail levels out and crosses several dirt roads.	24.7
7.8	Turn left (south) onto a gravel road, then go immediately right (west) back onto the signed trail.	22.4
	Northbounders: *Be careful, this turn is easy to miss.*	N
8.4	Cross FR 205 to the Murray Trailhead parking lot; there are restrooms and primitive camping spots nearby. Leaving the trailhead, you will cross a faint road and begin rolling in and out of drainages.	21.8
10.4	After crossing a dirt road, you will reach a caution sign that warns bicyclists of steep grades ahead. Check your brakes before dropping down a series of tight switchbacks.	19.8
10.8	At the bottom, enjoy some smooth single track through a charming narrow canyon.	19.4

Arizona "Lakes"

It will surprise some of you to see what passes for a "lake" in Arizona. A porous layer of limestone underlies the surface of the Kaibab and Coconino Plateaus. This rock layer allows water to soak through the surface. Because water rarely settles above ground, few permanent streams can form. The water instead forms caverns and tunnels that lie hidden underneath the surface. When these caverns collapse, they leave behind depressions called "sinkholes." Sometimes these sinkholes fill up with water and become what Arizonans call "lakes." Don't laugh. These stagnant ponds are an important source of water for wildlife as well as campers.

Southbound		Northbound
11.0	Now you must begin a painful climb out of the canyon by ascending an eroded section of trail.	19.2
12.0	Leave FR 418A and cross a dirt road. You will descend into a drainage and then begin another climb.	18.2
12.7	As you near the top of the ridge, look back (north) for views of the Vermilion Cliffs and Navajo Mountain. Begin a rolling ride on an old roadbed with more uphill grade for southbound riders.	17.5
16.6	At FR 241, AZ 67 is only 0.25 mile to the west. Begin a gradual ascent up Telephone Ridge.	13.6
17.1	Just uphill of the sign, you can see a tree that was once used as a fire lookout. A wooden ladder is still attached to the trunk of the large ponderosa pine. Get your camera ready. The scenery keeps getting better as you continue north.	13.1
19.4	A short, steep descent brings you off of Telephone Ridge and onto the meadow at Crane Lake. AZ 67 is within sight. Crane Lake is one of the area's few good water sources (filter first) so fill up your water bottles here. Ride to the south side of the bumpy meadow, where the trail ascends up through a corral. The AZT now parallels AZ 67 as it travels in and out of forest-lined meadows.	10.8
	Northbounders: *The sign that says FR 241 is 2 miles ahead is wrong; it is more than 3 miles to the road.*	

Trees of Gold

Quaking aspen (Populus tremuloides), *the stunning beauty queens of the boreal forests, are found between 8,000 and 9,100 feet. Aspen are a pioneering species, trees that reclaim areas cleared by fire, weather, or humans. Aspen roots send shoots up to grow into trees that protect the forest floor from the harsh sun, giving shade-loving seedlings like spruce and fir a chance to grow. Eventually, the evergreens will grow taller than the aspen and the aspen trees will die. The aspen roots lie dormant until another disturbance clears the land, and the cycle can continue.*

As you travel across the Kaibab Plateau you will see areas in various stages of forest progression. Many of the groves of thick "dog hair" stands of aspen are evidence of lightning-caused forest fires that plague the Kaibab Plateau during summer and fall. At the edges of the meadows, you might notice that the aspens appear to have been groomed with precision. Deer browse the leaves, evenly clipping the lower branches.

44 Biking the Arizona Trail

Southbound		*Northbound*
20.3	After passing a grassy camp with a meadow view, begin traversing up and down several ridges.	9.9
21.1	The trail gets loose and steep as you descend the ridge.	9.1
21.5	Pass a small pond, then join a road that goes to the right (west).	8.7
21.7	You can camp at the site next to the corral if you don't mind the company of cows. At the end of the meadow, you'll find a stock pond with water. This is Little Pleasant Valley. The AZT curves into the trees and continues to roll in and out of meadows.	8.5
23.0	A large pine tree frames an expansive view of Pleasant Valley. Go down the old road to the bottom of the grassy slopes. At the "Trail #101" sign, begin a 0.7-mile climb.	7.2
23.6	The trail follows a faint road through an aspen forest. The fall colors are unbeatable as the trail goes through an area scorched by the DeMotte forest fire in 1977. Since then, the aspens have grown thick as they start the process of reclaiming the land.	6.6
24.9	Cross FR 213 into a beautiful forest of aspen, fir, and spruce. The trail soon crosses FR 221 and then passes a stock tank with scummy water.	5.3
25.7	After crossing a dirt road, go through a wooden fence before descending into Tater Canyon.	4.5
26.3	The trail joins up with an old road along Tater Canyon. This pleasant section rolls over an easy grade through a meadow lined with dark evergreens. Morning riders might get to see the flocks of turkeys that inhabit the area.	3.9
27.7	You will pass a sign that says "East Rim View 2 miles." Leave Tater Canyon via a rocky series of switchbacks. When you spook blue grouse out of the brush, don't let the explosive sound of their thumping wings give you a heart attack.	2.5
28.2	After FR 610, the trail crosses a faint road and then drops down into another scenic meadow.	2.0

Southbound			Northbound
29.3	In the center of the meadow, the trail reaches a four-way intersection of dirt roads. Signs will direct you to stay on course to the other side of the meadow, where you begin a gradual ascent.		0.9
29.7	This pretty, although slightly scummy, pond is called Dog Lake.		0.5
29.9	Pass through the wooden gate and across FR 611. East Rim View parking is to the right (west) but continue on the trail for the scenic route. You will soon pass a dry camp with a view.		0.3
30.2	The paved path to the right (northwest) leads a short distance to the East Rim View parking lot.		0.0

Day Rides

East Rim View to Crane Lake
Total Distance: 22 miles
Difficulty: Easy
Technical Rating: Beginner

Day riders can park at East Rim View and ride north to Crane Lake for an out-and-back ride that samples the best scenery on this route. To get to the East Rim View parking lot, see Trail Access: Northbound.

Segment 3A/B — *EAST RIM VIEW to NORTH KAIBAB TRAILHEAD*

Idyllic camping spots are plentiful along the AZT in the Kaibab National Forest.

Total Distance: 17.4 miles

Distance from Utah: 51.1 miles

Distance to Mexico: 652.8 miles

Difficulty: Easy to Moderate

Technical Rating: Beginner

Trail Status: Official AZT and a road connection around a short section of incomplete trail.

Season
Spring to fall. On the North Rim, the park roads shut down with the first significant snow accumulations and do not reopen until May or June.

Maps
USFS: North Kaibab Ranger District
USGS: DeMotte Park, Dog Point, Little Park Lake, Bright Angel Point
Trails Illustrated: Grand Canyon National Park

Signage
Good: AZT stickers on Carsonite posts and Kaibab Trail #101 brand on wooden signs.

Water Sources
Crystal Spring, North Kaibab Trailhead

Trail Access
SOUTHBOUND: East Rim View
From Jacob Lake, drive 23 miles south on AZ 67 to FR 611. Turn left (east) onto FR 611 and go 4 miles to East Rim View where there is parking and a restroom but no water.
NORTHBOUND: North Kaibab Trailhead
Drive south on AZ 67 into Grand Canyon National Park. The North Kaibab Trailhead is 2 miles north of the Grand Canyon Lodge and the southern end of AZ 67. A biker/hiker campground and a store for campers are about 1 mile south of the trailhead off of AZ 67.
FROM THE MIDDLE: Park Entrance Trailhead
Drive south on AZ 67. Just past the park entrance station is a pullout on the east side of the road. The AZT starts on the south end of the parking area.

Trail Overview
The gentle grades, convenient water sources, and awesome scenery make Segment 3 a prime spot for bikepacking. Groups with vehicle support will find several primitive campsites along the Forest Service roads near the trailheads. The fall colors usually peak sometime between the middle of September and the first week of October. A connector trail at the park boundary remains incomplete at this time. Until the National Park Service (NPS) cuts a path, thru-bikers will have to detour back on FR 610 and FR 611 to AZ 67 for about 7 miles to reach the NPS Multi-Use Trail.

When you get on the trail south of the park boundary, you will be riding a section of single track that was cut in 2001. At the time of this printing, the NPS had not decided on the official AZT route through the park. The route given here is one of the options being considered. (You might see some Arizona Trail signs, however, until a decision is made.)

Southbound riders will enjoy some fast trail on their way to where the Kaibab Plateau drops away to the depths of the Grand Canyon. Northbounders will have more climbing, but the overall downhill grade they will get north of the park boundary should make up for it.

48 Biking the Arizona Trail

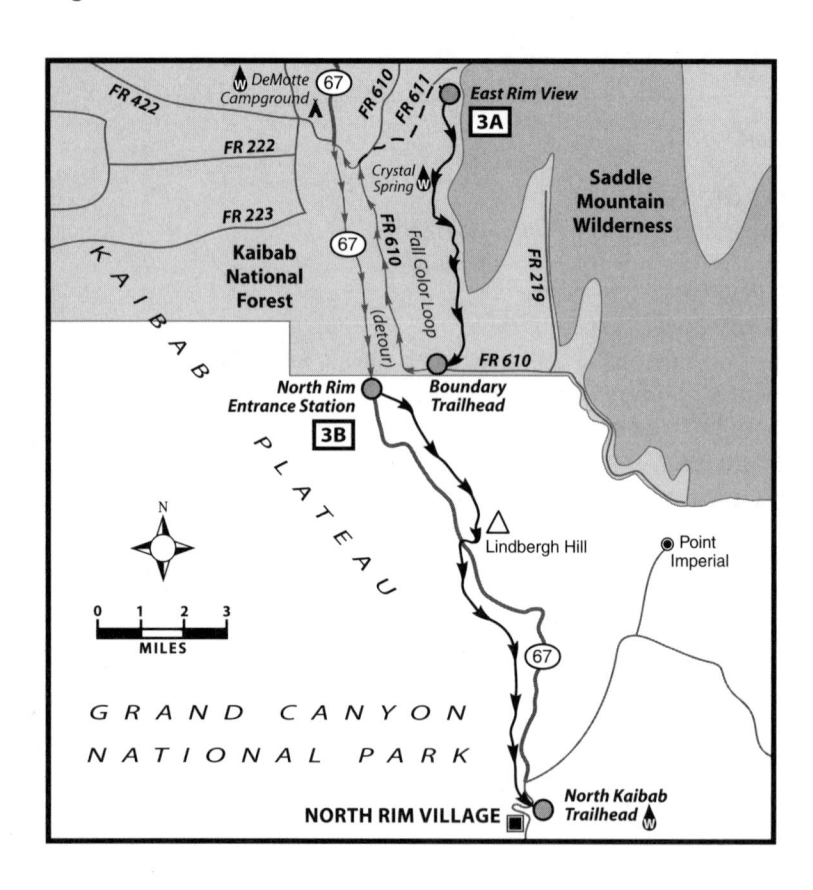

Segment 3A Total Elevation Gain: 300 Feet
Total Elevation Loss: 100 Feet
Change in Elevation: 200 Feet

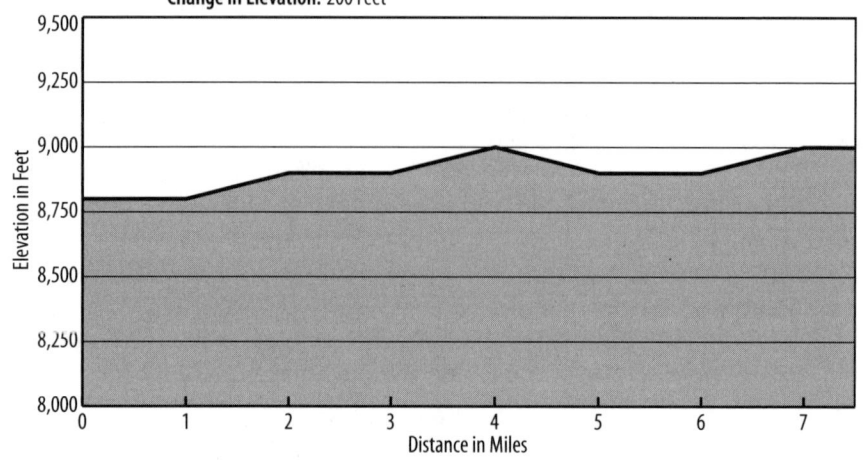

Route Description
3A: East Rim View to Boundary Trailhead

Southbound			Northbound
0.0	From the gravel parking lot, take the paved path to the overlook. Southbounders go right (south) on a fast section of single track that skirts the rim. Don't go so fast that you miss the views of Saddle Mountain, Marble Canyon, Tilted Mesa, and the Painted Desert.		7.3
0.9	The trail winds through a forest of large aspen trees.		6.4
1.1	As you drop off the East Rim, the trail gets loose, rocky, and steep.		6.2
2.4	Crystal Spring is contained in a small concrete tank behind a wood fence. This is an excellent water source (make sure to filter). You should camp at least 100 yards away from the spring.		4.9
	Northbounders: *You can fill up on water here and continue south to the dry camp just north of East Rim View.*		N
3.3	The trail leaves a faint road and jumps onto single track before ascending a steep section through a forest of aspen and Christmas-tree-sized evergreens.		4.0
3.7	Cross a gravel road, then in 0.2 mile cross a dirt road that is marked only with a rock cairn. Stay on the single track and go across a series of beautiful meadows.		3.6
4.1	As you leave the meadows, get ready for two steep ascents through forests of large white-barked aspen.		3.2
5.0	You might find some water in the sinkholes just south of Sourdough Well. The well is covered with a concrete cap. A road comes in but you'll stay on the well-marked single track that travels through a long, narrow meadow.		2.3
5.9	Continue a gradual ascent up a canyon on a well-defined trail.		1.4
7.0	After you cross FR 610, look for a signed trail heading up to your right (northwest) to the Boundary Trailhead.		0.3
7.3	There is a restroom and parking at the Boundary Trailhead.		0.0

Segment 3B Total Elevation Gain: 200 Feet
Total Elevation Loss: 900 Feet
Change in Elevation: 900 Feet

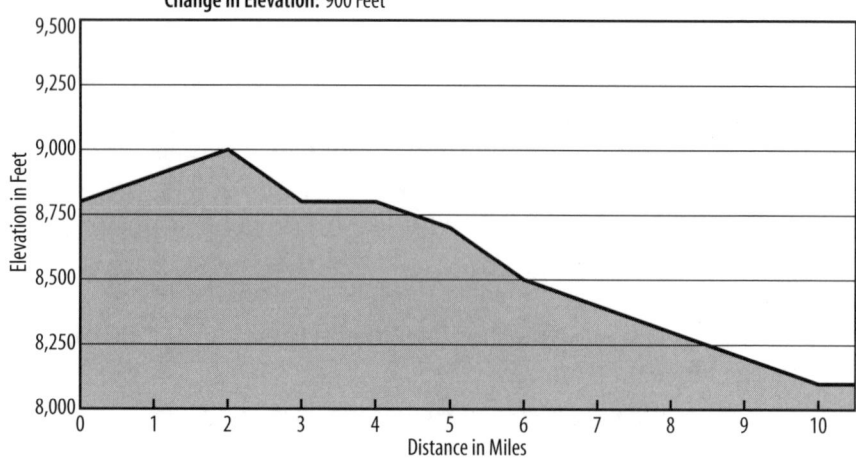

Route Description
3B: North Rim Entrance Station to North Kaibab Trailhead

Southbound		*Northbound*
0.0	Take the groomed trail that heads southeast from the pullout on the east side of the road.	10.1
0.5	Begin a difficult climb up an old road. The NPS plans to improve the trail here in the future.	9.6
0.9	The first climb ends here but you have a couple of shorter versions of the same thing ahead of you.	9.2
2.9	Look west for views of the heavily forested Kaibab Plateau. You'll pass several green boxes that are electric relay stations. They are called "coffin boxes" for good reason. Don't touch them!	7.2
3.4	The trail leaves the old road as it descends a series of switchbacks through a dark forest of evergreens. Climb up the other side of the drainage and get back on the old road. The trail condition improves as you continue southbound.	6.7
4.0	Turn right (north) onto a gravel road then cross the paved AZ 67. A signed trail goes into the forest and parallels a dirt road.	6.1

Southbound			Northbound
7.9	Enjoy a yahoo-fun gradual descent through aspen and pine. You'll go through some areas that have been burned to a crisp by forest fires.		2.2
8.6	Cross the road again before making a steep descent.		1.5
	Northbounders: Steep climb ahead!		N
8.9	At the bottom you are in Harvey Meadow. Turn left (south) on a dirt road and follow the signs.		1.2
9.3	The Widforss Trailhead parking lot has a restroom.		0.8
9.6	Leave the dirt road for a primitive road that ascends to the right (south).		0.5
10.1	The AZT jumps onto AZ 67. Watch for vehicle traffic as you cross the highway to the North Kaibab Trail parking lot and to the beginning of Trekking Segment 4. A water fountain is hidden behind some evergreens to the east of the trailhead sign.		0.0

Thru-Bikers

At this printing, a short section of trail connecting the Boundary Trailhead with the NPS Multi-Use Trail is incomplete. Most likely the connector will not be completed until 2003. Until then, thru-bikers will have to detour 7 miles back to AZ 67 and travel south to the entrance station to Grand Canyon National Park.

From the Boundary Trailhead, go west on FR 610 for 5 miles to FR 611. Take FR 611 to the west for 1.4 miles to AZ 67. Then go south on AZ 67 to the entrance station. The AZT starts on the east side of AZ 67 from the pull-out just south of the entrance station.

Mountain Lying Down

The Paiute word for the Kaibab Plateau translates into "mountain lying down." The first white settlers called the same area Buckskin Mountain. Surrounded by deep canyons and cliffs, the Kaibab Plateau is cut in half by the Colorado River and the Grand Canyon. From the South Rim to the edge of the Mogollon Rim, the same broad ridge is called the Coconino Plateau. The largest ponderosa pine forest in the world covers both plateaus.

Day Rides

Fall Color Loop (3A)
Total Distance: 15–22 miles
Difficulty: Easy
Technical Rating: Beginner

For an incredibly scenic loop ride, park at East Rim View and take the AZT to the south as outlined in the 3A Route Description. At the Boundary Trailhead, take FR 610 for 5 miles to the four-way intersection. Turn right (east) onto FR 611 and go 3 miles back to East Rim View. This 15-mile loop will take you through some of the best scenery the Kaibab Plateau offers.

If you want a longer 22-mile ride, at the four-way intersection continue on FR 610 for about 5 miles to where the road hits the AZT near Tater Canyon. Then ride the AZT for 2.4 miles south to East Rim View. Morning riders will have an excellent chance of spotting wild turkeys, mule deer, and blue grouse.

Multi-Use Trail (3B)
Total Distance: 10.1 miles (one way)
Difficulty: Easy
Technical Rating: Beginner

Arrange for a shuttle to drop you off at the park entrance station and ride south on the Multi-Use Trail for an excellent 10 miles of mostly downhill single track back to the North Kaibab Trail parking lot. The Multi-Use Trail starts at the pullout just south and east of the park entrance station (see Trail Access: From The Middle) and follows the 3B Route Description.

Segment 4: NORTH RIM to SOUTH RIM (Trekking)

Most Novel Place to Buy a Cold Drink:
Phantom Ranch Cantina, Grand Canyon

Total Distance: 24.0 miles
Distance from Utah: 68.5 miles
Distance to Mexico: 635.4 miles
Difficulty: Strenuous
Technical Rating: N/A
Trail Status: Proposed AZT route.

Season
The trail remains open all year. However, access to the North Kaibab Trailhead is closed once snow closes the roads to the North Rim. The upper portions of the trails might require the use of crampons during the winter months. In the summertime, avoid hiking during the heat of the day by starting your hike well before sunrise or just before sunset. Take a flashlight.

Hikers use a bridge to cross the Colorado River in Grand Canyon National Park.

Maps
Trails Illustrated: Grand Canyon National Park

Signage
Good

Water Sources
North Kaibab Trailhead, Supai Tunnel, Roaring Springs, Cottonwood Campground, Bright Angel Creek, Phantom Ranch, Colorado River, Pipe Creek, Garden Creek, Indian Garden, Three-Mile House, Mile-and-a-Half House. Some water sources are seasonal; refer to the route description.

Shuttle Service
The Trans-Canyon Shuttle (928-638-2820) runs between the North and South Rims once each day. Travel time is about 4 hours each way. The cost is $65 per person. Call to see if you can make arrangements to get bicycles shuttled across. Currently there are no facilities on either rim for storing your bikes as you hike across the canyon. If you can, make arrangements for someone to pick up your bikes.

Permits and Fees
Reservations are recommended (definitely get them before hiking in) for bunk or campground space in the cross-canyon corridor. For Phantom Ranch call Grand Canyon Lodges at (303) 297-2757 for advanced reservations or (928) 638-2631 for same-day accommodations. Bunk spaces at Phantom Ranch can include dinner and breakfast, which will make for some lightweight hiking. For information on how to get a camping permit, go to the trip-planning section of the National Park Service (NPS) web page www.nps.gov/grca/grandcanyon/index.htm or contact the Backcountry Information Center at (928) 638-7875. Mention that you are an AZT thru-hiker/biker on your permit request so that they can help facilitate your needs. The camping fee is $4 per person per night plus a $10 processing fee.

Trail Access
SOUTHBOUND: North Kaibab Trailhead
Drive south on AZ 67. The North Kaibab Trailhead is about 2 miles north of Grand Canyon Lodge. Water is available at the trailhead.
NORTHBOUND: Bright Angel Trailhead
Find the Bright Angel Trailhead in Grand Canyon Village, just off of AZ 64 between Bright Angel Lodge and West Rim Bus Stop. The trail starts behind Kolb Studio.

Trail Overview
Bicycles are prohibited on most trails inside Grand Canyon National Park. Bicycle purists can take US 89A from Jacob Lake to US 89 then take AZ 64 west to the Grand Canyon's South Rim—a 171-mile detour on dangerous paved highways. I don't recommend it. Besides, you'd miss out on the opportunity to do one of the most famous treks in the world. Why not give your rear end a break and walk across the canyon?

With an elevation gain and loss of almost 2 miles, this hike is best experienced in at least two days. Make reservations for one of the three campgrounds or splurge on a bunk at Phantom Ranch. At the ranch you'll find a cantina where you can purchase cold beer, lemonade, and snacks. Postcards and "packable" T-shirts are also for sale. After you cross the Colorado River, you will begin the tough grunt of a hike out of the canyon. Look up to see if any condors are flying overhead as they search for potential food. Don't become buzzard food! Bring plenty of snacks and water. Hike during the coolest parts of the day. Take rest breaks and prepare to hike after dark if necessary. Study the hiker safety information in the *Backcountry Trip Planner* (pick it up at the visitor center) and at all the trailhead signs as if your life depended on it. It does. The Grand Canyon is as unforgiving as it is beautiful.

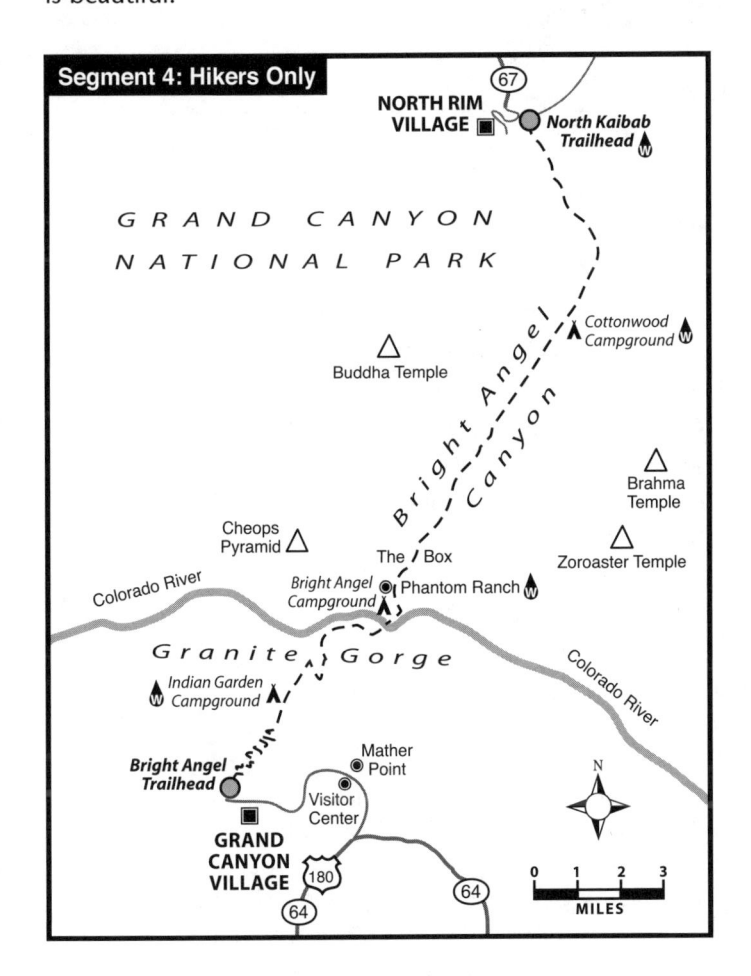

Segment 4

Total Elevation Gain: 4,400 Feet
Total Elevation Loss: 5,800 Feet
Change in Elevation: 5,800 Feet

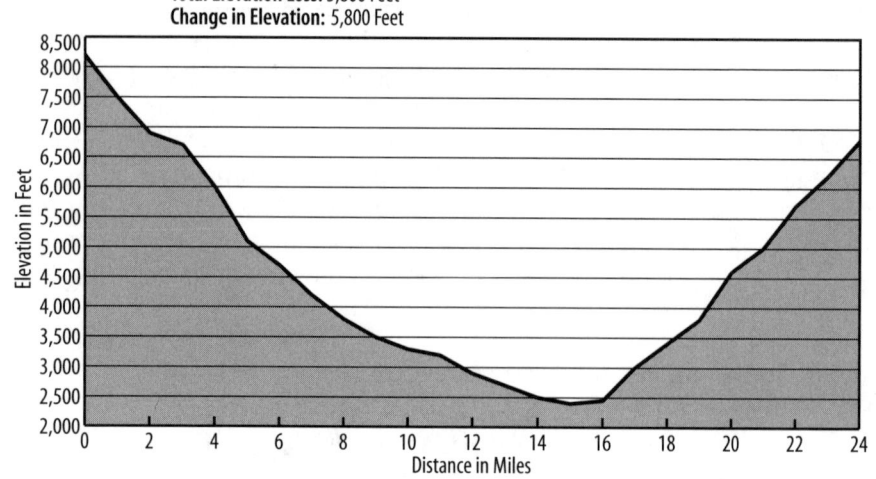

Route Description

Southbound / Northbound

Southbound		Northbound
0.0	Start at the North Kaibab Trailhead.	24.0
2.0	Go through a tunnel in the Supai rock layer.	22.0
4.7	At Roaring Springs, there is a trail to a day-use area that has water during the summer. Water is also available at the pump operator's residence.	19.3
6.9	Cottonwood Campground requires a permit. Drinking water is available during the summer. You can treat water from Bright Angel Creek all year round.	17.1
8.4	Take in the view of Ribbon Falls.	15.6
14.0	Phantom Ranch offers water, lodging, snacks, gifts, and a cantina. Reservations are required for lodging and meals.	10.0
14.2	Bright Angel Campground is on other side of the creek. Continue south. Take the right (west) fork at the trail sign. Water is available in front of the restrooms. Continue past the restrooms and cross the Colorado River over the silver bridge. On the other side of the bridge go right (west) onto the River Trail.	9.8
14.8	Follow signs to the left (south) past the stone structure called River Rest House. After leaving Pipe Creek, you begin the grueling climb up the Devil's Corkscrew. The trail levels out for a bit before you reach Indian Garden.	9.2

Southbound   *Northbound*

19.5	Indian Garden Ranger Station and Campground has benches in a nice shady spot. Water is available at the rest area near the trail sign. If you reach Indian Garden during the hottest part of the day, rest here until the upper canyon is in the shade.	4.5
21.0	Three-Mile Rest House provides water from spring through fall.	3.0
22.5	Mile-and-a-Half House is hidden in the trees above the trail. Drinking water is available here from spring through fall.	1.5
24.0	Whew! You made it to the Bright Angel Trailhead. The bus station is just down the hill to the west. If you're hungry, walk east along the Rim Trail to the grill and soda fountain at Bright Angel Lodge.	0.0

The California Condor

The Arizona Trail between Utah and Grandview Lookout travels through the habitat of a species that once seemed destined for extinction. In 1987, the last three condors living in the wild were captured and placed into a captive breeding program at the San Diego Zoo. After the successful reintroduction of condors in California, the Vermilion Cliffs were selected as a release site. Today more condors live in Arizona than existed in the world in 1982. About 22 of the largest birds in North America now make the Grand Canyon their home. Fossil evidence found in caves indicates that the Grand Canyon was a historical nesting area for these scavengers as well.

Condors can travel as far as 100 miles in a day and can have up to 10-foot wingspans. Unlike vultures, condors use vision instead of smell to find the carcasses on which they feed. These gregarious birds travel together in flocks and are extremely curious about human activity. You might get the thrill of having one fly overhead while you trek across the canyon. Sightings are common along the rim near the Bright Angel Trailhead as these magnificent birds hover on the thermal air currents that rise from the depths of the Grand Canyon. Photo by Ron Shaffer.

Grand Canyon National Park. Photo by Ron Shaffer.

Know **T**he **C**anyon's **H**istory, **S**tudy **R**ocks **M**ade **B**y **T**ime

That's the acronym memorized by park rangers in order to keep track of the Grand Canyon's geologic layers. **K**aibab limestone, **T**oroweep, **C**oconino sandstone, **H**ermit shale, **S**upai layer, **R**edwall limestone, **M**auve, **B**right Angel shale, and **T**onto layer. At the very bottom lies the 2-billion-year-old Zoroaster granite. Today, Grand Canyon geology remains an enigma to both sides of the faith vs. science debates. The seventh natural wonder of the world remains unfathomable to both young-earth creationists, who believe the world is less than 10,000 years old, and to secular geologists who cannot completely explain how the canyon was formed. It might be best to leave the human need to classify to the scientists as you descend into the depths that Reverend C. B. Spencer described in 1900 as:

"Horror! Tragedy! Silence! Death! Chaos! There is the awful canyon in five words."

Hopefully, like most of the 5 million visitors who come to the Grand Canyon each year, you will have a different experience.

Segment 5: TUSAYAN to GRANDVIEW LOOKOUT

Total Distance: 16.7 miles
(Thru-bikers add 9 road miles from Bright Angel Trailhead.)

Distance from Utah: 92.5 miles

Distance to Mexico: 611.4 miles

Difficulty: Easy

Technical Rating: Beginner

Trail Status: One of several proposed routes for the AZT.

Season
All year except when the trail is snow covered or extremely muddy.

Maps
USFS: Kaibab/Tusayan Ranger District
USGS: Tusayan East, Grandview Point NE
Tusayan Bike Trail Map: Can be found at ranger station or at the trailhead sign.

Riders can find fun trails through ponderosa pines between Tusayan and Grandview Lookout.

Signage
Good: Bicycle stickers on brown Carsonite posts.

Water Sources
Watson Tank is not recommended. Fill up at South Rim Village or Tusayan. Grandview Lookout is a convenient place to cache water.

Trail Access
THRU-BIKERS:
Until the National Park Service completes the proposed greenway path between the rim and Tusayan, thru-bikers will have to use AZ 64 to get to the start of Segment 5. From Bright Angel Trailhead, cross the railroad tracks and follow the signs to the park exit. On your way out, you will pass access to the campground and the general store. Go past Mather Point Overlook, then go through the Desert View intersection staying on AZ 64

south to Tusayan. The entrance station is about 7.5 miles from the Bright Angel Trailhead, and 1.2 miles south of the park entrance you'll find the Tusayan Trailhead on the right (west) side of AZ 64.

SOUTHBOUND: Tusayan Bike Trailhead
Trailhead parking is just north of Tusayan and 1.2 miles south of the park entrance station on the west side of AZ 64. The trailhead sign has maps and a trail register.

NORTHBOUND: Grandview Lookout
(See Southbound, Segment 6, p. 64)

Trail Overview
At the time of this printing, there is no route designated for the AZT between Grand Canyon Village and Grandview Lookout. However, this segment is the perfect mountain bike connection between the village of Tusayan and Grandview Lookout. From the Tusayan Bike Trailhead, you can enjoy a fun section of single track and old roads through pines and shallow limestone canyons. You have a good chance of spotting elk on this rarely traveled segment. Loop opportunities from 3 to 32 miles in length are available for day riders. An ascent with tight switchbacks might force some riders to dismount, but most of the route is built for bicycles. At Grandview Lookout, you can climb the fire tower for views of the canyon and the San Francisco Peaks. Southbound thru-bikers will be on the other side of those peaks in two or three days.

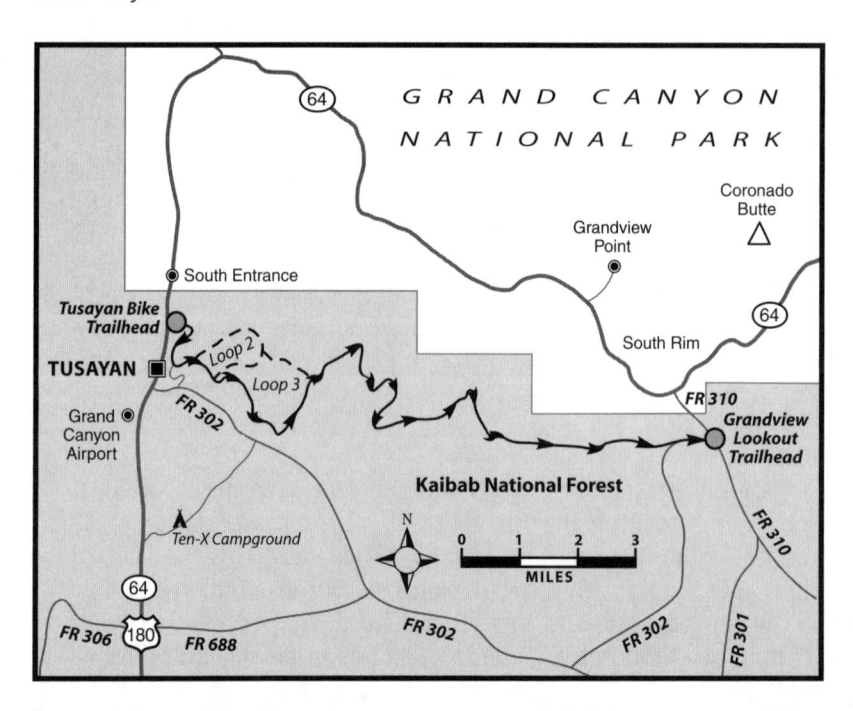

Segment 5 Total Elevation Gain: 900 Feet
Total Elevation Loss: 50 Feet
Change in Elevation: 900 Feet

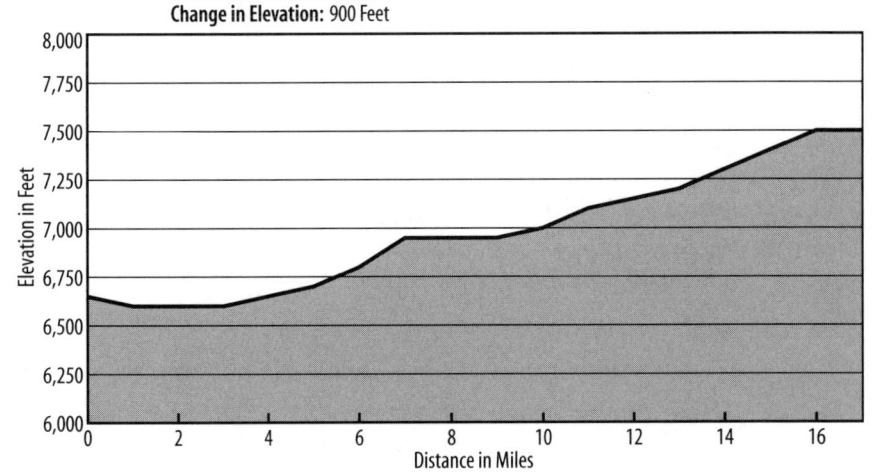

Route Description

Southbound / *Northbound*

Southbound		Northbound
0.0	Take the path to the north of the trailhead sign.	16.7
0.3	Go through the tunnel under AZ 64, then get on a trail that weaves through the pine forest.	16.4
1.1	Take the right (west) fork onto Loops 2 and 3. Look for the brown posts with bicycle stickers that mark the trail. Stay on the south (right) side of the loops.	15.6
1.9	Behind the town of Tusayan, the trail goes left (east) onto an old road and through a shallow limestone canyon.	14.8
2.4	Stay on Loop 3 when Loop 1 comes in from the left (northeast).	14.3
4.7	Stay left (northeast) of the fence around the refuse transfer station. Look for signs directing you onto a faint road that climbs gradually to the north.	12.0
5.9	Cross FR 2709 at the wooden sign that says it's 10 miles to Grandview Lookout. You are leaving Loop 3 now for Trail #4. This trail heads east and is marked by brown posts with bicycle stickers. You will follow these signs all the way to Grandview Lookout.	10.8
Loop	*Tusayan Bike Trails:* At the wooden sign, you can take Loop 3 back to the Tusayan Bike Trailhead for a 9-mile loop.	

Southbound		*Northbound*
8.2	Look for the signs that direct you to the left (northeast) onto a faint trail along a fence.	8.5
8.7	The trail might be faint where you leave the fence just before an earthen dam (Upper Ten-X Tank). Go up the slope for a short distance. Look for a sign that directs you onto a dirt road near a "Closed to Motorized Vehicles" sign.	8.0
9.2	You'll come to a fork. Follow the signs to the right and down.	7.5
9.9	Begin a mile-long ascent.	6.8
11.1	Descend, and look for the trail sign at the bottom.	5.6
12.3	After passing Watson Tank (poor water source) go through the gate and take the single-track trail.	4.4
12.8	Begin a short ascent with tight switchbacks. At the top of the hill, continue on the bumpy single track that will take you into Grandview.	3.9
15.4	Cross a dirt road.	1.3
16.1	Go through a wire gate.	0.6
16.7	Cross the gravel road to Grandview Lookout parking where there is a restroom, a fire lookout tower, and an interpretive sign. (No water.)	0.0
Loop	*Take AZ 64 or FR 302 back to Tusayan for a 34-mile loop.*	

Day Rides

Tusayan Bike Trails (Loops)
Total Distance: 3–9 miles
Difficulty: Easy
Technical Rating: Beginner

The USFS has built some fine mountain bike trails in this area. Start from the Southbound trail access at the Tusayan Bike Trailhead. Maps for the three loops are usually available at the trailhead, or you can follow the route description.

Segment 6 — GRANDVIEW LOOKOUT to MOQUI STAGE STOP

Best Historical Trail

Total Distance: 18.3 miles
Distance from Utah: 109.2 miles
Distance to Mexico: 594.7 miles
Difficulty: Easy
Technical Rating: Beginner
Trail Status: Official AZT.

Season
All year except when snow covers the route.
Can be muddy during wet weather.

Maps
USFS: Kaibab National Forest, Tusayan Ranger District
USGS: Grandview Point NE, Harbison Tank, Peterson Flat

Signage
Good: AZT stickers on Carsonite posts and AZT brand on wooden posts.

Water Sources: Russell Tank

Rabbitbrush bloom under the Arizona sky near Moqui Stage Stop.

Trail Access
SOUTHBOUND: Grandview Lookout via Grand Canyon
From Grand Canyon National Park, take AZ 64 east toward Desert View. About 2 miles east of the Grandview Point turnoff, take FR 310 south for 1.3 miles to Grandview Lookout parking area. The AZT starts behind the trailhead display sign. A pit toilet and trash cans are available, but there is no water. You can reach Russell Tank Trailhead by continuing south on FR 310, then taking FR 311 south to the trailhead.

You can avoid paying the park fee by reaching the trailhead via dirt roads. From AZ 64, just south of Tusayan and 0.8 mile north of the airport entrance, take FR 302 east and follow signs for 16 miles to Grandview Lookout. Except during muddy conditions, these gravel roads are accessible by two-wheel-drive vehicles. There are several primitive camping spots in the area.

NORTHBOUND: Moqui Stage Stop
(see Southbound, Segment 7, p. 69)

Trail Overview
At Grandview Lookout, the AZT begins to follow a historic stagecoach route all the way to Flagstaff. This section travels through pine-oak woodland and is good for beginners wanting to practice self-contained bikepacking. Primitive campsites with sunrise views can be found along the route and several loop options exist. Beginners might need to dismount on a few short, steep climbs but most of the trail is rolling with a gradual grade. Cattle gates will force you on and off your bike many times, but the views of the Painted Desert as the trail skirts the Coconino Rim should make up for it. Watch for signs of elk and deer.

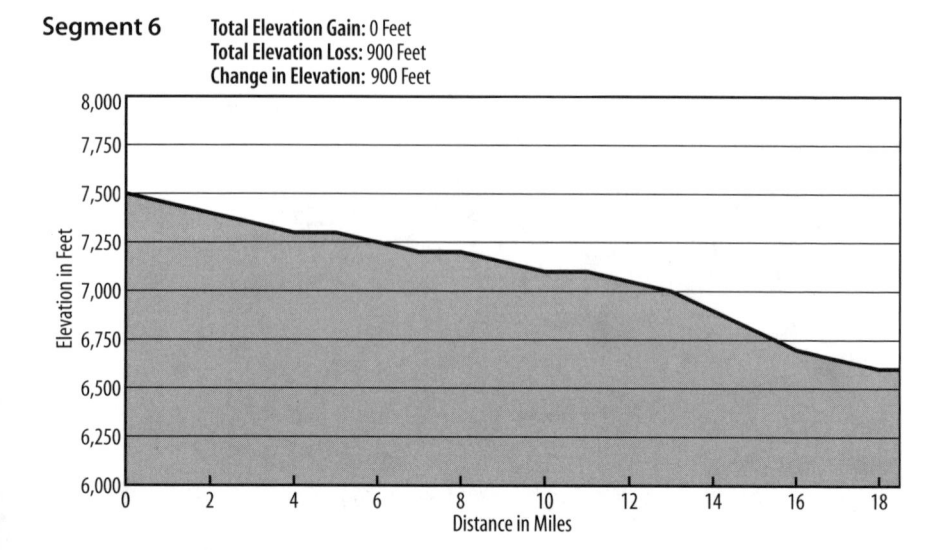

Segment 6
Total Elevation Gain: 0 Feet
Total Elevation Loss: 900 Feet
Change in Elevation: 900 Feet

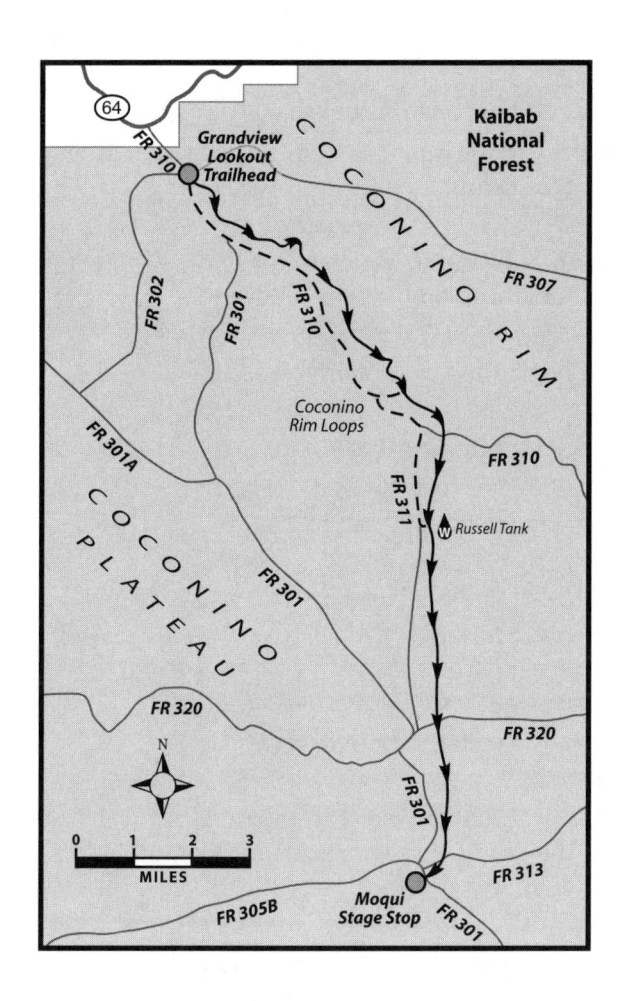

Route Description

Southbound *Northbound*

0.0	Go under the AZT sign onto a gravel nature path.	18.3
0.2	At the "Will mistletoe be wiped out?" sign, leave the nature trail by taking the dirt path to the left (east).	18.1
0.3	Cross FR 307.	18.0
1.9	Look for a nice view to the east as you ride through a cleared area.	16.4
2.9	The primitive (no water) campsite has a sunrise view over the Coconino Rim.	15.4
3.3	Take in the best view of the Painted Desert on this route and more primitive campsites with views.	15.0
6.5	Pass through the first of many cattle gates.	11.8

Southbound			*Northbound*
7.3	Travel over a series of short steep sections.		11.0
8.3	Take the double track to the right (west) as directed by signs. This is a bike detour around steep switchbacks.		10.0
8.4	Leave the double track by taking a path to the left (south). There is a dry camp on the slope above this intersection.		9.9
10.3	Cross FR 310 and begin the Russell Wash section of the AZT.		8.0
Loop	**Coconino Rim Loop #1:** *Take FR 310 north for 6.8 miles back to Grandview Lookout.*		
12.0	Go through a cattle gate. Russell Wash parking is on the right (west). Russell Tank (treat the water) is on the left (east) side of the trail.		6.3
Loop	**Coconino Rim Loop #2:** *Take FR 331A right (west) from parking area to bottom of hill then take FR 311 and FR 310 north for 9 miles back to Grandview Lookout.*		
15.1	Cross a road. There is a metal stock tank in this area that might have water.		3.2
16.4	South of the cattle gate, take an old road to the right (west). Watch for the brown Carsonite posts marking the AZT.		1.9

Moqui Stage Stop

From 1892 to 1901, the Flagstaff–Grand Canyon Stagecoach transported people and supplies to the Grand Canyon. The trip took all day and stopped at three staging areas along the way so that passengers and horses could rest before continuing on the dusty, kidney-busting ride. At Moqui Stage Stop, a cistern held water for thirsty horses and passengers. Remains of this stone tank can still be seen next to the Arizona Trail, but you won't find any water at this lonely outpost today. When the Grand Canyon Railroad was completed in 1901, the stage route was abandoned.

By riding from Grand Canyon to Flagstaff along the stage line, you are continuing a 100-year tradition. In 1896 a group of Flagstaff bicycle enthusiasts established the Coconino Cycling Club. Since then, the club continues to bike the entire 70-mile route nearly every fall. In 1897, the hardy bikers won a race against the six-horse stagecoach to the Grand Canyon. They were riding single speeds and in those days there was no such thing as a suspension fork. For more information on the history of the Flagstaff–Grand Canyon Stagecoach Line, see Suggested Reading in Appendix F.

Southbound   **Northbound**

18.0   Cross a road then take a trail up a short steep section. You are now in piñon-juniper forest.   0.3

18.3   After crossing under a power line, take a signed trail that descends to the right (west) for 0.25 mile to Moqui Stage Stop. Another trail sign points a way to the National Forest boundary that is 5 miles to the south. This trail is faint and will hit FR 301 in less than 1.6 miles. Bikers should follow the path to Moqui Stage Stop. You will pass a dry campsite and what remains of the cistern that provided water for horses and passengers on the stagecoach route. There is an interpretive sign where the trail hits FR 301. This is the beginning of Segment 7 and a good place to cache water or to meet vehicle support. North of the sign, look for the foundations of other buildings associated with the historic rest stop.   0.0

Day Rides

Coconino Rim Loops
Total Distance: 17–21 miles
Difficulty: Easy
Technical Rating: Beginner

These loops provide views of the Painted Desert from the edge of the Coconino Rim, as well as opportunities to see elk. Refer to the route description for directions.

Russell Tank to Moqui Stage Stop
Total Distance: 12.6 miles
Difficulty: Easy
Technical Rating: Beginner

The portion of the AZT described in Segment 6 runs along a historic stagecoach route with great views of the San Francisco Peaks. Park at either the Russell Tank Trailhead (see Trail Access: Southbound, this segment) or Moqui Stage Stop (see Trail Access: Southbound in Segment 7, p. 69) and ride out and back, or set up a shuttle and bike the 6.3 miles one way.

Segment 7: MOQUI STAGE STOP to FOREST ROAD 523

Total Distance: 35.1 miles
Distance from Utah: 127.5 miles
Distance to Mexico: 576.4 miles
Difficulty: Moderate
Technical Rating: Beginner
Trail Status: Official AZT.

Season
All year except during periods when the trail is snow-covered. Rainy weather can make some parts of the route muddy to the point of being unridable.

Maps
USFS: Coconino National Forest and Kaibab National Forest, Tusayan District
USGS: Peterson Flat, Lockwood Canyon, Chapel Mountain, SP Mountain, White Horse Hills

Signage
Good: AZT stickers on Carsonite posts and AZT brand on wooden posts.

Expect the company of cattle while biking near Babbitt Ranch.

Water Sources
Muddy water at Lockwood Tanks, and access to water at Tubs and Cedar Ranches if urgently needed. The junction of the trail with FR 417 at Cedar Ranch is a good spot to meet vehicle support or cache water.

Trail Access
SOUTHBOUND: Moqui Stage Stop
From Flagstaff, go north on US 180 to AZ 64. Head north on AZ 64 toward the Grand Canyon. Near milepost 223, turn right (east) onto FR 320. Follow FR 320 past Red Butte to the intersection with FR 301. Then drive south on FR 301 to the Forest Service sign for Moqui Stage Stop. From Grandview Lookout (see Segment 6, p. 64), you can drive south on FR 301 all the way to Moqui or you can go south on FR 311 from Russell Tank to FR 301 and then to Moqui.
NORTHBOUND: Intersection of FR 523 and FR 416
(see Southbound, Segment 8, p. 74)

Trail Overview
Welcome to cattle country. As you continue paralleling the stagecoach route, this segment will take you through a working cattle ranch. Babbitt Ranches, Inc. has granted access to users of the AZT on a series of dirt roads between the Kaibab and Coconino Forest boundaries. Respect the rules as stated on the Babbitt Ranches signs. Leave gates as you found them and keep alert for vehicles, as these roads are open to motorized travel. You probably won't see many trucks or people. Cattle and pronghorn antelope are more likely to keep you company on this lonely stretch of trail. The San

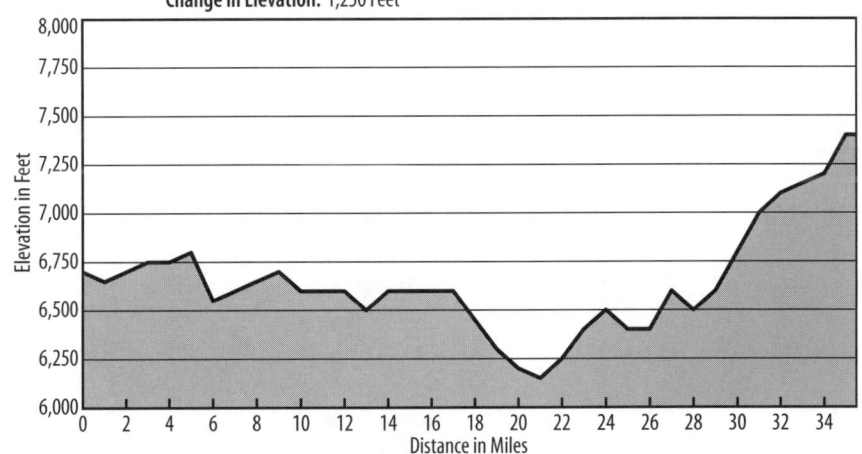

Segment 7 Total Elevation Gain: 1,800 Feet
Total Elevation Loss: 1,100 Feet
Change in Elevation: 1,250 Feet

Francisco Peaks get bigger and closer as Southbounders cut the distance to Flagstaff. If you camp in this area, elk and coyote might serenade you to sleep. This section is rated moderate because it has long flat sections between several steep climbs. The 600-foot climb over the saddle at Missouri Bill Hill will probably involve some pushing, and the route is rocky. You might find the wide-open spaces and piñon-juniper forest boring after a while. Don't worry; the scenery is going to change significantly on the next segment.

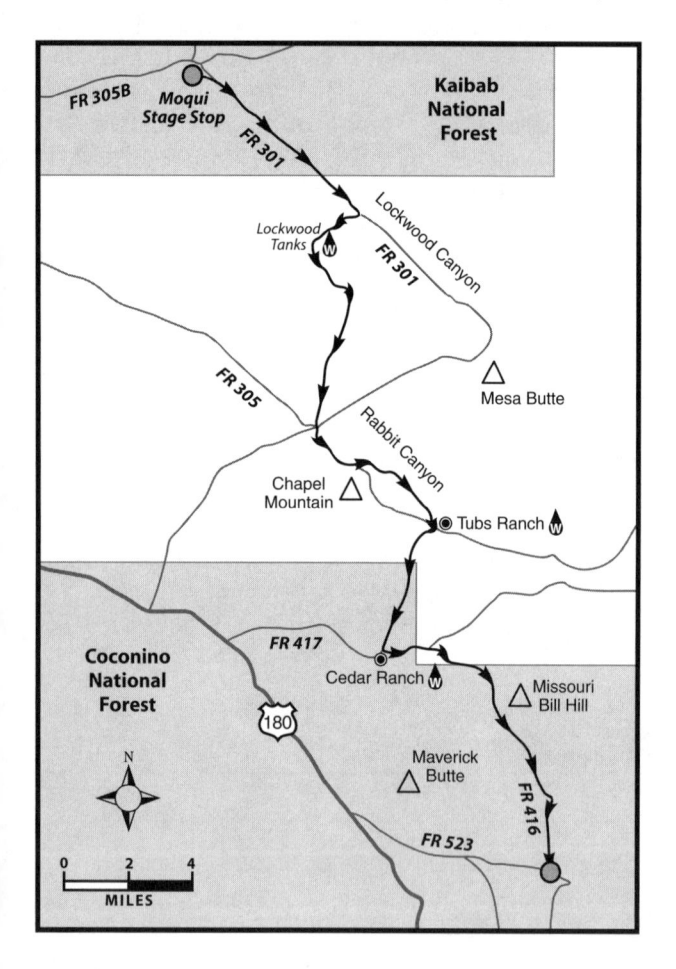

Route Description

Southbound		Northbound
0.0	At the Moqui Stage Stop interpretive sign go left (east) on FR 301.	35.1
1.5	A faint AZT path crosses here, but bikers should stay on the road.	33.6
3.4	Several roads will come in from both sides, but stay on FR 301. Begin a gradual descent to Lockwood Tank.	31.7
4.7	Cross the cattle guard at the Kaibab National Forest boundary. The trail travels through a combination of state and private lands for the next several miles.	30.4
6.3	At Lockwood Tank, go right (southwest) through a gap in the fence. Look for a faded AZT post. Stay to the right and head into a shallow canyon on a rutted double track. Expect to see cattle in the area.	28.8
8.2	Make the short, steep climb on the other side (west) of Upper Lockwood Tank.	26.9
11.5	Stay on course as several roads come in from the left (west).	23.6
12.5	Pass a rusty water tank.	22.6
14.8	Go under a power line. This is a confusing area. Look for AZT signs on the other side of the water tank here.	20.3
16.1	Follow a flat section of double track with views of Red Mountain to the west.	19.0
16.7	Begin a mile-long descent down a drainage into Rabbit Canyon.	18.4
18.4	Go through a metal gate. The road improves over the next 7 miles.	16.7
19.7	Begin a descent down graded switchbacks to Tubs Ranch with views of the San Francisco Peaks and volcanic cinder cones.	15.4
20.4	Go uphill towards the right (west).	14.7
20.6	Go through a gate near a water tank. This is Tubs Ranch (private property). The stock tank should have water. You will get on the well-maintained FR 9008A.	14.5
20.9	At the cattle guard, follow AZT signs and bear left (east).	14.2
23.6	Cross another cattle guard.	11.5

Southbound		Northbound
24.8	Just north of the metal gate, look for a wooden sign for the Babbitt Ranch Passage of the AZT at Cedar Ranch on FR 417. Turn left (east) onto a rocky road marked with AZT posts.	10.3
25.2	Stay on course as several roads intersect the one you are on. Keep looking for the AZT posts that mark the route.	9.9
25.9	Go through a metal gate. A sign will indicate that you are on FR 417.	9.2
26.1	Begin a 0.5-mile ascent. Can you tell that you are traveling through an ancient volcanic field?	9.0
27.2	Go through another gate and continue along a fence line.	7.9
28.0	After a short, rocky ascent, follow signs to the right (south) onto FR 416.	7.1
28.8	Begin a climb to and over the saddle to the right (west) of Missouri Bill Hill.	6.3
30.0	At the metal gate, the toughest part of the climb is over.	5.1
30.6	FR 900SB comes in from the west. Continue on FR 416 as you weave through the piñon-juniper forest.	4.5
31.5	Check out the nice piñon in the grassy area to the east. Continue on course. The road surface will get smoother over the next 3 miles.	3.6
32.3	Cross a dirt road.	2.8
32.9	Go through a gate.	2.2
33.8	The scenery will change as you enter a ponderosa forest.	1.3
35.1	Cross a cattle guard just before you reach the intersection with FR 523 and the beginning of Segment 8.	0.0

Ancient Volcanoes

Missouri Bill Hill is one of the 400 cinder cones that make up the area known to geologists as the San Francisco Volcanic Field. The cone-shaped hills you see at the foot of Humphreys Peak are what remains from the basaltic lava eruptions that occurred over 900 years ago. About a million years ago, a major eruption created the San Francisco Peaks, including Arizona's tallest mountain, Humphreys Peak. The lava flows left behind a surface of jagged rocks that make portions of Segment 7 unpleasant for bikers. So blame it on the volcanoes.

Segment 8 FOREST ROAD 523 to BUFFALO PARK

Total Distance: 32.6 miles

Distance from Utah: 162.6 miles

Distance to Mexico: 541.3 miles

Difficulty: Moderate

Technical Rating: Intermediate

Trail Status: Near a route proposed for the AZT.

Season
Spring, summer, and fall. In winter, much of the route can be covered in snow. In summer, this area is prone to severe afternoon thunderstorms.

Maps
USFS: Coconino National Forest, Mount Elden/Dry Lake Hills Trail System
USGS: White Horse Hills, Humphreys Peak, Sunset Crater West, Flagstaff East

The views of the San Francisco Peaks fill up the sky as a biker pedals south to Flagstaff.

Signage
Fair: AZT stickers and FS road numbers on Carsonite posts. Some areas are signed poorly.

Water Sources
Snowbowl Ski Area, Schultz Tank, Buffalo Park

Trail Access
SOUTHBOUND: Forest Road 523 and FR 416
Take US 180 north from Flagstaff for approximately 13 miles. 1.5 miles north of the Kendrick Park picnic area and 0.3 mile south of mile marker 339 look for FR 523 on the right (east). Take FR 523 for 4.8 miles east to the intersection with FR 416. Look for a wire gate and AZT signs.
NORTHBOUND: Buffalo Park
From downtown Flagstaff, take San Francisco Street or Fort Valley Road (US 180) north to Forest Avenue. Turn right (east) on Forest Avenue. Go through two stoplights, and continue about 0.6 mile to Gemini Drive. Take a left (north) on Gemini and proceed to the end of the road where you'll find parking, a rest area, and a water fountain.

Trail Overview
At this printing, the AZT remains undesignated from Kelly Tank to Buffalo Park. An equestrian bypass goes around the east side of the peaks and hits the AZT south of Fisher Point. Segment 8 follows a route near the proposed San Francisco Peaks Passage by connecting several prime mountain biking trails including a section of the epic Around the Peaks Ride. There are no AZT signs south of Kelly Tank so use your map and Forest Service markers as you follow the trail description. Southbounders will ascend to the cool aspen and fir forests the likes of which haven't been seen since leaving the north rim. You will be treated to spectacular vistas of the San Francisco Peaks along the way. Starting at the north end, the dirt and gravel road surface is relatively easy riding until you leave Hart Prairie (FR 151) and start up a trail local mountain bikers call "the rock garden." South of Freidlein Prairie road, you begin riding a series of challenging single-track trails. Weatherford, Sunset, Brookbank, and Lower Oldham are part of the Mt. Elden/Dry Lake Hills Trail System. You'll see why Flagstaff is a favorite with mountain bikers. Expect some company. Northbounders will face a few mile-long climbs that require portages (pushing). An easier alternative is given in the route description. If you can suffer through the climbs, you will be rewarded with sections of smooth single track through shady alpine forests, views of Flagstaff, and wildflower-filled meadows. Several day-ride options are available, and there are many primitive camping opportunities as you continue to follow the stagecoach route to Hart Prairie. Anybody with energy left over for summit bagging can hike a strenuous 4.5 miles to the top of Humphreys Peak (12,633 feet) from the ski lift at Snowbowl.

Segment 8 75

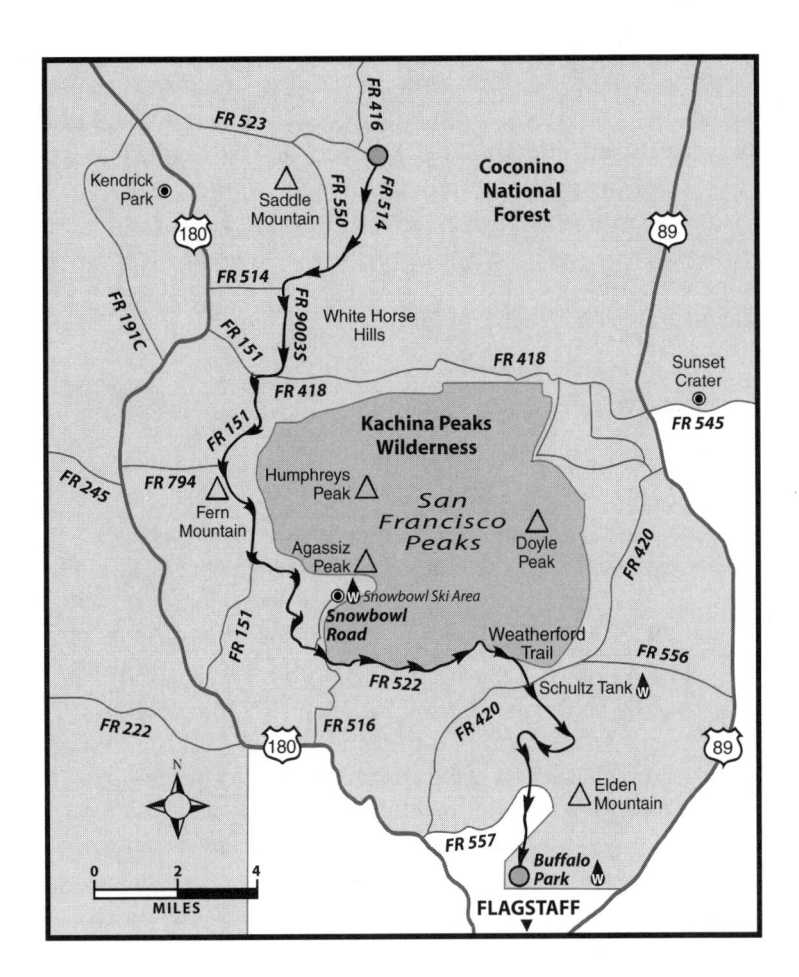

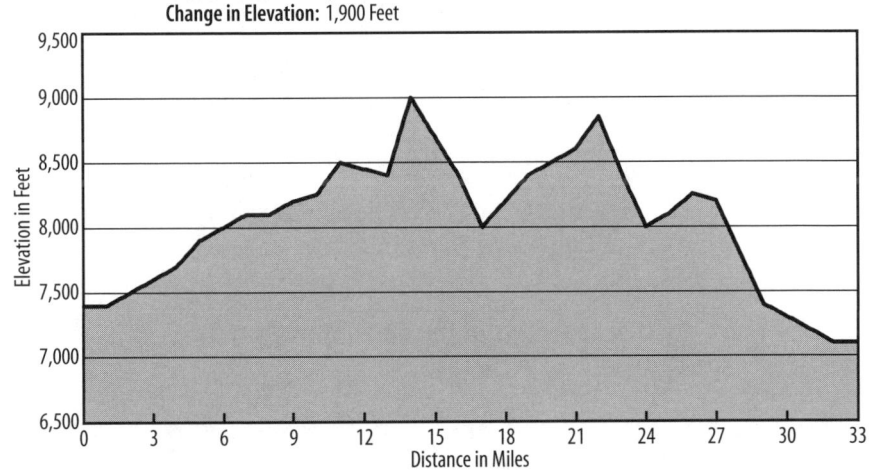

Route Description

Southbound   *Northbound*

0.0	At the intersection of FR 523 and FR 416, the AZT goes cross-country to the south. Bicyclists should continue east on FR 523 for 0.7 mile to FR 514.	32.6
0.7	Turn right (south) onto FR 514.	31.9
2.0	Travel south over a red gravel road through an area burned by forest fires with expansive views of the San Francisco Peaks to the southeast.	30.6
3.7	Pass Kelly Tank (an unreliable water source) on the left (east).	28.9
4.1	FR 550 comes in from the right (west).	28.5
4.9	As the scenery opens up, look for the "Kendrick Park" sign. Near here the Forest Service has a cabin available for rent through the "Room with a View" program. Call (928) 526-0866 for reservations and directions.	27.7
5.1	Just past the "Kendrick Park" sign but before (north of) the cattle guard, take primitive FR 9003S. Follow this unsigned road into the pines and toward the view of the peaks. You will go through an area burned by a forest fire. As you travel through Horsethief Pass for 2.4 miles, the road braids around rough areas. Stay southbound.	27.5
7.5	At FR 418, go right (west) and follow the dirt road for 0.5 mile to FR 151.	25.1
8.0	Take FR 151 to the left (south), following the sign that says "Hwy 180, 9 miles." You are now on the Around the Peaks Ride. Begin a long ascent.	24.6
9.9	The route intersects a trail to the historic Little Spring Relay Station. Campsites can be found 0.25 mile down FR 418B.	22.7
10.0	Begin ascending as you enter an aspen forest shading a lush, fern-covered floor. Fall colors here are unbelievably beautiful.	22.6
10.2	Begin descending.	22.4
11.4	Look up to see views of the Snowbowl ski runs on the peak to the south.	21.2

Segment 8

Southbound		**Northbound**
13.1	Immediately after crossing a cattle guard, look for a road with a metal gate to the left (east), just north of a cattle chute. Parking is on the right (west) side of FR 151. Head up this road onto a route known as the "rock garden."	19.5
13.7	This is a confusing area, so stay alert. When the dirt road comes in from the southwest, stay left on the uphill side of the meadow. The trail is rocky and steep.	18.9
14.0	Near the small pond, the trail might be faint and covered by grass. Look for bike tracks as you move up and toward the forest edge on the southern end of the meadow. Along the forest edge, you will find a defined trail that heads uphill towards the peaks.	18.6
14.3	Reach a parking area on the paved Snowbowl Road. Turn right (south) and downhill. You are on the highest point of the route here as you reach 9,000 feet in elevation.	18.3
Hike	*Arizona Snowbowl side hike:* Snowbowl Ski Area is 1.4 miles uphill from where this route crosses the paved road. Memorial Day through Labor Day, you can eat at the restaurant and take the ski lift up to 11,500 feet for some impressive views (10 a.m. to 4 p.m). Pay phones, restrooms, water, and a gift shop are available during business hours. From Labor Day through mid-October, the ski lift is open on Friday, Saturday, and Sunday only.
17.5	Turn left (east) onto dirt FR 522 (Freidlein Prairie Road).	15.1
17.6	Roads to the right (south) lead to primitive campsites (no water). Stay to the left (north) on the road that looks the most traveled.	15.0
18.2	Pass a corral and peak views to the left (east).	14.4
18.8	There are nice dry campsites in this area.	13.8
20.5	The road switchbacks up a grassy hill.	12.1
21.3	FR 6273 comes in from the right (west). Continue on FR 522 to the parking area. Take a non-motorized road at the end of the parking lot.	11.3
21.7	Pass the Kachina Trail sign, and then follow along the Wilderness boundary for the next few miles.	10.9

Southbound			Northbound
22.1	At the wooden sign, take Weatherford Trail down to the right (southwest). Begin a winding descent with some rocky sections.		10.5
23.7	Cross over the pipeline route and follow the sign to Schultz Tank.		8.9
24.0	At Schultz Pass Road (FR 420), go west (right) to the parking lot on the south side of the road. (See loop/alternate route described at mile 29.4) You are leaving the Around the Peaks Ride at this point. Schultz Tank has water (treat first). From the southwest side of the parking lot, take the Sunset Trail. Stay on Sunset past the intersection with Little Elden Trail. Begin a steep climb. Don't forget to look back to catch the views.		8.6
25.7	At the top of the climb, look for a sign explaining forest-fire ecology. Now you get to coast for a while.		6.9
26.0	At the trail intersection, go right (south) onto Brookbank Trail. A sign says that Buffalo Park is 5.7 miles from here. Roll down over the rocks and roots.		6.6

Taking a break near the volcanic cinder cones north of the San Francisco Peaks.

Segment 8

Southbound		Northbound
27.0	After the meadow, the trail levels out some as you traverse a ridgeline. This shady section of single track through alpine forest makes the climbs worth the effort.	5.6
27.9	An unmarked trail comes in from the right (west). This trail leads to the Dry Lake Hills area, which would make a scenic place to camp if you filled up with water at Schultz Tank.	4.7
28.0	At the benchmark, check your brakes before you start descending the rocky switchbacks of Lower Brookbank Trail.	4.6
28.3	**Northbounders:** *Be careful here. Avoid the eroded trail that comes in from the left (west).*	N 4.3
28.4	There are views of Flagstaff to the south. The big white structure is the Northern Arizona University (NAU) Sky Dome.	4.2
29.2	Leave Brookbank Trail and go right (west) onto FR 557 (Elden Lookout Road).	3.4
29.4	Leave FR 557 at the trailhead sign on your left (south), and begin a gradual descent down the Lower Oldham Trail.	3.2
Loop	**Alternate and Loop Route:** *Northbound bikers wanting to avoid the steep switchbacks on Brookbank and day riders looking for a challenging day loop might return to Schultz Tank by following these directions. Take FR 557 down (west) for 2.7 miles to FR 420. Make a 6-mile gradual climb up FR 420 to Schultz Tank. Expert mountain bikers can choose to ride down the Rocky Ridge Trail instead of FR 557.*	Loop
29.6	Go down a rocky trail along the base of a boulder field. When you reach the bottom, look for funky boulders that resemble gigantic beach balls.	3.0
30.2	At the junction with the Rocky Ridge access trail, follow signs to Buffalo Park and start a 0.4 mile ascent through some technical terrain.	2.4
31.4	Cross a pipeline route and then a wide dirt path. Stay on the course marked by brown posts with white bicycle stickers.	1.2
31.7	At the 0.7 mile to Buffalo Park sign, climb a short technical section.	0.9

Southbound		*Northbound*
32.1	Go through a gate at the Coconino National Forest sign, then bear right (west) onto a gravel path on the other side of the pump station.	0.5
32.6	The Buffalo Park parking area is on the other side of the park entrance shelter. A water fountain is on the north side of the shelter.	0.0

Day Rides

> ### *Schultz Tank to Buffalo Park*
> ***Total Distance:*** 8.6 miles
> ***Difficulty:*** Moderate
> ***Technical Rating:*** Intermediate
>
> Get someone to drop you and your bike off at the Sunset Trailhead at Schultz Tank and ride the route (from mile 24.0 as detailed in the route description) down to Buffalo Park/Flagstaff. This will be a mostly downhill ride on fine mountain biking trails through extremely scenic forests. To get to the Sunset Trailhead, go 2.5 miles north of Flagstaff on US 180 to FR 420 (Schultz Pass Road). Continue west on FR 420 for about 5 miles to the parking area at Schultz Tank.

Segment 9: BUFFALO PARK to FLAGSTAFF URBAN TRAIL

Summer flowers on the mesa at Buffalo Park.

Best Trail Town: Flagstaff

Total Distance: 2.8 miles
Distance from Utah: 195.2 miles
Distance to Mexico: 508.7 miles
Difficulty: Easy
Technical Rating: Beginner
Trail Status: A proposed urban route for the AZT.

Season
All year.

Maps
USFS: Coconino National Forest
Flagstaff city maps

Signage
Good: Use city road signs.

Water Sources
Buffalo Park, many sources in town.

Trail Access
SOUTHBOUND: Buffalo Park
Trailhead parking is off of Gemini Drive (see Northbound, Segment 8, p. 74).
NORTHBOUND: Flagstaff Urban Trail System
Access is on Babbitt Way (see Southbound, Segment 10, p. 74).

Trail Overview
This section is for thru-bikers and follows an urban route connecting Buffalo Park with the AZT on the south side of Flagstaff. Several restaurants, hotels, and resupply opportunities exist right on or near the trail. A paved bikeway along Historic Route 66 (Business I-40) provides easy access to downtown Flagstaff.

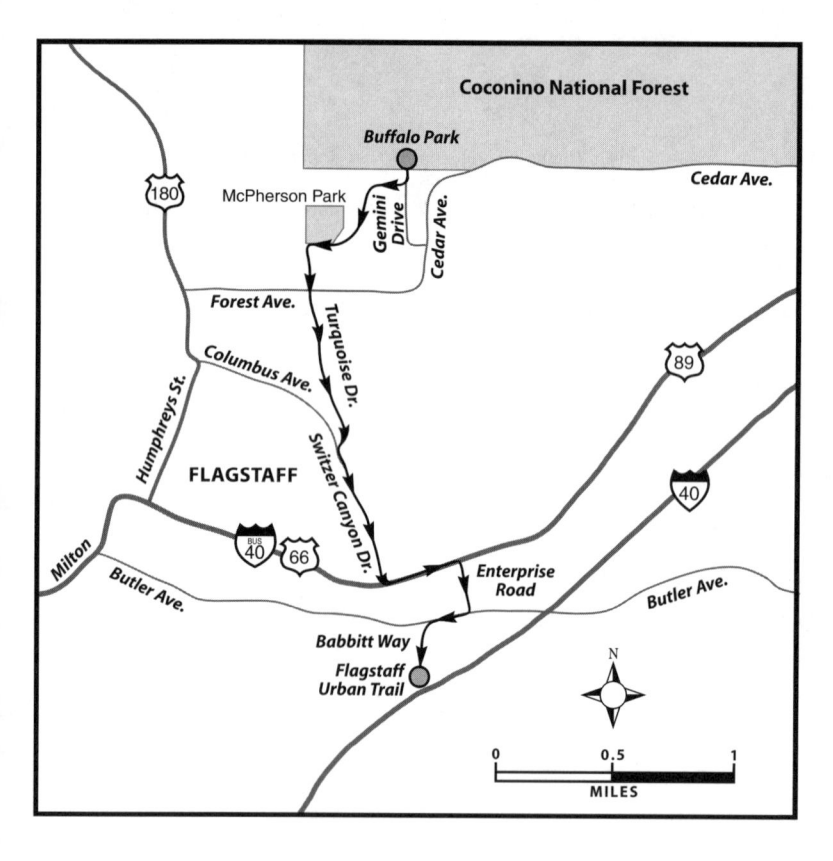

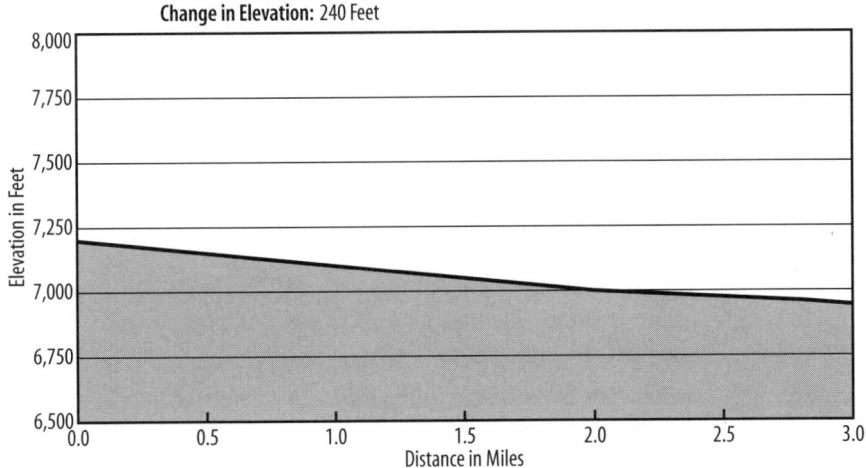

Segment 9 Total Elevation Gain: 0 Feet
Total Elevation Loss: 240 Feet
Change in Elevation: 240 Feet

Route Description

Southbound *Northbound*

0.0	Take the path to the right (west) and just south of the parking area.	2.8
0.6	At the bottom of the gravel path, you will come to a stoplight at the intersection of Turquoise and Forest Roads. Cross Forest Road at the crosswalk and go downhill on Turquoise.	2.2
0.9	Go straight at the first stop sign.	1.9
1.2	Go left (south) at the second stop sign onto Switzer Canyon Drive.	1.6

Trail Town

Flagstaff has long been a favorite for mountain bikers and other outdoor enthusiasts. While in the largest town on the Arizona Trail, consider taking what Appalachian Trail thru-hikers call a "zero day" (zero miles) to enjoy the benefits civilization offers. A paved bicycle path follows Route 66 and conveniently connects the AZT with the downtown area. Bicycle shops, outdoor outfitters, cafés, and grocery stores are all within easy biking distance. Thru-bikers can take advantage of the inexpensive mom-and-pop motels that line Route 66. Use the Flagstaff map in this guide to help you find other services listed in Appendix B and D.

84 Biking the Arizona Trail

Southbound			*Northbound*
1.8		At the stoplight, cross Route 66 (Business I-40) to the paved bicycle path on the south side. Go left (east). Grocery stores, restaurants, and inexpensive hotels can be found in this area. If you have time for a trip into downtown Flagstaff, follow the bicycle path to the right (west).	1.0
2.2		At the next light, turn right (south) onto Enterprise. Cross the railroad tracks.	0.6
2.4		At the traffic light, turn right (west) onto Butler. Several fast food restaurants and hotels can be found to the east on Butler.	0.4
2.5		Turn left (south) at next traffic light, in front of Ace Hardware and onto Babbitt Way.	0.3
2.8		Follow Babbitt Way to the dead end. At the west side of the cul-de-sac is the start of the Flagstaff Urban Trail System and Segment 10 of the AZT.	0.0

Segment 10 — FLAGSTAFF URBAN TRAIL to MORMON LAKE

Total Distance:
30.9 miles

Distance from Utah:
198.0 miles

Distance to Mexico:
505.9 miles

Difficulty: Moderate

Technical Rating:
Intermediate (With several opportunities for Easy/Beginner day trips.)

Trail Status: Official AZT and a connection route near where a trail is proposed.

Season
All year, except during periods the trail is snow-covered or after long periods of rain when the trail is extremely muddy.

Maps
USFS: Coconino National Forest
USGS: Flagstaff East, Lower Lake Mary, Ashurst Lake, Mormon Lake

A pine fence interrupts a field of flowers near Marshall Lake.

Signage
Good: Northern end is marked well with AZT stickers on Carsonite posts.

Water Sources
Flagstaff, Pine Grove Campground, and Mormon Lake. You can find water in Marshall Lake and Horseshoe Lake, but you should avoid using these sources to help protect wildlife habitat.

Trail Access
SOUTHBOUND: Flagstaff Urban Trail System/AZT Trailhead
From downtown Flagstaff, go east on US Route 66 to Enterprise Road. Turn right (south) at stoplight and cross the railroad tracks. At the next light turn right (west) onto Butler, then immediately go left at the next light onto Babbitt Way. Go past Sam's Club to where the road ends. Park at the cul-de-sac or in the Sam's Club parking lot. The AZT starts at the gated paved road. This road is also an access point to the Flagstaff Urban Trail System.

NORTHBOUND: Mormon Lake Post Office
From Flagstaff, go south on Lake Mary Road (FR 3) for about 20 miles to FR 90. Go right, (west then south) on the paved FR 90 for 8.5 miles to the village of Mormon Lake. The Mormon Lake Post Office is on the left (east) next to the general store. Park in the village. The route description begins at the post office.

Trail Overview
This segment is both a joy and a struggle. Leaving the modern conveniences of Flagstaff, you will have a pleasurable 5 miles of smooth single track through scenic meadows. Enjoy it while it lasts. To get to Marshall Lake, you will have to climb up a series of steep hills. Beginners and thru-bikers should expect to push their bikes some. At the top of Anderson Mesa, you can catch inspiring views along with your breath. South of Marshall Lake, the route eases up. You will ride past an observatory and get views of the San Francisco Peaks and Lake Mary. The section between Marshall Lake and Horseshoe Lake makes a nice day ride for beginners or those in the mood for some flat (although sometimes rocky) single track. Near Pine Grove Campground, you will run out of completed AZT. This guide will take you on a scenic detour near the proposed trail to the village of Mormon Lake, where you can stop at the saloon or the general store for a cold one. You'll deserve it by the time you finish this bumpy, roller-coaster ride.

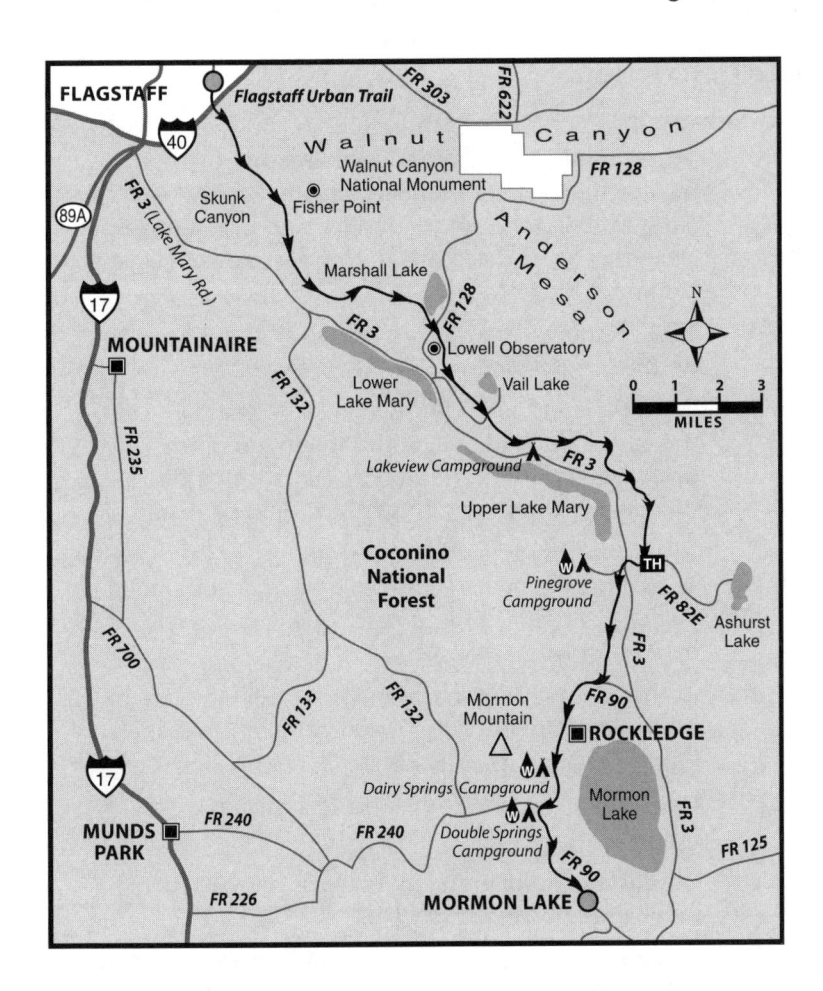

Segment 10

Total Elevation Gain: 1,100 Feet
Total Elevation Loss: 800 Feet
Change in Elevaion: 600 Feet

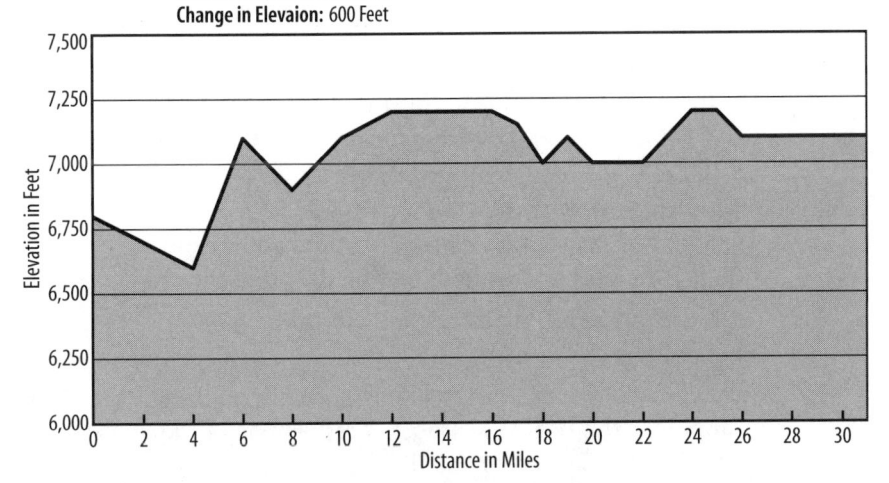

Route Description

Southbound   *Northbound*

0.0	At the cul-de-sac, take the paved road to the right next to the "Rio De Flag Reclamation Facility" sign. Go downhill, through the tunnel, and pass a trail to the right (west) that leads to the west side of Flagstaff. Go under the I-40 overpass.	30.9
0.4	Take the gravel road to the left (east) and stay on the northeast side of the pond.	30.5
0.5	Cross the creek and ignore the road coming in from the east. Before you reach the south end of the pond, turn left (east) onto the red gravel path that heads up the hill into the forest. This path should be marked with AZT Carsonite posts.	30.4
0.7	At the top of a steep climb, you will descend under a power line then go through an opening in a fence marked with AZT stickers.	30.2
1.4	At the south end of a meadow, you will hit a fork in the trail. (There is a large pine tree here.) Take the right (west) fork that heads slightly uphill.	29.5
2.0	Here is another fork at the end of a meadow. Stay right (west).	28.9
2.2	Go through an opening in a fence, then take the uphill road to the left (south).	28.7
3.1	Enjoy a long descent through meadows that explode with wildflowers during the summer. At the "T" intersection, take the single track to the right (west).	27.8
3.4	Pass a trail that heads west into Skunk Canyon.	27.5
4.0	The equestrian bypass ties back into the AZT here. If you have the energy, take the 1.2-mile (one way) hike to the top of Fisher Point to check out the views. This is a good day-ride destination for beginners.	26.9
4.9	Turn left (south) at the wooden sign that points the way to Marshall Lake. Leave the lazy meadows and begin the most challenging section of this segment.	26.0
5.1	After riding past the pretty, pink sandstone bluffs, begin the arduous climb.	25.8
5.4	Views reach out to the San Francisco Peaks (known simply as "the peaks" to Flagstaff residents) and down into Sandy's Canyon to the right (west).	25.5

Southbound		Northbound
5.9	Continue ascending as the surface becomes looser and rockier for the next 0.5 mile.	25.0
6.3	Cross the unsigned FR 1288 and begin a series of steep descents and ascents that are broken up by some shady and smooth flat sections.	24.6
8.2	Cross a faint two-track road at the bottom of a drainage.	22.7
9.1	Go through the cattle gate.	21.8
9.7	Surprise, surprise—another steep rocky ascent!	21.2
9.8	This is an unsigned trailhead. Leave the single track and go right (east) onto the gravel road.	21.1
10.0	Look across the road intersection for a signed trail that heads up the ridgeline. The trail climbs a ridge on a fun little section of single track that requires some technical maneuvering. Marshall Lake is the grassy field to the left (north) of the trail. (During dry years, you will have to travel north on the gravel road a bit to get to any water.)	20.9
10.7	At the top of Anderson Mesa, the trail crosses a paved road (FR 128) near the Anderson Mesa Lowell Observatory site. Follow the signs to the left (east).	20.2
10.8	Go right (south) through a gap in the fence between the Carsonite posts marking the AZT. Follow along a wooden fence. You'll get glimpses of the observatory to your right (west).	20.1
11.3	The trail heads right (west).	19.6

Farther Than the Eye Can See

Thru-bikers have probably already seen why Northern Arizona makes a good spot for an observatory. The abundance of undeveloped land decreases the amount of light pollution. With more than 200 cloudless nights and a wind flow that reduces heat distortion, Anderson Mesa provides some of the best night-sky viewing in the country. The facilities on Anderson Mesa (part of the Lowell Observatory operation) were built when the lights of town became too bright for the main observatory in Flagstaff. If the weather is nice, leave the tent in the stuff sack, snuggle into your sleeping bag, and fall asleep under the stars that fill up Arizona's sky. If you camp on Anderson Mesa, astronomers ask that you help protect the darkness by not building campfires.

Southbound *Northbound*

11.7	A fantastic view of Lake Mary opens up as the trail skirts the edge of Anderson Mesa. This is a scenic area to camp if you can find a spot that isn't too rocky. There is a short section of technical riding along the edge, but beginners should have little trouble getting through it.	19.2
12.2	The trail leads onto a faint road and continues south.	18.7
13.3	As you approach a "Dead End" sign and a three-way intersection of dirt roads, look for the single-track trail that goes south toward the metal gate. Take this trail.	17.6
13.6	Lost Tank is on the left (east) and might have some water. The trail continues to wind through grassy fields under scattered ponderosa pines. Look north for impressive views of "the peaks."	17.3
15.7	The AZT sign directs you to go right (west) onto the dirt road.	15.2
16.7	Go through the wire gate. Horse Lake is the wide grassy area just west of the trail. You might see some water shimmering in the distance. This area is important wildlife habitat. Behave accordingly. Follow the old road on the eastern edge of the "lake."	14.2
16.9	After crossing the cattle guard, bear right (west).	14.0
17.1	After the "Horse Lake" sign, the trail goes south. This area makes a good lunch stop or turnaround point for day riders.	13.8
17.6	An AZT sign directs you onto FR 129A. Continue south on this extremely rocky road.	13.3

More "Arizona Lakes"

Segment 10 will take you within view of several wide, flat, grassland marshes that Arizonans have the guts to call "lakes." Believe it or not, Mormon Lake is actually Arizona's largest natural lake, except during years when evaporation exceeds precipitation. In dry years, these lakes shrink, leaving behind wetlands that are important habitat for waterfowl populations. Bald eagles and osprey often use Mormon Lake as winter fishing grounds. Horse Lake is vital waterfowl-nesting habitat and the USFS has plans to build a bird-watching blind near the Arizona Trail. Be considerate of wildlife as you travel by the natural lakes of Arizona. Stay on the trail, camp away from water sources, and respect the posted rules and regulations.

Segment 10

Southbound		Northbound
19.0	Descend a short rocky section.	11.9
20.5	The trail leaves the road here as you get close to Ashurst Lake Road (FR 82E). Take the single track that heads right (west) and downhill toward FR 3. If you continue straight, you will hit Ashurst Lake Road in about 0.1 mile. There is trailhead parking where the AZT hits Ashurst Lake Road.	10.4
21.0	Cross the paved FR 3 (Lake Mary Road). Take the path that goes left (south) of the road that leads to Pinegrove Campground. The AZT is not developed from here to Mormon Lake. An alternative route near the proposed trail is given.	9.9
21.3	Go through the gate into the Pine Grove Quiet Area. This gate is locked from August 15 to January 1. You might need to lift your bike over the gate. After the gate, you will pass an old gravel pit on the left (east).	9.6
22.7	Leave FR 6078A and continue south onto FR 6078. The grade here is nice as you travel along the Walnut Creek drainage.	8.2
23.2	Leave FR 6078 as you go right and begin a gradual climb on FR 90E, which is a more improved dirt road.	7.7
24.4	After a gate, turn right (west) onto paved FR 90.	6.5
26.6	A road to Dairy Springs Campground (water) is to the west and views of Mormon Lake are to the east.	4.3
26.9	The Mormon Dairy historical marker will be on the right (west).	4.0
28.1	A road to Double Springs Campground (water) heads west.	2.8
30.9	Mormon Lake offers camping and lodging, a restaurant, saloon, and store, and water. Segment 11 begins at the post office.	0.0

Day Rides

Flagstaff to Fisher Point
Total Distance: 8 miles
Difficulty: Easy
Technical Rating: Beginner

A fun stretch of single track leads through grassy meadows and shady forests. At the end you can take a short hike to Fisher Point for views of the San Francisco Peaks. Start from the Southbound Trail Access and ride to mile 4.0.

Flagstaff to Marshall Lake
Total Distance: 21.4 miles
Difficulty: Strenuous
Technical Rating: Intermediate

Tough climbs reward you with fun sections of single track. Refer to the route description; start at Southbound mile 0.0 and turn around at mile 10.7.

Observatory Trailhead to Horse Lake
Total Distance: 13 miles
Difficulty: Easy
Technical Rating: Beginner

Park at the Observatory Trailhead and ride out and back to Horse Lake for a nice day ride that takes you past an excellent viewpoint. To get to the Observatory Trailhead from downtown Flagstaff, go south on Lake Mary Road (FR 3) for about 7 miles to the signed turnoff for Marshall Lake (FR 128). Park at the trailhead at the end of the paved road. See the route description, and start at Southbound mile 10.7.

Segment 11: MORMON LAKE to BLUE RIDGE RANGER STATION

Total Distance: 38.5 miles

Distance from Utah: 228.9 miles

Distance to Mexico: 475.0 miles

Difficulty: Moderate

Technical Rating: Intermediate

Trail Status: Official AZT and detours around areas where the trail is incomplete.

Wild West kitsch at Mormon Lake.

Season
All year, except after snowstorms or during extremely muddy conditions.

Maps
USFS: Coconino National Forest
USGS: Mormon Lake, Hutch Mountain, Jaycox Mountain, Turkey Mountain, Hay Lake, Blue Ridge Reservoir

Signage
Good to Poor: Some areas are signed well with AZT stickers and FR numbers on Carsonite posts, but you should also expect some confusing areas where map reading is necessary.

Water Sources
Mormon Lake, Camp Tank, Lane Tank, Pine Springs, Wild Horse Tank, Gonzales Tank, Blue Ridge Ranger Station

Trail Access
SOUTHBOUND: Mormon Lake
From Flagstaff, go south on Lake Mary Road (FR 3) for 23 miles to the turn-off to Mormon Lake. The post office is 2 miles west from the southern entrance on Mormon Lake Road (FR 90).

NORTHBOUND: Blue Ridge Ranger Station
From Payson go 50 miles north on AZ 87. The ranger station is 9 miles northeast of the intersection of AZ 87 and Lake Mary Road (FR 3).

Trail Overview

This segment takes you over newly established trail across the Coconino National Forest. Some sections of the AZT are signed but uncut at the time of this printing. Primitive roads provide scenic detours around undeveloped trail. You will need map skills and common sense to find your way through this area. The forest here is popular with Phoenix residents looking to escape the summer heat. Expect to share the route with ATVers and four-wheel-drive enthusiasts. Don't fret. Most are friendly and might even share some of the contents of their coolers with hardy adventurers such as yourselves. You will be grateful for refreshments after rolling over some painfully rocky sections. This segment has steep climbs that are technical but short. You might see elk as you travel through pine-oak forests and over grassy meadows. Wildflowers bloom into September and the aspen burst into shimmery golds by October. Water sources at Gonzales Tank, Wild Horse Tank, and Pine Springs make remote camping an inviting possibility. Happy Jack Lodge is a 9-mile ride from Bargaman Park if you want to get off the trail for some creature comforts.

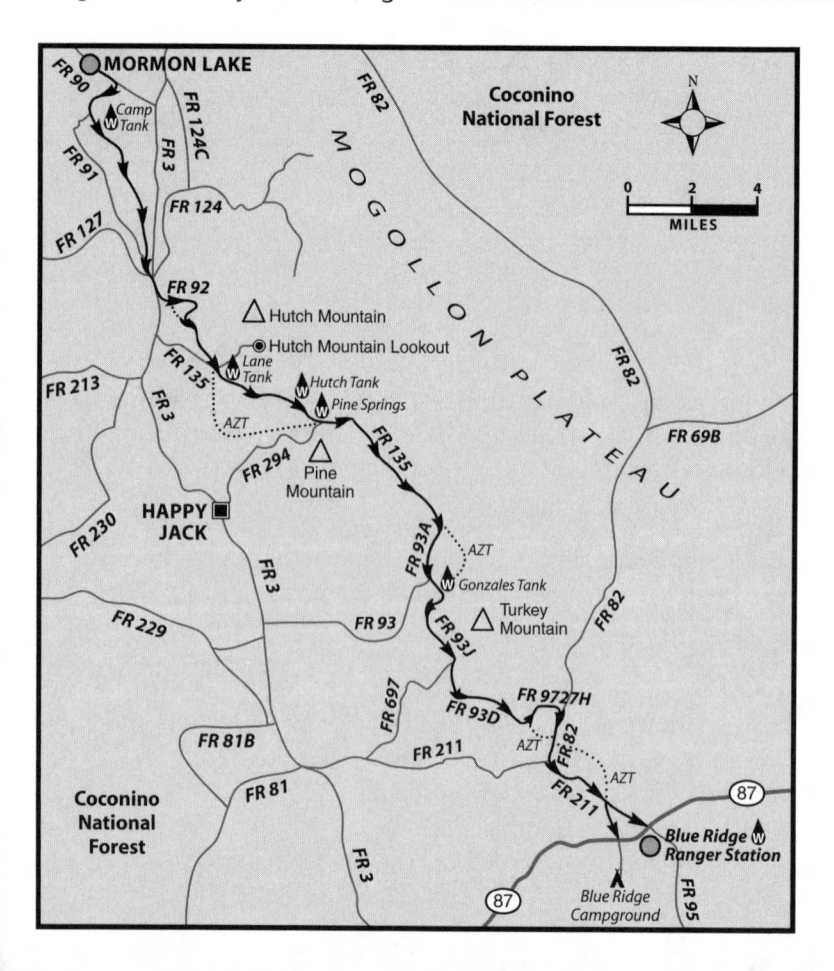

Segment 11

Total Elevation Gain: 1,450 Feet
Total Elevation Loss: 1,700 Feet
Change in Elevation: 1,100 Feet

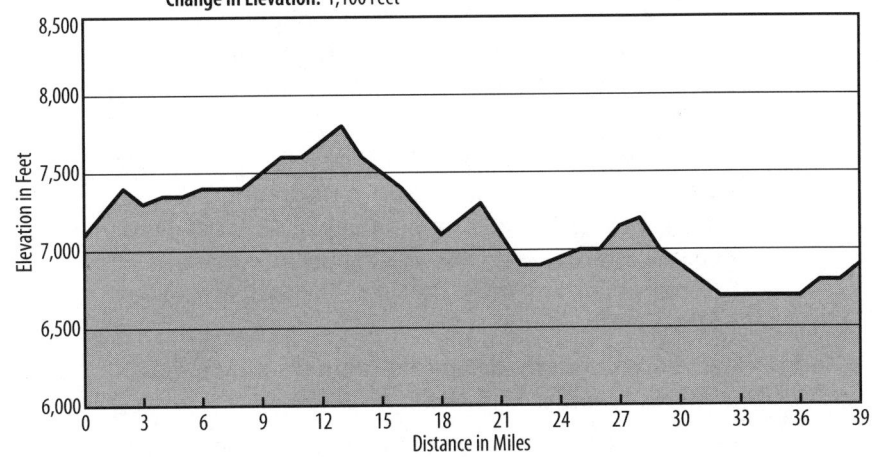

Route Description

Southbound		Northbound
0.0	From the Mormon Lake Post Office go south on paved FR 90 (Mormon Lake Road).	38.5
0.7	Leave the pavement and turn right (west) onto FR 219. Hopefully you ate a good meal back at the lodge, because you will immediately begin a steep climb up a rocky primitive road.	37.8
1.1	Go over a cattle guard.	37.4
1.4	Take the left (southeast) fork uphill.	37.1
1.9	At the top of the climb, go left (southeast) onto the signed FR 9486J. Soon you will pass Camp Tank (a decent water source) and cross another cattle guard.	36.6
2.5	Pass the muddier Airplane Tank. Stay right on the west side of the tank as you follow a graded road that traverses the right (west) side of a drainage. Continue to descend to a meadow at the bottom of the ridge.	36.0
3.3	Stay alert. Keep to the primitive road. Pass another unnamed stock pond on your left (east) and then cross a grassy drainage.	35.2

Southbound			Northbound
3.5	Follow alongside the rocky remnants of an old railroad track for about 0.2 mile. At the time of printing, the AZT is not signed here. Look for flagging and a faint path that goes up the ridge on the south side of the railroad grade.		35.0
3.8	Follow this faint path for a short distance until you see a sign that lets you know you are back on the AZT. After a short technical climb, the trail becomes obvious. Begin an enjoyable section of rolling single track that is used more by elk than humans. The AZT should be well signed for the next few miles.		34.7
4.1	Cross over a dirt road. You will go through two gates and cross another faint road.		34.4
7.0	Cross FR 91, an improved dirt road and a good place to meet vehicle support. Nice campsites are on the right (west).		31.5
7.1	After crossing FR 91, you will have a technical climb before you jump onto a section of mighty fine railroad grade. You'll pass a fenced spring (good water source). Decaying railroad ties line both sides of the trail.		31.4
7.8	Here you hit a dirt road. As directed by the AZT sign, go left (east) through the gate and then right (south) onto paved Lake Mary Road (FR 3).		30.7
8.3	Turn left (east) off of FR 3 and onto FR 92 (Gooseberry Springs Road).		30.2
8.6	Note the AZT post on the right (south) side of FR 92. The trail goes cross-country here at the time of this printing. Hopefully, as trail construction is completed, this section of the AZT will become biker friendly. For now, we will detour on scenic dirt roads. Stay on FR 92.		29.9
9.2	Begin a grunt-climb up the red gravel of FR 92.		29.3
9.7	Take the signed FR 92A to your right (south). You will switchback down, ignoring the first road that comes in from the left (south). The road will head west and pass several campsites popular with ATV enthusiasts on the weekends.		28.8
10.4	Here you will find an AZT post; you are back on the official trail.		28.1

Southbound   **Northbound**

10.5	Leave FR 92A by turning left (east) and following the AZT signs along a fence line. You are on FR 6048 as you follow a fence line through grassy oak and ponderosa forest.	28.0
11.0	Here you will find a small stock pond filled with muddy water.	27.5
11.4	Intersect with FR 135C. Go right (southwest) and slightly down. Then go left and down to FR 135. You will see an AZT post in the drainage.	27.1
11.6	The AZT goes cross-country again, so stay east on FR 135 for some pleasant spinning on hard-packed gravel.	26.9
12.2	Lane Tank has water and primitive camping nearby.	26.3
12.8	After climbing, you reach FR 135A and an elevation suitable for aspen trees. Stay on FR 135 to the left (northeast) following the sign to Bargaman Park.	25.7
13.3	Enter private property as indicated by signs. Respect the wishes of landowners. The aspen are gorgeous here in the fall. Descend for about a mile staying on FR 135.	25.2
14.9	After a flat section, descend again. Try to catch peek-a-boo views of the Mogollon Rim and Pine Mountain.	23.6
15.2	After crossing a cattle guard, go right (southwest) under a power line.	23.3
15.5	Hutch Tank has water.	23.0
16.0	Stay on FR 135 as you pass FR 2941 and then FR 294. Pine Springs is right off of the road here. Look for a concrete box filled with water on the north side just east of the intersection of FR 294 and FR 135. Go left (east) and you will soon see AZT signs where the cross-country route comes in from the north. Continue southeast on FR 135, now the AZT. FR 135 gets significantly rockier and rougher from this point south. If you are looking to escape the trail, you can take FR 294 for about 5 miles west to FR 3 then go south on FR 3 to Happy Jack Lodge. Happy Jack Lodge has rooms, a restaurant, laundry facilities, and showers.	22.5

Southbound			**Northbound**
16.5	Follow AZT signs over a series of rocky climbs and descents. Be sure your gear is strapped on tightly. The bumpy route here made me lose a tent and forced me to do the unthinkable—bike back to retrieve it.		22.0
17.7	Go right (south) onto a four-wheel-drive road as the AZT leaves FR 135 and gets onto FR 9361E toward Wild Horse Tank.		20.8
18.6	Wild Horse Tank is a muddy water source with two picturesque dead pines in the middle. After passing the tank, take a fork to the left (east). Look for an AZT post. Prepare yourself for more rocky riding as you climb up a primitive road. Although this climb is not terribly steep, you'll still be glad when it's over.		19.9
19.6	The trail twists and turns through pines that shade a grassy floor.		18.9
20.3	The trail levels out for a bit.		18.2
20.5	Go left (east) following AZT signs to FR 93A.		18.0
20.8	Descend for nearly a mile to a big meadow.		17.7
22.0	The trail intersects with FR 93A.		16.5
22.4	You'll see AZT signs going cross-country to the left (east). Stay on the road until you hit the AZT again on the south side of Gonzales Tank.		16.1
22.9	Cross the cattle guard.		15.6
23.5	Gonzales Tank is a large stock pond with water.		15.0
23.7	Just after (south of) Gonzales Tank, take a connector road left (east) to the road paralleling the one you are on. Go left (northeast) on FR 93. You will go to the east side of Gonzales Tank and climb gradually for 0.2 mile where you will find AZT signs and FR 93 markers. Continue up and east. You are now back on the AZT.		14.8
24.5	Leave FR 93 as the AZT sign directs you to the right (west) onto FR 93J.		14.0
25.9	Take a left (east) fork uphill and keep looking for AZT signs.		12.6
26.8	Get ready for another climb. The rocky terrain might be getting old now, but hang in there. You have 5 more miles of this stuff.		11.7

Segment 11

Southbound		*Northbound*
27.7	Here the trail hits FR 93 again. Go right (southwest). Shortly, you will reach an intersection with FR 697 where AZT signs will keep you on FR 93.	10.8
28.6	Follow the trail as it goes left (east) onto FR 93D.	9.9
31.1	AZT trail markers go cross-country up a ridge to the right (south). Stay on the road marked as FR 9727H on the Coconino Forest map. Between here and FR 82 the route gets unbelievably rocky.	7.4
32.6	Whew! Go right (south) onto the relatively smooth gravel of FR 82.	5.9
33.5	The AZT crosses FR 82 here. Again, this portion of the AZT is signed but not improved as of winter 2002. Stay on FR 82.	5.0
35.2	At the stop sign, turn left (east) on FR 211 towards AZ 87.	3.3
37.0	The AZT crosses FR 211 here, giving you two options. If you are planning to camp at the Blue Ridge Campground, go right (west) onto faint single track signed as AZT. In just over a mile, this trail will take you to AZ 87. Cross AZ 87 to FR 138. You can take the AZT single track or FR 138 for 1 mile to the campground. Between May 15 and September 15, Blue Ridge Campground offers water and shaded campsites with picnic tables for $5 a night. If you are planning to continue, and want to take the recommended thru-route (see Segment 12, p. 100), stay on FR 211 until you reach the pavement at AZ 87.	1.5
38.5	Cross AZ 87 onto FR 95 to begin Segment 12. If you need water or would like to stop by the ranger station for trail information, go right (southwest) on AZ 87 for a short distance and you will see the entrance to the Blue Ridge Ranger Station. A red-handled pump at the far end of the parking lot provides drinking water year-round. Inside the ranger station (Monday through Friday, 7:30 a.m. to 4:00 p.m.), you can get information and purchase maps for the next segment of your trip. After filling your water bottles, you can find plenty of primitive camping spots south on FR 95.	0.0

Segment 12: BLUE RIDGE RANGER STATION to GENERAL SPRINGS CABIN

Total Distance: 18.8 miles

Distance from Utah: 267.4 miles

Distance to Mexico: 436.5 miles

Difficulty: Moderate

Technical Rating: Beginner to Intermediate

Trail Status: Bicycle detour around a tough section of AZT.

Season
All year except when roads are closed because of snow or muddy conditions.

Maps
USFS: Coconino National Forest
USGS: Blue Ridge Reservoir, Dane Canyon

Signage
Good: FS roads signed with numbers on brown posts.

Getting water from the well at General Springs Cabin requires some creativity.
Photo by Beth Overton.

Water Sources
Blue Ridge Ranger Station, East Clear Creek, Pinchot Cabin, General Springs

Trail Access
SOUTHBOUND: Blue Ridge Ranger Station
The station is on AZ 87, approximately 50 miles northeast of Payson. The ranger station is 9 miles northeast of the intersection of AZ 87 and Lake Mary Road (FH 3).

NORTHBOUND: General Springs Cabin
Follow FR 300 for 11.5 miles east from AZ 87. Start at the Battle of Big Dry Wash marker or follow the signs to General Springs Cabin.

Trail Overview

The AZT travels from Blue Ridge Campground to the camping area at General Springs Cabin. Steep climbs and descents make this passage an extremely difficult thru-route for mountain bikers. Thru-bikers and beginners should take the detour or do the AZT sections as day rides. If you're up for a rugged challenge, you can make a long loop out of the AZT and the bicycle bypass. I have described the AZT route separately for those who want to try it.

The recommended thru-route will take graded gravel roads that lead you to the edge of the 200-mile-long escarpment called the Mogollon (moo-gee-yon) Rim. After bouncing over Segment 11, you will enjoy easier riding, but expect to climb in and out of several canyons including the dramatic East Clear Creek gorge. Elk are frequently seen among the tall pines and in the grassy meadows. Apparently, bear also live here at the southern end of the largest ponderosa pine forest in the world. But you're not likely to see one. Two historic ranger cabins, with natural water sources and pleasant camping nearby, are within 0.5 mile of the route. The graded roads and availability of water make this area a forgiving segment for beginners to try bike-packing. If you are doing a loop ride, plan on camping at one of the campsites at the edge of the rim on FR 300. Southbounders, savor the cool green forests while you can; soon you will be leaving the shady pines for the cacti of the Sonoran Desert.

Segment 12   Total Elevation Gain: 1,630 Feet
Total Elevation Loss: 950 Feet
Change in Elevation: 1,080 Feet

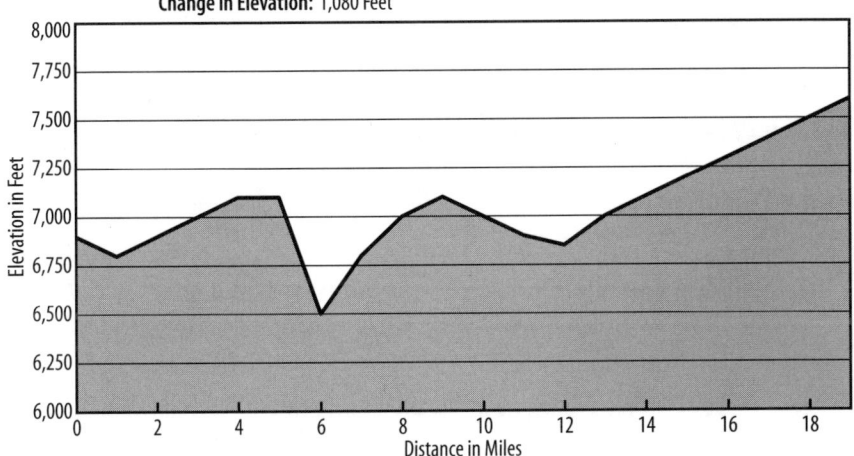

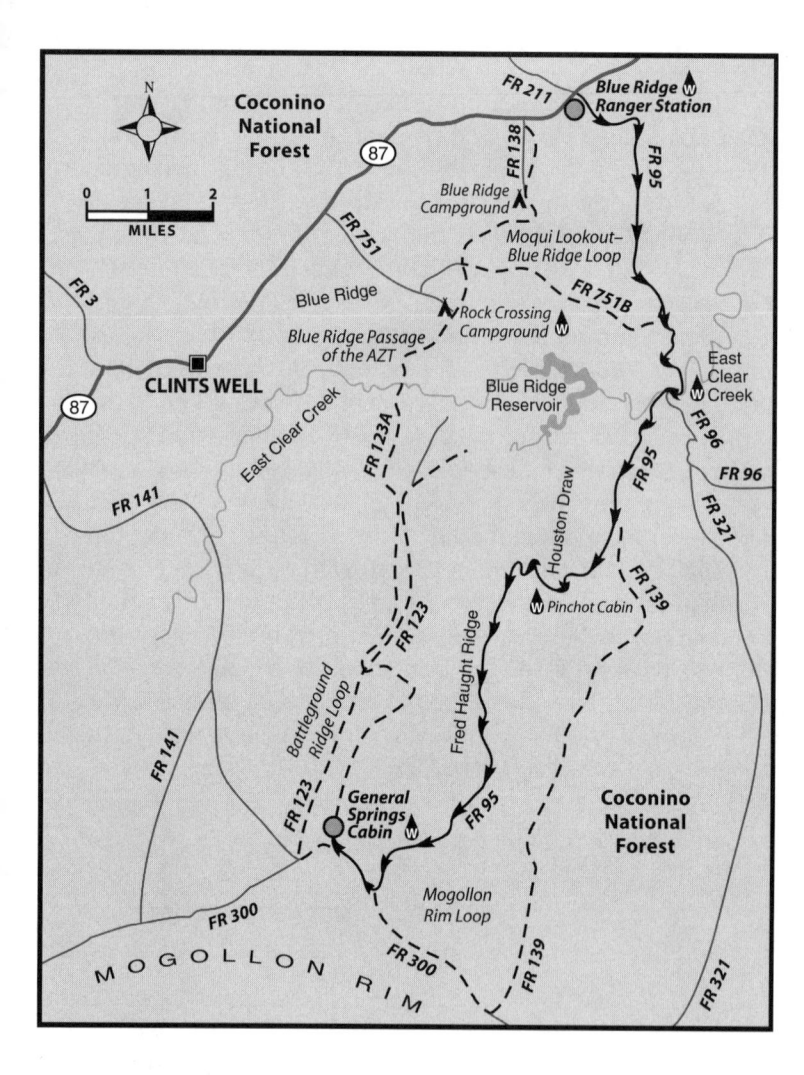

Route Description

Southbound   *Northbound*

0.0	From the Blue Ridge Ranger Station, ride a short distance north on AZ 87 to the intersection with FR 95.	18.8
0.1	Go right (south) on FR 95.	18.7
0.3	Stay on FR 95 as several roads come into this major gravel road.	18.5
1.2	FR 513 comes in from the east.	17.6
3.3	Make a short climb. You will pass several grassy areas that are good places to camp after filling your water bottles at the ranger station.	15.5

Southbound			Northbound
4.2	Moqui Lookout is 1 mile up the road (FR 751B) to the right (west).		14.6
5.0	Begin the 1.5-mile descent to East Clear Creek.		13.8
5.6	There's a campsite with a view up to your right where the road becomes exposed to the scenic gorge.		13.2
6.5	Cross the one-lane bridge. Campsites on the south side with access to East Clear Creek and views of the gorge make this area a good rest stop. After the bridge, take the right (west) fork. You will continue on FR 95 from here. The road will become less used, as most vehicle traffic will be going left toward Knoll Lake. The bad news is that now you have to ascend out of Clear Creek gorge.		12.3
7.9	You've reached the top of climb!		10.9
8.9	Barber Lake is a stock tank that should have water.		9.9
9.0	Stay to the right (west) on FR 95 when you hit an intersection with FR 139. A sign will say "Rim Road 10 miles." Descend to a meadow then roll in and out of several grassy drainages and pine forests.		9.8

Cabins of the Mogollon Rim

While the U.S. Military was distracted by the Civil War, Apache Indians took strategic control of the area along the Mogollon Rim. Later, General George Crook was sent to Arizona to force the Apache back to reservations. It was while hiding from a band of Apache that General Crook and his men found the springs near where General Springs Cabin is today. The cavalry soon completed a road along the rim from Fort Apache to Prescott and the Apache's tactical position was lost. Several battles were fought and the area became safe for white settlement.

Built in 1914, General Springs Cabin became a link in a network of patrol cabins for early forest rangers. Carrying little more than an axe or shovel, rangers patrolled the forests of the Mogollon Rim by horseback as they suppressed forest fires, enforced regulations, and conducted timber inventories. The cabin at General Springs was rehabilitated in 1989 and offers a nice camping area under large pines.

Pinchot Cabin sits in a grassy draw where the Houston Brothers Ranch outfit camped while ranging their cattle during the summer. In 1919, the Forest Service took over the area, built a cabin, and named it after their Chief Forester, Gifford Pinchot. The cabin you see today was built in 1930 by the fireguard who lived in the old cabin with his family.

Southbound   *Northbound*

11.3	After you pass the "Houston Draw" sign, you can take FR 139A to the left (southeast) for 0.25 mile to Pinchot Cabin. There is water in the creek here and the grassy area near the cabin makes a peaceful camping spot.	7.5
12.1	Cross a creek that cuts through an interesting narrow canyon. Check out the Douglas fir trees growing in the shelter of the canyon walls.	6.7
12.3	A hiking trail goes up the ridge to the left (west). Stay on the road.	6.5
12.8	The road levels out a bit. Continue on top of Fred Haught Ridge.	6.0
18.5	The stock tank on the right (west) has water.	0.3
18.8	At FR 300 (Rim Road), go down to the right (west) in the direction of AZ 87 and General Springs Cabin.	0.0

Day Rides

Moqui Lookout–Blue Ridge Loop
Total Distance: 12 miles
Difficulty: Moderate
Technical Rating: Beginner

You can make a loop by parking at the Blue Ridge Campground near the Ranger Station (see Trail Access: Southbound) and taking the AZT north to AZ 87. Go northeast on AZ 87 to FR 95. Turn right (south) on FR 95 to FR 751B (Moqui Lookout Road) at Southbound mile 4.2, and go west until the AZT crosses the road. Take the AZT back; a difficult descent brings you down to the Blue Ridge Campground. Expect lots of rocks. By going this direction you can ride up the ridge on the road and down the ridge on the trail, which is more enjoyable.

Blue Ridge Passage of the AZT
Total Distance: 24.4 miles
Difficulty: Strenuous
Technical Rating: Intermediate

From the Blue Ridge Campground (see Trail Access: Southbound), take the signed AZT. The trail begins to climb immediately and will soon get even steeper. At the top of the ridge, you will have a flat but rocky ride to Rock Crossing Campground. The trail is signed with Carsonite posts and crosses FR 751B and then FR 751 just before the campground. Rock Crossing Campground is a nice site with water (summer only) and is about 3.2 miles from Blue Ridge Campground. South of Rock Crossing, you can ride the AZT along the edge of a canyon. This mile of AZT is rocky and provides a technical challenge that intermediate riders might enjoy. When the trail begins to descend sharply, you have reached the difficult portion across East Clear Creek. Day riders can hike their bikes across to the other side but you might want to turn around before descending to the bottom. The graveled bed of East Clear Creek is worth seeing, but pushing your bike in and out of the canyon is not fun. Large steps and log water bars make the pushing even more difficult. Thru-bikers carrying weight will hate this section. In the future, there are plans to improve this trail for mountain bikers. Until then, I recommend that thru-bikers use the thru-route on FR 95.

Mogollon Rim Loop
Total Distance: 25 miles
Difficulty: Moderate
Technical Rating: Beginner

Only 0.5 mile of this loop is part of the AZT, but this ride is excellent for beginners wanting to practice bikepacking skills. Park at General Springs Cabin (see Trail Access: Northbound). Take the AZT south to FR 300. Go left (east) on FR 300 to FR 95. Go left (north) on FR 95 to the intersection with FR 139. Go right (south) on FR 139 for 9 miles to FR 300 and go right (northwest) back to General Springs Cabin. Between FR 139 and General Springs Cabin, you will pass by rim-side campsites with spectacular views.

Battleground Ridge Loop
Total Distance: 17 miles
Difficulty: Moderate
Technical Rating: Intermediate

From General Springs Cabin (see Trail Access: Northbound), ride south on the AZT to FR 300. Go right (west) on FR 300 for 0.9 mile to FR 123. Go north on FR 123, a mostly level dirt road through the pine and fir forest. Take FR 123 for 7.8 miles to the fork at the end. Take the left (westernmost) road (FR 123A on the Coconino Forest Map). There will be a corral near where the road splits. The AZT hits the road about 0.2 mile north of this intersection. You can continue north on the AZT/FR 123A for 1.5 miles to the end of the road. This is where the AZT begins the steep drop-off into East Clear Creek. At the end of FR 123A, you will find a fence with a hiker gate and a primitive camping area.

Southbound day riders should now turn around and head south on the AZT/FR 123A. Just before the intersection of FR 123 and FR 123A, find where the AZT leaves the road to the right (southwest). The AZT will now parallel the road for 2 miles before crossing to the east side of FR 123. The crossing is marked with Carsonite posts and rock cairns. (Beginners might want to get to General Springs by taking FR 123 from here, as there are some particularly steep, rocky sections on the next portion of the trail.) Soon after crossing the road, the trail will merge with a primitive logging road. Once you pass the gate, be on the lookout for where the trail leaves the primitive road to the southwest. A large rock cairn marks the point. The single track will now begin a series of steep, rocky switchbacks with tight turns that are extremely difficult for northbound riders. Northbound thru-bikers carrying weight will find this section extremely unpleasant. Once off of Battleground Ridge, the trail goes south on the Fred Haught Trail/AZT for 2 miles to General Springs. This portion of the trail has some nice sections to ride but should be considered an intermediate route because of the technical sections along the creek. (Trail realignment is planned for this area. Be prepared to see changes from what is described here.)

Segment 13 — GENERAL SPRINGS CABIN to PAYSON

Total Distance:
20.3 miles

Distance from Utah:
286.2 miles

Distance to Mexico:
417.7 miles

Difficulty:
Moderate

Technical Rating:
Beginner (with one tough descent off of the rim)

Trail Status:
Official AZT and a bicycle detour around a tough section.

The Mazatzals can be seen in the distance from the edge of the Mogollon Rim. Bikers experience dramatic lifezone changes when they descend from the Coconino Plateau.

Season
All year. Colonel Delvin Trail can be unsafe during lightning storms.

Maps
USFS: Tonto National Forest
USGS: Dane Canyon, Kehl Ridge, Payson North, Payson South

Signage
Good: Use FS road and city street signs.

Water Sources
General Springs, East Verde River at several locations, Houston Mesa Campground, Payson

Trail Access
SOUTHBOUND: General Springs Cabin
From AZ 87, follow FR 300 for 11.5 miles east. At the Battle of Big Dry Wash marker, go north following the signs 0.5 mile down to the parking area at General Springs Cabin, where the route description begins.
NORTHBOUND: Payson
The Payson Chamber of Commerce is at the corner of Main Street and AZ 87 just south of the intersection with AZ 260.

Trail Overview

This segment starts with a rough descent down the Colonel Devin Trail. You will lose 1,000 feet in elevation in 2 miles. Notice the changes in vegetation as you leave the ponderosa forest and get closer to the deserts of central Arizona. At Washington Park, the recommended thru-route leaves the AZT where the trail takes the Highline Trail to AZ 87 before entering the Mazatzal Wilderness area to the west. In *Along the Arizona Trail* (Westcliffe Publishers), M. John Fayhee describes the Highline Trail as "one of the rockiest stretches of trail it has ever been my displeasure to stumble..." For advanced mountain bikers who might take that description as a dare, a loop ride that includes the Highline Trail is provided. You can take the AZT/Highline Trail to AZ 87, then go south on AZ 87 to Payson. AZ 87 between Pine and Payson is a narrow, curvy highway with blind corners that I find intimidating. The bike detour described here is a quieter alternative that goes by several camping opportunities. Although 13 miles of this segment are paved, the rollercoaster hills and river fords provide enough challenges to keep things interesting.

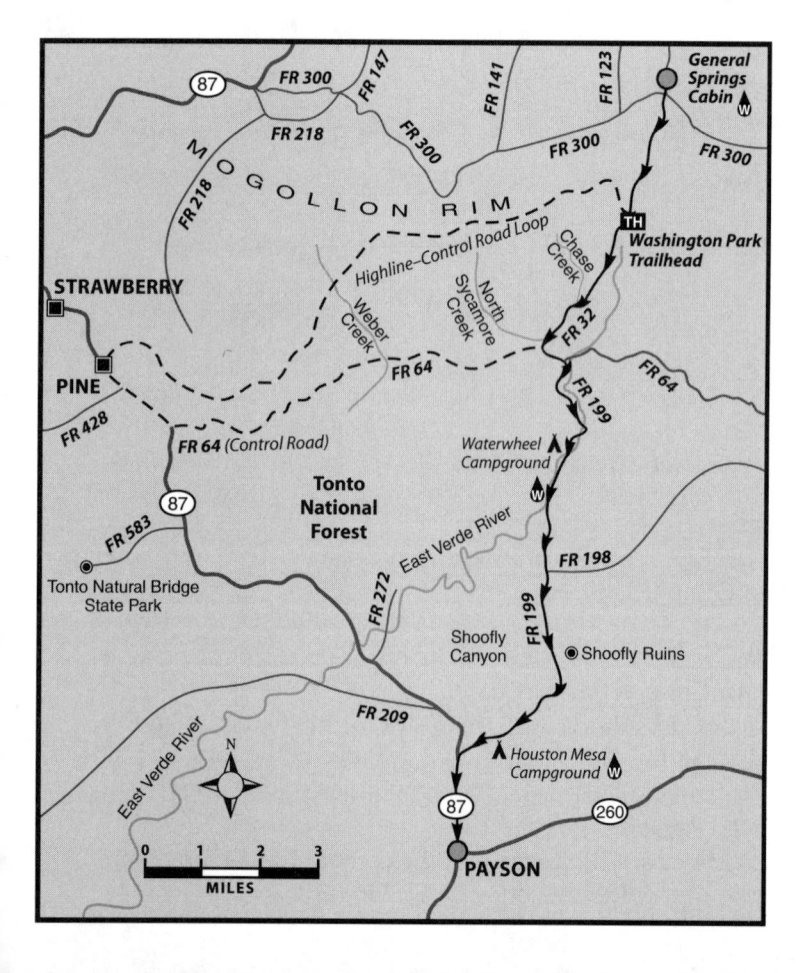

Riverside camping sites, expansive views, and a nature path to prehistoric ruins are the highlights of the recommended thru-route. Thru-bikers will appreciate the easy access to resupply, restaurants, and bike repair found in Payson.

Segment 13 Total Elevation Gain: 400 Feet
Total Elevation Loss: 2,600 Feet
Change in Elevation: 2,400 Feet

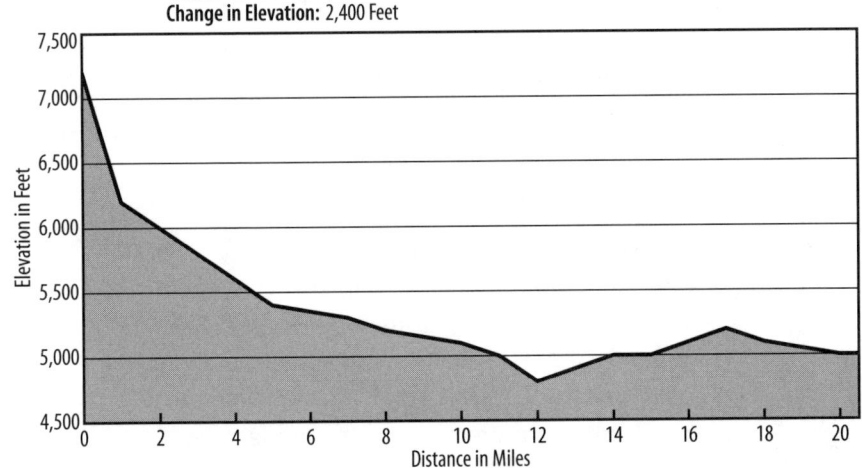

Route Description

Southbound *Northbound*

0.0	From General Springs Cabin ride 0.5 mile up the hill to FR 300. At the historic marker for the Battle of Big Dry Wash, take the Colonel Devin Trail #290 on the north side of FR 300. The trail gets steeper and more difficult as you follow a drainage under a power line. Be prepared to push your bike over some slabs of sandstone that can intimidate beginners.	20.3
0.5	At the sign for the Tunnel Trail, you can hike 0.25 mile up to the site of an abandoned railroad tunnel project. The 75-yard tunnel was part of a failed attempt to build a railroad from Globe to Flagstaff. A house and a campsite with views are at the site.	19.8
0.7	Continue down through an area scorched by the Dude fire.	19.6
1.2	Cross several creeks. Lush watercress grows in the seeps that feed the headwaters of the East Verde River. If you prefer solitude, and it's a weekend, you should camp along the trail before you reach the trailhead.	19.1

Southbound			Northbound
2.0	There is a horse corral at the Washington Park Trailhead and parking area where you will cross the Highline Trail. The AZT goes east (right) on the Highline Trail to AZ 87, but the thru-route will continue on forest roads.		18.3
	Northbounders: *Beware—the Colonel Devin Trail will be a grunting hike-a-bike to the top of the Mogollon Rim. If a vehicle supports you, you should consider shuttling your bikes around. The trail to the rim is interesting though. If you're up for some exertion, cowboy up and get yourself to the top of the Colorado Plateau and the start of Segment 12.*		N
2.4	Shady overused campsites line the East Verde River as you continue south on FR 32 from Washington Park.		17.9
3.1	At the yield sign, turn right, then go down to the left (south) onto a gravel road.		17.2
3.4	Stay on FR 32, signed as "Rim Trail 32." FR 199 descends into a residential area to the left. FR 32 descends steadily through pines on a good gravel road.		16.9
5.1	Cross Chase Creek.		15.2
6.4	Turn left (south) following the sign that says "FR 199 1 mile."		13.9
7.1	FR 32 ends at an intersection with FR 64 and FR 199. Go straight on FR 199. The gravel turns to pavement as you enter the Whispering Pines residential community. There is a pay phone at the East Verde Baptist Church.		13.2
8.2	After passing a fire station, check out the lawn with the funky yard sculptures.		12.1
8.4	Ford the East Verde River. Do not attempt to cross during periods of significant flooding. There are campsites on the right.		11.9
9.2	Ford the river again. More camping on the right. Expect roller-coaster hills that give you views of the Mazatzals to the southwest and the Mogollon Rim to the north.		11.1
9.8	Waterwheel crossing and camping area. The remains of a water mill can be found above the easternmost campsites. The campsites along the sycamore- and cottonwood-lined river are popular on weekends.		10.5

Southbound		Northbound
10.4	Cross a bridge and continue the roller coaster.	9.9
14.6	On the left (south), Shoofly Ruins is an appealing rest stop with shaded picnic tables. Take the short self-guided nature path to ruins of an ancient community built by prehistoric inhabitants of the area.	5.7
15.6	Houston Mesa General Store has a pay phone, snacks, and cold drinks—well-deserved treats after cranking up and down all those hills.	4.7
17.4	Houston Mesa Campground is a Forest Service camping area and charges $12 a night. Coin-operated showers are available if you want to freshen up before venturing into town.	2.9
17.6	FR 199 ends at AZ 87. Watch traffic and turn left (south) onto this busy highway.	2.7
19.6	At the stoplight where AZ 260 intersects with AZ 87, you are in the center of town. Restaurants and lodging choices are plentiful. If you need bike gear or repair, take AZ 260 east to the second strip mall on the right. Manzanita Cycling is next to the Safeway on the south side of AZ 260.	0.7
20.3	After passing the post office on your right (west), turn left on Main Street to the Payson Chamber of Commerce parking lot and the start of Segment 14.	0.0

General Springs Cabin.

Day Rides

Highline–Control Road Loop
Total Distance: 28 miles
Difficulty: Strenuous
Technical Rating: Intermediate

The AZT portion of the Highline Trail is a rocky, roller-coaster ride for mountain bikers looking for a scenic challenge along the base of the Mogollon Rim. Take the AZT/Highline Trail east from the Washington Park Trailhead for 17 miles to AZ 87 at the Pine Trailhead. (Geronimo Camp Trailhead is 9.5 miles west of Washington Park, and then it will be 8 miles farther to Pine Trailhead.) From there, go left (south) on AZ 87 for 1.6 miles to FR 64 (Control Road). Take FR 64 left (east) back to Washington Park.

To reach the Washington Park Trailhead, take AZ 87 north from Payson to FR 199. Go east on FR 199 for 10.3 miles to FR 64. Go west on FR 64 for less than a mile to FR 32, then go north on FR 32 for 3.3 miles to FR 32A. Take FR 32A for 0.5 mile to the trailhead.

Day riders can also be picked up and dropped off at the Pine Trailhead. To access the Pine Trailhead from Payson, drive north on AZ 87. Just south of the community of Pine and about 15 miles from Payson, the trailhead is on the east side of the highway on FR 297. The trailhead is well signed.

Segment 14 — PAYSON to JAKE'S CORNER

Total Distance:
30.0 miles

Distance from Utah:
306.5 miles

Distance to Mexico:
397.4 miles

Difficulty: Moderate

Technical Rating:
Beginner

Trail Status:
Bike detour around the Mazatzal Wilderness.

The Mazatzal Mountains along the road to Rye Creek.

Season
Fall, winter, spring. Summers will be hot. If you hit this segment during rainy weather, wait or take the highway. Although they dry quickly, the dirt roads become so muddy that the riding will be tedious and miserable during rainstorms.

Maps
USFS: Tonto National Forest
USGS: Payson South, North Peak, Gisela

Signage
Fair: FS road numbers on brown posts.

Water Sources
Payson, Rye Creek businesses on AZ 87, Rye Creek at bridge, Jake's Corner Store

Trail Access
SOUTHBOUND: Payson Chamber of Commerce
The Payson Chamber of Commerce is at the corner of Main Street and AZ 87 just south of the intersection of AZ 260 and AZ 87.
NORTHBOUND: Jake's Corner
Take AZ 87 then AZ 188 for about 23 miles south of Payson to the facilities at Jake's Corner.

Trail Overview

Southwest of Payson, the AZT travels into the rugged terrain of the Mazatzal (mah-zaht-zall) Mountains. Since bicycles are prohibited in the Wilderness Area, this bike route will stay east of the Wilderness boundary. You will ride through manzanita shrub, piñon-juniper forest, semi-desert grasslands, and a stand of Arizona cypress. Be ready for several steep climbs interspersed between some long sections of nice grade. The first half of the ride takes you up to the eastern foothills then follows Rye Creek back to AZ 87. You cross AZ 87 and then continue along Rye Creek to AZ 188. Jake's Corner has just about everything a thru-biker needs—food, pay phones, camping, laundry facilities, showers, and even a bar.

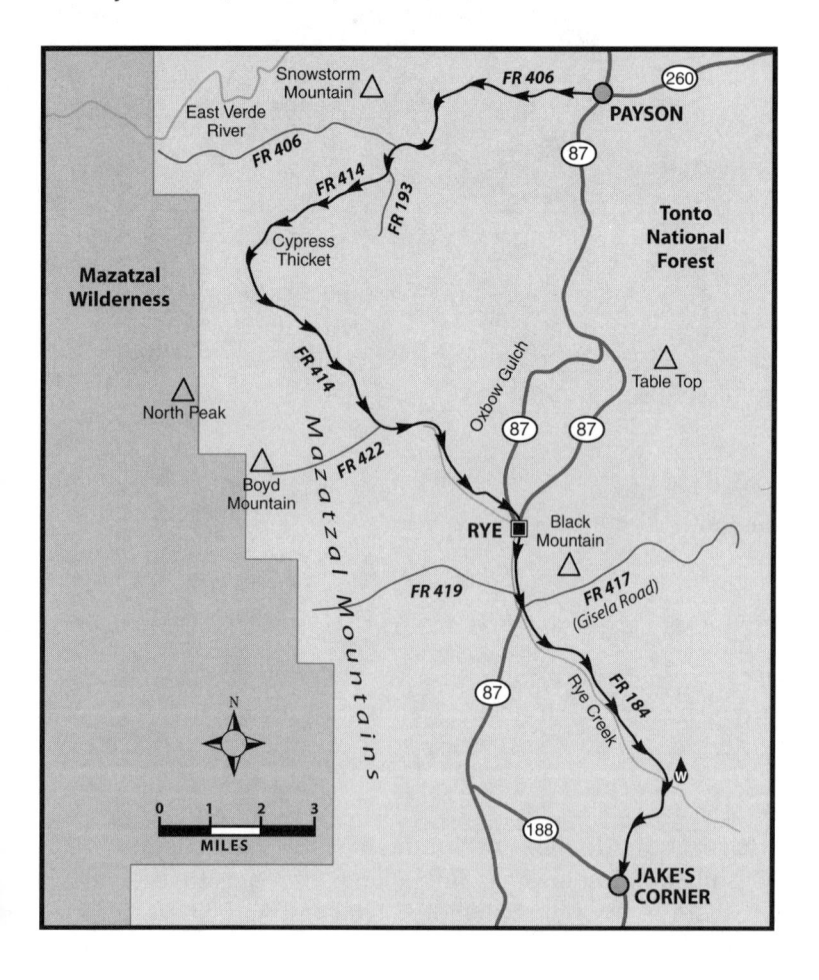

Segment 14 **Total Elevation Gain:** 650 Feet
Total Elevation Loss: 2,850 Feet
Change in Elevation: 2,250 Feet

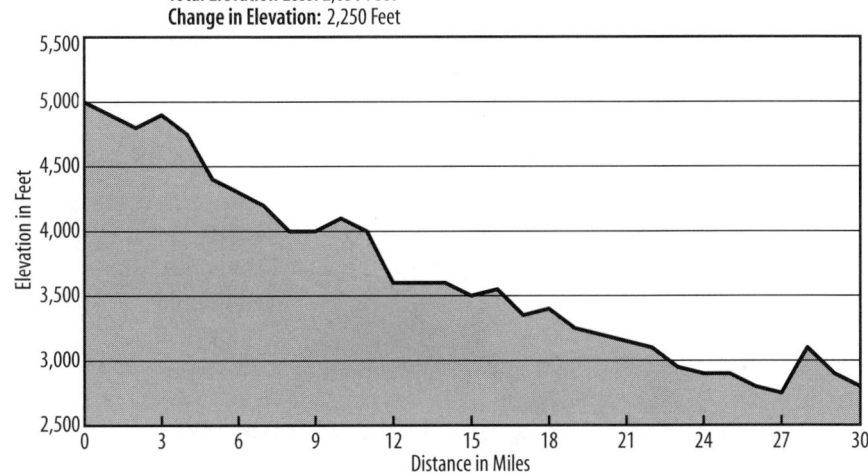

Route Description

Southbound *Northbound*

0.0	Go west on Main Street from the Chamber of Commerce parking lot.	30.0
0.6	The Public Library has Internet access.	29.4
1.1	Stop and take a break on the grassy lawns of Green Valley Park or check out the Rim Country Museum. Continue west as Main Street turns into Country Club Road. Wave to the golfers as you roll by the golf course.	28.9
2.4	At the sewage treatment plant leave the pavement for FR 406.	27.6
2.7	Cross a cattle guard and enter the Tonto National Forest.	27.3
3.2	Try to ignore the smell of the sludge-drying beds as you begin an arduous climb.	26.8
3.7	At the top, you'll get views of the eastern side of the Mazatzal Mountains.	26.3
4.2	You might find water in a stock tank hidden behind the junipers on the west side of the road.	25.8
4.5	At the bottom of a descent, stay on FR 406 as you pass by the road leading to Peach Orchard Springs.	25.5
4.7	More views of the Wilderness Area. Check your brakes. You have a steep descent ahead.	25.3

Southbound			Northbound
5.3	Turn left (south) onto FR 193/414. The road gets rougher and steeper as it goes in and out of several washes that are prone to flash floods.		24.7
6.1	Take FR 414 to the right (west).		23.9
7.3	Cross another cattle guard and pass a rocky campsite with a view.		22.7
8.7	Wind through a thicket of Arizona cypress. The tree has long strips of papery bark that peel off of smooth, red trunks.		21.3
10.5	At the top of a climb, you'll reach a spur road that leads to the Mineral Creek Trailhead. A Forest Service sign tells you that AZ 87 is 8 miles ahead. Drop down the ridge, and then follow alongside Mineral Creek (usually dry).		19.5
13.1	FR 193 comes in from the left.		16.9
Loop	*Alternate and Loop Route:* Day riders can take FR 193 back to the intersection at mile 5.3 for a 20-mile ride.		
14.7	The landscape opens up and displays the east range of the Mazatzals.		15.3
14.9	The corral on the left is made of juniper posts.		15.1
15.6	Cross a creekbed of purple and gray rocks lined with sycamore trees. This is Rye Creek, named after the wild rye plants that once grew along the banks. When FR 422 comes in from the west, stay on FR 414.		14.4
16.0	Rattle over another cattle guard. Notice the change in vegetation. You are in an area of semi-desert grassland with more mesquite trees than juniper.		14.0
16.5	Stay on the signed FR 414 at the intersection, then begin a long climb.		13.5
	Northbounders: *stay on a straight course and look for a FR 414 sign to check that you got on the right road.*		N
18.0	Reach an intersection with FR 517. Turn right (south) staying on FR 414.		12.0
20.2	Continue on FR 414 at this intersection. Brown signs with "414" will let you know you are on the right road.		9.8

Southbound **Northbound**

20.6	Roll onto the pavement in the tiny community of Heberville just before FR 414 hits AZ 87. Rye Creek Restaurant and Bar is across the highway if you need refreshments. Be careful of traffic as you turn right (south) onto the wide shoulder of AZ 87.	9.4
22.0	Carefully turn left (east) following the highway sign to Gisela. The farmer's market here has cold drinks and fresh produce but limited hours of business. Go west on Gisela Road for a short distance.	8.0
22.2	Turn right (south) onto dirt FR 184. A sign says AZ 188 is 8 miles south of here.	7.8
23.0	The Old Rye Creek Mill site is on the right (west). Travel the easy grade along the wide creekbed.	7.0
27.0	Cross the one-lane bridge over a gorge. Rye Creek might have water here, but it will take some effort to get to it. After crossing the bridge, start climbing up a ridge.	3.0
28.2	Near the top, you will get views to the west of the rugged, eroded slopes below.	1.8
30.0	FR 184 meets AZ 188 and Segment 14 ends. Across the street, you'll find the facilities at Jake's Corner.	0.0

Segment 15: JAKE'S CORNER to ROOSEVELT LAKE DAM

Total Distance:
29.2 miles

Distance from Utah:
336.5 miles

Distance to Mexico:
367.4 miles

Difficulty: Easy

Technical Rating: Beginner

Trail Status:
Bike detour around Mazatzal and Four Peaks Wilderness Areas.

Although Segment 15 is on paved highway, the views of Roosevelt Lake framed by saguaro cactus will make up for it.

Season
Fall, winter, spring.
Summers will be insanely hot. This segment is a perfect choice for a winter-season ride.

Maps
USFS: Tonto National Forest
USGS: Gisela, Kayla Butte, Tonto Basin, Theodore Roosevelt Dam
Any Arizona state road map

Signage
Good: Use road signs.

Water Sources
Jake's Corner Store, several small communities along the way, and Cholla Campground will sell or provide water to bicyclists.

Trail Access
SOUTHBOUND: Jake's Corner
Take AZ 87 then AZ 188 about 23 miles south of Payson to the parking lot at Jake's Corner.
NORTHBOUND: Roosevelt Dam Overlook
At the intersection of AZ 188 and AZ 88 (the Apache Trail), Segment 15 ends in the overlook parking lot east of Roosevelt Dam and west of the bridge.

Trail Overview

Segment 15 is the longest paved section on this route. The hiking route of the AZT leaves the Mazatzal Wilderness and enters the Four Peaks Wilderness Area north of Roosevelt Lake. Bicycles are prohibited in both areas. The thru-route has a wide shoulder and the traffic is relatively light. Wear bright clothing, and avoid riding this section in low light. For Southbounders, the landscape becomes more exciting as the route enters the Sonoran Desert for the first time. Several campgrounds and small stores offer plenty of opportunities for rewarding rest stops. The bright blue waters of Roosevelt Lake glisten like an oasis in the dryness of the Tonto Basin. Perched on the ridge above the lake, Cholla Campground is a thru-biker's dream. The Forest Service facility has showers and well-maintained campsites for $11 a night. Near the end of this segment, you'll ride over what made the Top 12 list of most outstanding bridges in 1995. The Roosevelt Bridge was built in 1990 in order to take vehicle traffic off the dam. From the overlook, you can see that the bridge was painted pale blue so that the support arch would blend in with the lake and the Arizona sky.

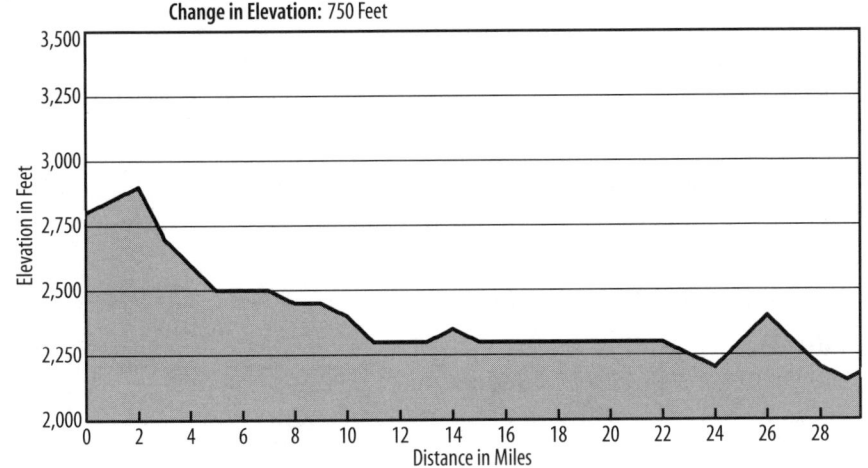

Segment 15   **Total Elevation Gain:** 360 Feet
Total Elevation Loss: 1,000 Feet
Change in Elevation: 750 Feet

Route Description

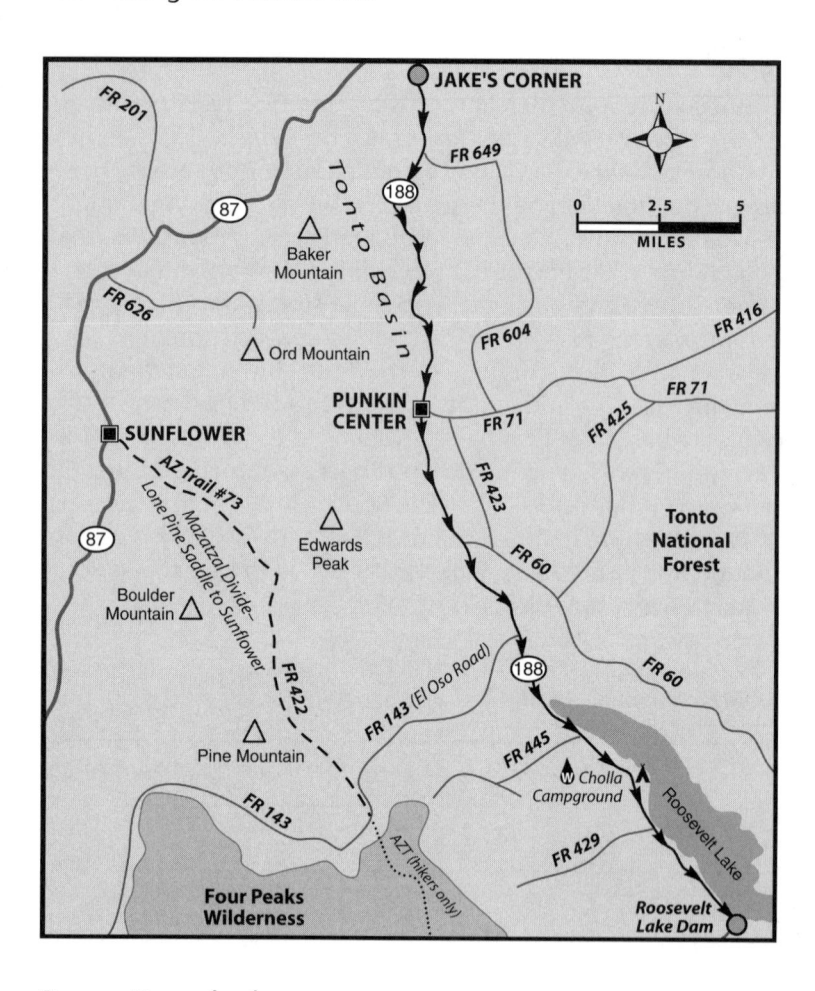

Southbound   Northbound

0.0	At Jake's Corner go south on AZ 188. The route is self-explanatory and involves some ascending but has tolerable grades.	29.2
2.4	When you come out on the south side of the road cut, do you notice anything different? There they are! Saguaro cactus. Congratulations—you've just entered the Sonoran Desert.	26.8
10.3	At Punkin Center, you can stop by the store or restaurant on the east side of the road.	18.9
12.9	Look for the Tonto Basin Inn.	16.3
19.5	You start to get views of Roosevelt Lake to the southeast.	9.7

Southbound   **Northbound**

21.9	Bermuda Flat will appear.	7.3
24.0	The entrance to Cholla Campground, a good camping spot for bikers with or without vehicle support, is on the left (east).	5.2
26.7	The USFS overzealously charges a fee for picnicking at the Vineyard Picnic Area, but the shaded tables with views of the lake make it a nice rest stop.	2.5
29.2	After crossing Roosevelt Bridge, turn right (west) onto AZ 88—The Apache Trail. The road is paved at first. Go a short distance west on AZ 88 to the first overlook and the beginning of Segment 16.	0.0

Saguaro, King of the Desert

Nothing irritates Arizonans more than seeing a movie with fake saguaro cactus in a scene that is supposed to be taking place in Texas. Outside of the Hollywood stage set, Arizona is the only state in the union where the king of cacti grows. Pronounced "suh-wah-ro," the noble plant symbolizes the Wild West and is revered by the Tohono O'odham tribe. Saguaro are the largest cactus in North America, grow from sea level to 4,000 feet, and are comprised of 90% water. From mid-May to June, waxy white flowers appear at the tops of the tall branches called "arms." The flowers remain open at night, to accommodate the nectar-sucking bats that pollinate them. By July, the flowers turn into red fruits that are an important food source for animals, birds, and people. Using poles, the Tohono O'odham knock the fruit to the ground, and then boil them down to syrup used for making jam and wine. Apparently, the fruit would make excellent energy food. Studies have shown them to be balanced at 10% protein, 60% carbohydrates, and 30% fat. Hopefully, you won't find yourself in a situation where you are forced to rely on saguaro fruit for food. Each fruit has over 2,000 seeds.

Day Rides

Mazatzal Divide—Lone Pine Saddle to Sunflower
Total Distance: 17.5 miles
Difficulty: Strenuous
Technical Rating: Advanced

This AZT passage is bypassed by the thru-route, but experienced riders might want to try this section which links the Mazatzal and Four Peaks Wilderness Areas. This ride involves a tough climb over the Mazatzal Divide if you come in from the north. When I rode part of this section, I could not find where the trail leaves FR 1452, so I ended up taking FR 524. This involved a heinous climb and descent in order to get from AZ 87 to AZ 188. If FR 524 is any indication, the AZT route from FR 1452 to FR 422 will be extreme and unpleasant for those going southbound. The best portion of this passage for bikes is the section along FR 422 that follows along the Mazatzal Divide, offers primitive camping areas, and gives you great views of the Tonto Basin and Roosevelt Lake. Day riders can do this as a one-way trip and should turn around before descending Boulder Creek Trail #73. Advanced mountain bikers who want to try the route should go south to north and have transportation waiting for them where the AZT hits AZ 87. This area is too hot in the summer, offers little shade, and has no reliable water sources.

To get to FR 422, take AZ 188 about 20 miles south of the intersection with AZ 87. FR 143 (El Oso Road) is just north of mile marker 255. Drive (high-clearance vehicle recommended) up FR 143 for 8.2 miles until you reach the intersection with the AZT/FR 422. To the south, the AZT will soon head into the Four Peaks Wilderness Area (bicycles prohibited). Take the AZT/FR 422 to the right (north). You can ride for 9 miles until the trail drops off of the Mazatzal Divide. You will pass several campsites and should expect some steep, loose, and rocky climbs. If you take the AZT/Boulder Creek Trail down to FR 1452, it will involve a 2,000-foot loss in elevation. Follow the AZT signs along FR 1452 to FR 22 then to AZ 87, where hopefully you have a vehicle waiting for you. (The trail is in the process of being rerouted near Sunflower. Contact the ATA for updated route information.)

Segment 16 — ROOSEVELT LAKE DAM to LOST DUTCHMAN STATE PARK

Best Ice Cream Stop: Tortilla Flat

Total Distance: 42.7 miles

Distance from Utah: 365.7 miles

Distance to Mexico: 338.2 miles

Difficulty: Strenuous

Technical Rating: Beginner

Trail Status: Bicycle detour around the Superstition Wilderness.

An impressive view of Roosevelt Dam, the largest masonry dam in the world, from the Apache Trail.

Season
Fall, winter, spring. Summers will be insanely hot. A good winter-season ride.

Maps
USFS: Tonto National Forest
USGS: Theodore Roosevelt Dam, Pinyon Mountain, Horse Mesa Dam, Mormon Flat Dam, Goldfield

Signage
Good: Use road signs.

Water Sources
Burnt Corral Campground (0.5 mile from the route), Canyon Lake Resort, Tortilla Flat, Lost Dutchman State Park

Trail Access
SOUTHBOUND: Roosevelt Dam Overlook
Segment 16 starts from the overlook parking lot at Roosevelt Dam, west of the bridge, on the Apache Trail (AZ 88).

NORTHBOUND: Lost Dutchman State Park
From Phoenix, take US 60 to Apache Junction. From the town of Apache Junction, follow signs to the Apache Trail (AZ 88). Lost Dutchman State Park is about 5 miles east of Apache Junction, and the trail description starts from the parking area at the Siphon Draw Trailhead.

Permits and Fees
Lost Dutchman State Park has a $1 entrance fee for bicyclists, $6 for cars. It costs $12 to camp. Call (480) 982-4485 for more information.

Trail Overview
Just south of Roosevelt Bridge, the AZT heads south into the Superstition Wilderness Area. The bicycle route will skirt the northern end of the Wilderness by taking the Apache Trail. The speed limits are slow, the motorists are pleasant, and the vistas are extraordinary, but stay alert as you go around the blind corners and tight curves. Frequent hills will make this long stretch of road challenging for most riders. You'll earn the right to stop for some prickly-pear ice cream at Tortilla Flat. Tortilla Flat (population 6) has a general store, a post office, and a saloon. There are several opportunities for camping along the way. A short but very sweet section of single track will take you to the campground in Lost Dutchman State Park, where hot showers, awesome views, and colorful sunsets await you.

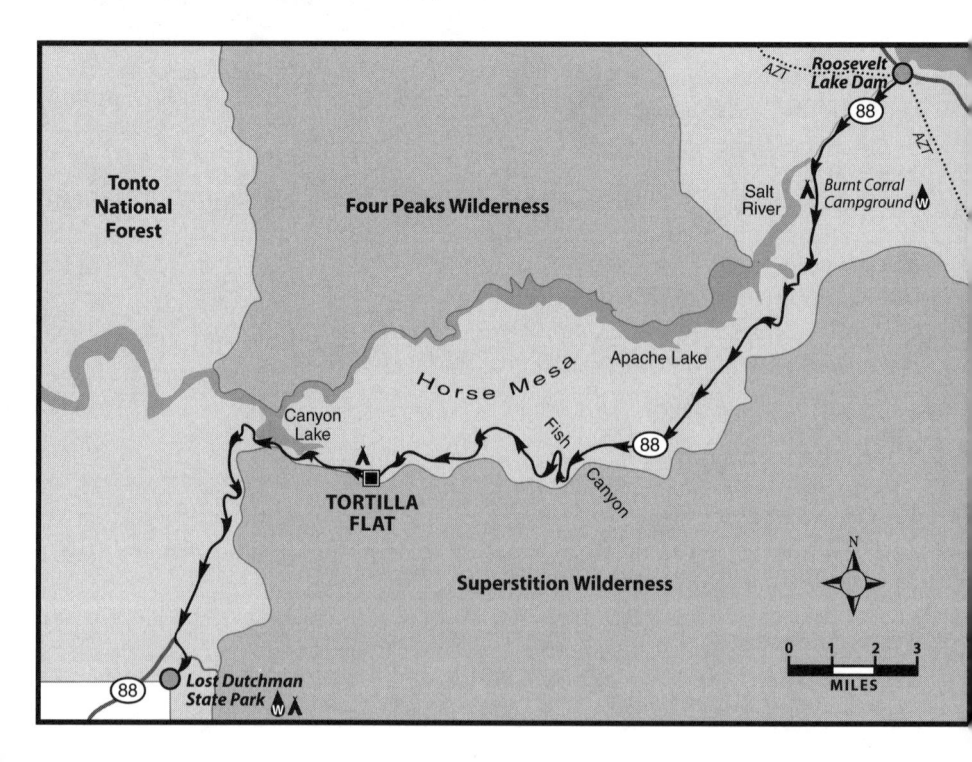

Segment 16 Total Elevation Gain: 3,450 Feet
Total Elevation Loss: 3,520 Feet
Change in Elevation: 1,350 Feet

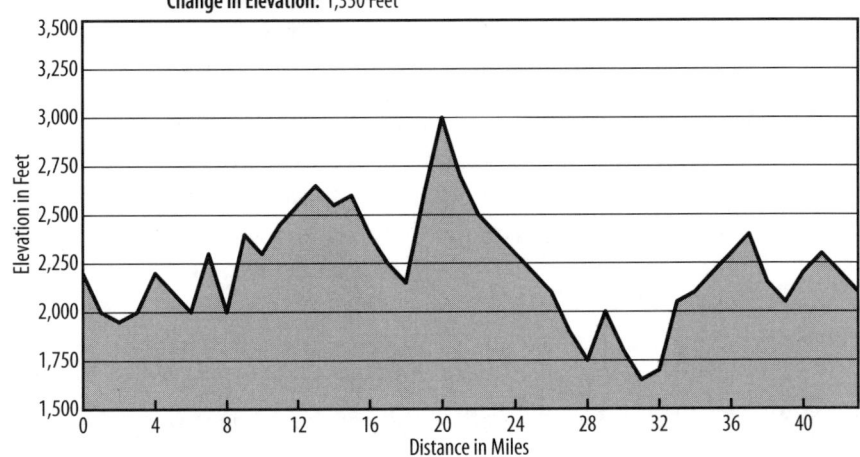

Route Description

Southbound *Northbound*

0.0	From the overlook parking lot at the dam, go west on the Apache Trail (FR 88). Roosevelt Dam is the largest masonry dam in the world.	42.7
0.8	Stop at the second lookout on the west side of the dam. There are breathtaking views of the dam along the short trail to the overlooks.	41.9
1.4	Pavement ends and you begin a section of up-and-down biking. The hills and curves are too numerous to list. Expect a long day of roller-coaster riding on dirt and pavement for the entire length of this segment.	41.3
5.3	Stay on the major road. You'll pass several primitive roads that head north to the mountains or south to the river. Try to watch the road more than the scenery, as the road plunges sharply off the shoulders in several places.	37.4
6.0	A road to the right leads 0.5 mile to Burnt Corral Campground and shady campsites by the water.	36.7
8.5	Cross a bridge over Pine Creek.	34.2
10.4	At Davis Wash you can pull off the road if you need a safe place to take a break.	32.3

Southbound   **Northbound**

12.9	This road leads to Apache Lake Resort. At the Apache Lake Overlook you can see views of the lake and the resort with the Four Peaks Wilderness Area in the background. A short nature trail with interpretive signs leads to another viewpoint. The resort has air-conditioned rooms, campsites, a restaurant, and boat rentals.	29.8
17.9	Stop at the pullout on the right (north) side of the road and contemplate the bluffs rising above you to the west. You will be riding on a road cut into the beige-yellow cliff that towers above you.	24.8
18.6	Cross a scenic canyon at Fish Creek just before beginning an 800-foot climb in just over a mile.	24.1
20.3	You did it! Take a breather and check out the views at the Fish Creek Vista. After taking the nature path to the best views, begin some enjoyable coasting down the other side of the mesa you just climbed.	22.4
22.1	Leave the dirt road for the paved portion of this segment. Be careful—the shoulder is narrow.	20.6
27.7	Be sure to stop at Tortilla Flat and have a soda or an ice-cream cone on the porch.	15.0
30.0	Canyon Lake has grassy waterside campsites and a small store.	12.7
31.6	Cross the one-lane bridge over a finger of Canyon Lake. Acacia Picnic Area has shaded picnic tables, but camping is not permitted. Begin climbing.	11.1

The Apache Trail

Sounds like a road with a rich and romantic western history, doesn't it? I hate to break it to you, but the name, Apache Trail, is little more than a marketing tool to attract tourists. Native American tribes did have trails along the Salt River, but the road traveled today was built to haul supplies and personnel for the construction of Roosevelt Dam, the largest masonry dam in the world. The Roosevelt Dam project in 1903 was the first step toward harnessing the Salt River to supply the Phoenix area with water. It was soon followed by the construction of Mormon Flat Dam and Horse Mesa Dam. By 1920, the Salt River had been thoroughly tamed. When dam construction was finished, the haul road was named "The Apache Trail" and promoted as a tourist attraction. The road snakes along the edge of ridges exposing travelers to panoramic scenes of shimmering lakes framed by majestic saguaros. You'll also get impressive views of the Four Peaks, Goat Mountain, the Painted Cliffs, and the Superstition Mountains.

Southbound | | **Northbound**

32.6	After passing Canyon Lake Vista, the road begins to snake down the ridges in a series of tight curves.	10.1
37.2	At Needle Vista, you can get a peek-a-boo view of Weaver's Needle to the south. Weaver's Needle is 4,535 feet tall. The road flattens out here as you ride past some expansive views of the Superstition Mountains to the south.	5.5
39.5	Just before the brown sign that says "Lost Dutchman State Park 1/4 mile," turn left (south) on FR 78. Pass a sign for the Crosscut Trailhead as you go up the gravel road.	3.2
40.1	Just past the Crosscut Trailhead sign, turn right (south) into the trailhead parking lot. Get on the Jacob's Crosscut Trail #58. This section of single track will lead you to the campground at Lost Dutchman State Park. Go through a gap in the fence, then cross a soft sandy wash. Climb up on the other side of the wash and you should see a sign indicating that you are on the Jacob's Crosscut Trail and that the Broadway Trailhead is six miles ahead.	2.6
40.4	At the top of a steep rise, you will pass a fence and a faint old road. Begin some fun single track that winds through a forest of saguaro and cholla. There are outstanding views of the Superstitions to the south. The riding is pretty easy but there are a few technical climbs and tight switchbacks.	2.3
41.4	The trail crosses the Treasure Loop Trail several times. Stay on Jacob's Crosscut Trail.	1.3
42.2	Bear right at the intersection with Prospector View Trail #57. You should be heading northwest toward the bright green roof of the campground bathhouse.	0.5
42.3	Get on Siphon Draw Trail #53 which will lead you to the trailhead parking area.	0.4
42.5	Leave Tonto National Forest as you go through two gates and enter Lost Dutchman State Park.	0.2
42.7	This is the Siphon Draw Trailhead parking lot and the beginning of Segment 17. Turn right onto the one-way, paved road and ride a short distance to the bathhouse of the campground.	0.0

Segment 17: LOST DUTCHMAN STATE PARK to US 60

Total Distance: 24.3 miles

Distance from Utah:
408.4 miles

Distance to Mexico:
295.5 miles

Difficulty: Easy

Technical Rating: Beginner

Trail Status: Bicycle detour around Superstition Wilderness Area.

Season
Fall, winter, spring. Summers will be hot.

Maps
USFS: Tonto National Forest
USGS: Goldfield, Superstition Mountains, Florence Junction

Excellent singletrack through the Sonoran Desert at the base of the Superstition Mountains.

Signage
Good: The roads are signed at all major intersections.

Water Sources
Lost Dutchman State Park, various businesses along US 60, Florence Junction

Trail Access
SOUTHBOUND: Lost Dutchman State Park
From Phoenix, take US 60 to Apache Junction. From the town of Apache Junction, take AZ 88 and follow signs to the Apache Trail. Lost Dutchman State Park is about 5 miles east of Apache Junction. The trail description starts from the park entrance station.

NORTHBOUND: Mineral Mountain Road
This segment ends where Mineral Mountain Road heads south from US 60, 3.6 miles east of Florence Junction. There is an ORV (Outdoor Recreation Vehicle) information sign and you might see a red flag for the military firing range at the start of the road.

Permits and Fees
Lost Dutchman State Park has a $1 entrance fee for bicyclists, $6 for cars. It costs $12 to camp. Call (480) 982-4485 for more information.

Trail Overview
The recommended thru-route in this section continues to bypass the Superstition Wilderness passage of the AZT. The land west of the Wilderness Area, close to the urban sprawl of Phoenix, continues to experience rapid development. State and county planners are considering the development of a recreational trail through the area this segment travels. But until a trail is built, riders wanting a thru-route will have to use the wide shoulder of US 60. (If you want to help preserve some of this area from overdevelopment, contact the Superstition Area Land Trust, (480) 983-2345, www.azsalt.org).

Segment 17 will bypass the center of Apache Junction by taking a "shortcut" on a suburban road and a power-line road before using US 60 to get to the start of Segment 18. Even though this segment involves mostly paved riding, the scenery is outstanding. You can stop at one of the kitschy, mining-camp tourist attractions as you ride this easy (if it isn't windy) tour though Sonoran desert back-dropped by the Superstition Mountains. Be sure to take advantage of the restaurants and resupply options on this ride. Segments 18 and 19 will make up for this segment's lack of remoteness.

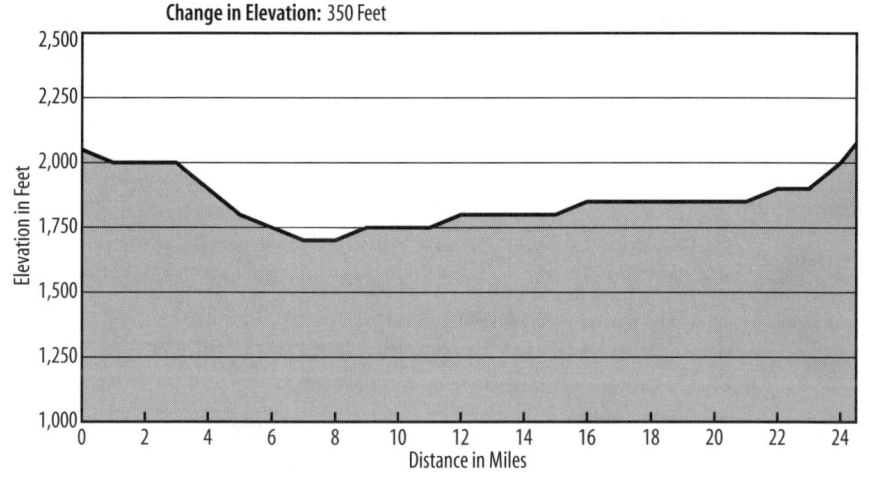

Segment 17 **Total Elevation Gain:** 345 Feet
Total Elevation Loss: 350 Feet
Change in Elevation: 350 Feet

Route Description

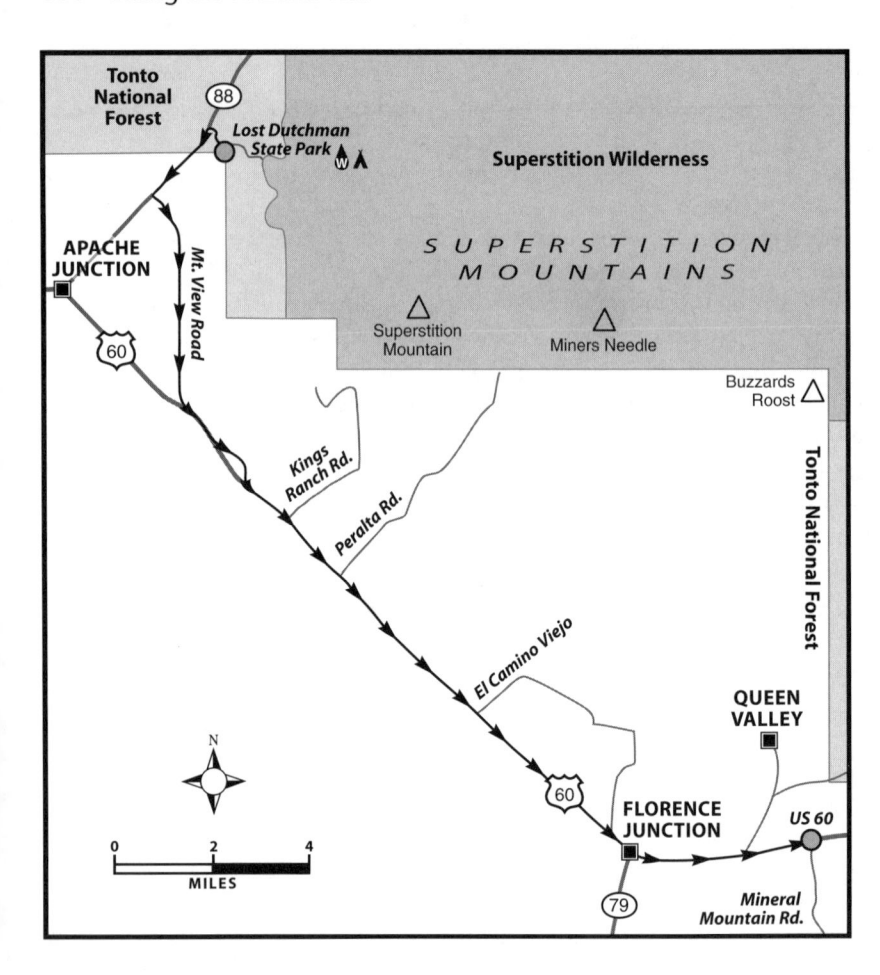

Southbound   Northbound

0.0	From inside Lost Dutchman State Park, leave the park via the park road.	24.3
0.9	Exit the park, then head west on AZ 88. You'll pass the Goldfield Ghost Town with gift shops, a saloon, and a bakery that serves real coffee.	23.4
2.7	Turn left (south) onto Mountain View Road. The road is graveled at first as it travels through a growing residential area.	21.6
4.0	The road becomes paved here at the intersection with Pioneer. Continue south on Mountain View until it reaches US 60.	20.3

Southbound *Northbound*

7.4	When you see US 60, look for the dirt road that goes south under the power lines. Follow this road over some easy grade that is much quieter than the highway. You'll cross Silly Mountain Road as it climbs up the mountain to the east.	16.9
9.0	The power-line road hits Gold Canyon Road across from a shopping center. A golf course puts a stop to our use of this dirt route, so go right (west) then immediately take US 60 to the south. You can bike along the wide shoulder or use the dirt road that parallels the highway.	15.3
10.7	There is a coffee shop 0.3 mile east on Kings Ranch Road if you need a boost.	13.6
13.3	During February and March, you can stop here and check out the Renaissance Festival.	11.0
20.7	Veer left (east), stay on US 60, and go through Florence Junction. Soon you'll see a gas station and your last chance for water before the Gila River.	3.6
22.6	Cross the railroad tracks and pass the entrance road to the community of Queen Valley.	1.7
24.3	On the south side of US 60, 3.6 miles east of Florence Junction, look for a major dirt road that heads south. There will be an information sign for ORV users and danger signs for the military firing range. If you see a red flag, the military is conducting live-fire exercises in the area, but you can still travel the road described in Segment 18.	0.0

The Lost Dutchman Mine

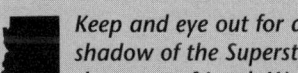

Keep and eye out for a one-armed paloverde while traveling underneath the shadow of the Superstition Mountains. According to legend, a Dutchman by the name of Jacob Waltz found an entrance to one of the richest gold mines in the country. Waltz obsessively protected the mine's location until he was on his deathbed. One version of the story claims that Waltz described the mine as being between a one-armed paloverde and Weaver's Needle. After over 100 years, the legend still inspires prospectors to search for the Dutchman's lost gold. All have failed—some after losing their lives. You'd probably be safer and would have better odds by buying Powerball tickets.

Segment 18   US 60 to GILA RIVER

Best Sonoran Desert Scenery

Total Distance: 18.8 miles

Distance from Utah: 432.7 miles

Distance to Mexico: 271.2 miles

Difficulty: Strenuous

Technical Rating: Intermediate

Trail Status: Detour around White Canyon Wilderness and near proposed route for AZT.

Season
Fall, winter, spring. Summers will be hot. Wet weather can make the roads muddy and subject to flash flooding. Do not enter the Box Canyon Narrows when there is a risk of flooding!

Gorgeous desert vistas await bikers along this beautiful segment of the Arizona Trail.

Maps
BLM: Mesa
USGS: Florence Junction, Florence NE, Mineral Mountain, North Butte, Florence

Signage
Poor: No road numbers and very few road signs. Rely on maps, route description, and landmarks. Carrying topographic maps is recommended.

Water Sources
Florence Junction, Gila River

Trail Access
SOUTHBOUND: Mineral Mountain Road at US 60
The beginning of Segment 18 is 3.6 miles east of Florence Junction at the intersection of US 60 and Mineral Mountain Road. If the red flag is up, it means the military is conducting live artillery firing, but you can still travel the road described in this section.

NORTHBOUND: Diversion Dam Road or Price Road
From Florence, drive north on AZ 79 for 2 miles to a wide graveled road that heads east between the Gila River drainage and the railroad tracks. This road is labeled "Price Road" on some maps and is just south of the railroad tracks. Follow this road for about 9 miles to the diversion dam and the end of Segment 18.

Permits and Fees
Signs indicate that the Arizona State Trust requires permits to use the area. However, as long as you keep your use to the dirt road, no permit is required. Contact: Arizona State Land Department/Public Record, 1616 West Adams, Phoenix, Arizona 85007, (602) 364-2753, www.land.state.az.us.

Trail Overview
The AZT route between US 60 and AZ 77 is still in the development stage. A section of trail has been built that heads south from the Superstition Wilderness to the proposed White Canyon Wilderness Area. Although it is legal to bike some portions of the AZT in this area, the trail is not practical as a thru-route. Day-ride options for those interested in attempting the portions of the trail open to bikers are described in Day Rides. Those satisfied with trying the thru-route won't be disappointed. Segment 18 is an exciting ride through lush Sonoran Desert and the Box Canyon Narrows. The beige walls, brightened with yellow patches of lichen, tower above a gravel-bottomed canyon. You will encounter off-road vehicles on this route but the traffic will not be excessive. Mountain bikers can often make better time than four-wheel-drives on the technical sections of this route. Roads are not signed, so route-finding skills are essential. Water sources are scarce, so plan accordingly. Do not enter the Box Canyon Narrows during stormy weather or when there is risk of a flash flood. If the Gila River is flowing, take the high-water road detour to Florence. Most of the route is on graded dirt roads, but because of the technical sections in Box Canyon Narrows and the steep climbs and descents, Segment 18 is rated as intermediate.

134 Biking the Arizona Trail

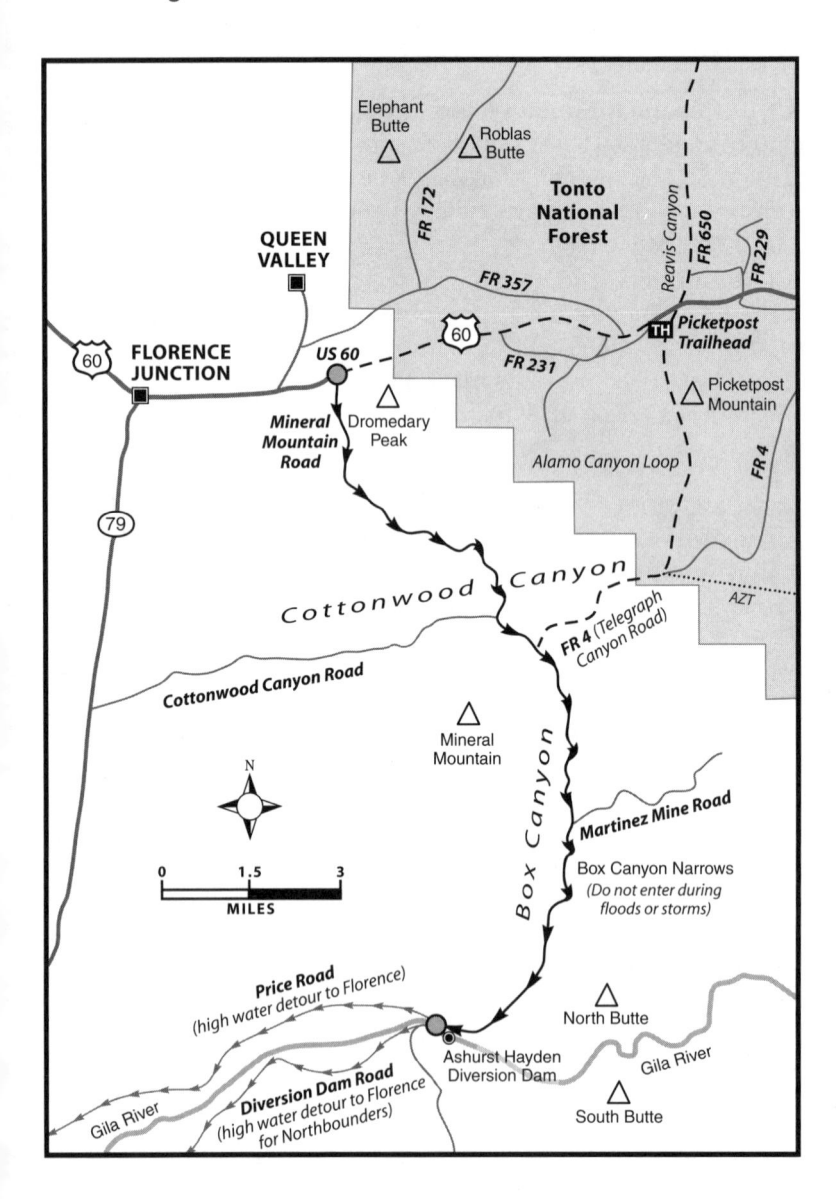

Segment 18 Total Elevation Gain: 750 Feet
Total Elevation Loss: 1,385 Feet
Change in Elevation: 1,400 Feet

Route Description

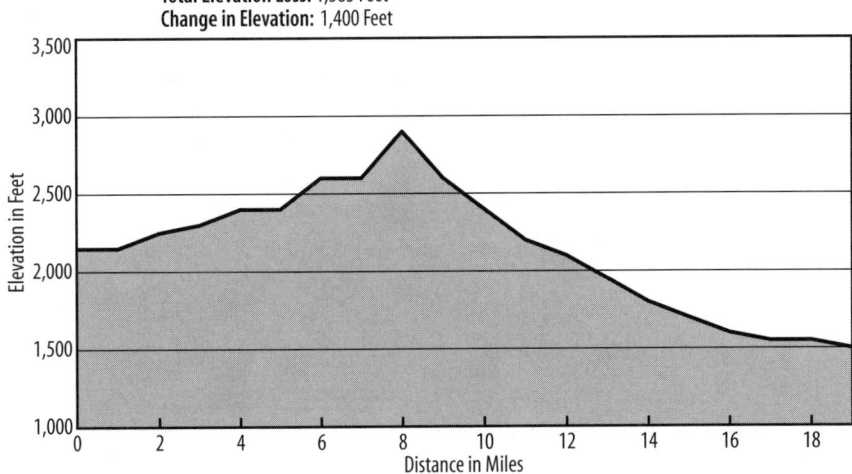

Southbound / *Northbound*

Southbound			Northbound
0.0	Head south on the Mineral Mountain Road. The route starts out well graded. Several roads will come into this one as you continue south and east on the road that shows the most use.		18.8
3.5	The climbing is gradual at first as you head deeper into the desert.		15.3
4.9	You'll cross a cattle guard and a campsite shaded by a large tamarisk before you begin another climb.		13.9
6.0	Descend into Cottonwood Canyon.		12.8
6.6	At a fork in the road, there is a cactus with the way back to US 60 painted on it. Take the left (east) fork. You will cross a wash several times as the road travels through Cottonwood Canyon.		12.2
7.4	Three roads come in from the left (north), but you will stay right. After crossing the wash for the last time, start a long, steep ascent.		11.4
8.5	As you crest a hill, you will get a 360-degree view of the surrounding area that includes Mount Lemmon and the Rincons to the southeast and Weaver's Needle to the north.		10.3
9.1	The road enters a wash and continues down toward Box Canyon.		9.7

Southbound		*Northbound*
10.5	Check out the old adobe dwelling with a fence made of ocotillo branches.	8.3
11.5	The road to Martinez Mine heads left (northeast). Stay right (south) and continue down-canyon. You will soon cross a cattle guard just before you enter the narrowest part of the canyon. Do not enter the canyon if there is a danger of flash flooding.	7.3
13.0	1.5 miles after you pass Martinez Mine Road, you exit the narrow part of the canyon. Continue down and south. The canyon will open up and you will see several camping areas.	5.8
16.6	A railroad comes in from the east as you near the Gila River drainage. You will follow the road to the west along the railroad tracks.	2.2
18.8	When you see the buildings on the south side of the Gila River drainage, you have reached the end of Segment 18. If the Gila River is running with water (the river is usually dry) you should take the high-water detour by continuing west for 9 miles on Price Road to AZ 79 and the town of Florence. If the riverbed is dry and you plan to continue, walk your bike across the area below the dam to the road on the south side, then start Segment 19.	0.0

Day Rides

Reavis Canyon
Total Distance: 14.7 miles
Difficulty: Strenuous
Technical Rating: Intermediate

This section of the AZT is for day riders interested in biking a portion of the trail that is open to bicycles. From Picketpost Trailhead (see directions in the Alamo Canyon Loop), take the AZT to the north. The trail goes under US 60 and then travels along FR 650 to the Reavis Canyon Trail. After the AZT joins with the Reavis Canyon Trail, the route gets rugged and steep as it climbs to Rogers Trough Trailhead. You can bike up the trail for 14.7 miles before the AZT enters the Superstition Wilderness Area near Montana Mountain. The climb is tough so ride until you stop having fun, and then return the way you came. You'll find desert views, campsites, and access to hiking trails on this challenging ride.

Alamo Canyon Loop
Total Distance: 20 miles
Difficulty: Strenuous
Technical Rating: Advanced

This is an extremely challenging loop for advanced riders. To get to the Picketpost Trailhead, take FR 231 (0.4 mile east of milepost 221 and approximately 5 miles west of Superior on US 60). Follow the signs for about 1.6 miles to the well-signed trailhead. Park here then ride back (north) to US 60. Go west on US 60 until you reach the turnoff for Mineral Mountain Road as explained in the Segment 18 route description. Continue south on Mineral Mountain Road until you reach Cottonwood Canyon. Just before the thru-route climbs out of the canyon, take the road to the left (northeast) that parallels the west side of a wash that heads northeast. This is FR 4 (Telegraph Canyon Road). You will pass a metal tank and a mine site before you climb up a steep road that traverses the edge of a canyon. Near the top of the climb (4.3 miles from where you turned off of Mineral Mountain road), you will see an AZT post and a trail that heads northwest.

From where the Arizona Trail leaves FR 4, it is about 5 miles north to Picketpost Trailhead. Follow this rugged trail down the ridge and into a wash. The trail travels through a gravel-bottomed canyon that is marked by rock cairns. The bed of the wash can be soft at times, forcing you to hike your bike. The desert scenery is beautiful and quiet. You will pass a windmill and a stock tank that might have water. The AZT eventually leaves the wash and follows primitive roads back to the trailhead where you started at the base of Picketpost Mountain.

Segment 19 — GILA RIVER to ORACLE

Total Distance: 59.2 miles
Distance from Utah: 451.5 miles
Distance to Mexico: 252.4 miles
Difficulty: Moderate
Technical Rating: Beginner
Trail Status: Bicycle route west of a proposed AZT route.

Season
Fall, winter, spring. Summers will be incredibly hot. Wet weather can make the roads muddy and subject to flash flooding.

Maps
USGS: North Butte, Ninetysix Hills NW and NE, Black Mountain, Fortified Peak, North of Oracle, Oracle

Signage
Fair: Ranch roads often have street signs but this route requires map-reading skills.

Water Sources
Gila River, Oracle

Contemplating the climb ahead. To the south, Mount Lemmon waits for thru-bikers.

Trail Access
SOUTHBOUND: Diversion Dam Road
From Florence, drive north on AZ 79. Just outside of town turn east onto the signed Diversion Dam Road. Five miles east of AZ 79 is the Ashurst Hayden Diversion Dam.

NORTHBOUND: Oracle
Oracle is about 20 miles north of Tucson on AZ 77. Turn south on American Avenue and drive 2 miles to the intersection with Mount Lemmon Control Road.

Trail Overview
This segment involves a long stretch of ranch roads. From the Gila (hee-la) River at the Kelvin Bridge to AZ 77 near Oracle, the AZT is still in the planning stage. Although some sections of trail have been built, as of 2002 a continuous route does not exist. Until this segment of trail is complete, thru-bikers can use the dirt roads. Do not expect much company. The desert here is remote and isolated. Flash floods can make the roads impassable during storms. Be prepared to wait in case you are trapped by floodwaters. Use the high-water detour if the Gila River is flowing. Views of the Tortilla and Catalina Mountain ranges and a look at a Sonoran Desert ecosystem are among the highlights. If you time it right, you might catch the dramatic flower blooms that occur in the early spring after wet winters.

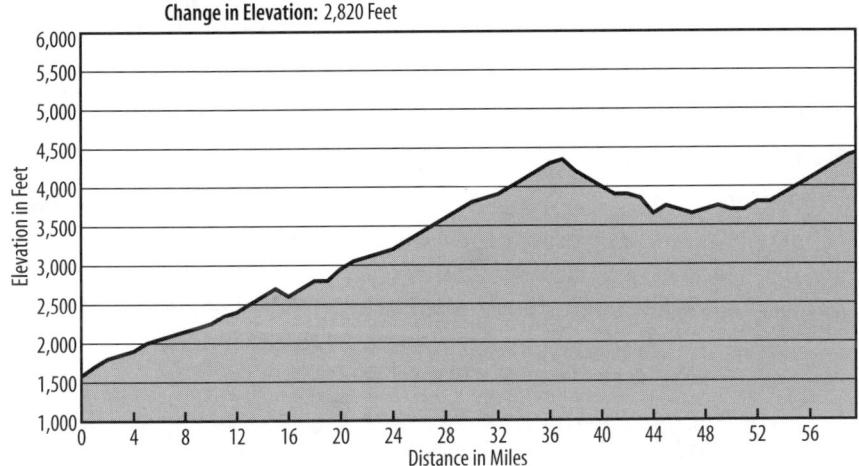

Segment 19 Total Elevation Gain: 3,780 Feet
Total Elevation Loss: 950 Feet
Change in Elevation: 2,820 Feet

Route Description

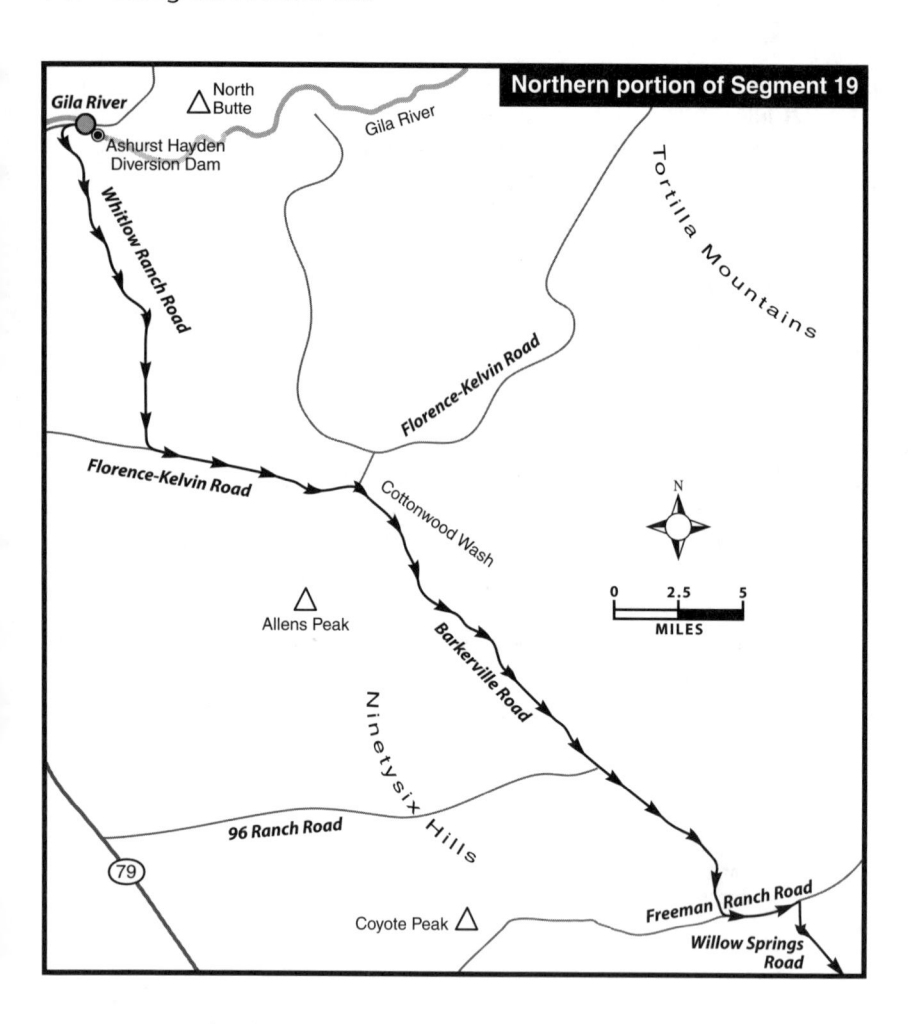

Southbound   *Northbound*

0.0   On the south side of the Gila River, take the road   59.2
      leading up the ridge above the canal. The river is
      channeled and water should be available (filter). Head
      south and climb up the ridge past the abandoned
      buildings with graffiti-covered walls.

Northbounders: *If the Gila River is running with water,*   N
don't cross here. Take the road west for 5 miles to
Florence, then go north on AZ 79 to Price Road as
described in the previous segment.

Segment 19

Southbound *Northbound*

0.3	Cross a cattle guard at the top of a hill. To the east are views of North Butte and the Tortilla Mountain Range. Follow the dirt road as it curves through a forest of saguaro. Stay to the right (southeast) on the most improved road. You will climb several hills and descend into dry washes that can flood during wet weather. Do not cross areas that are flooded!	58.9
4.6	Go around a working ranch and under a power line.	54.6
6.0	After crossing a cattle guard, stay right (east) along the fence and power line until you reach an improved gravel road. Turn south and start rolling over a series of hills.	53.2

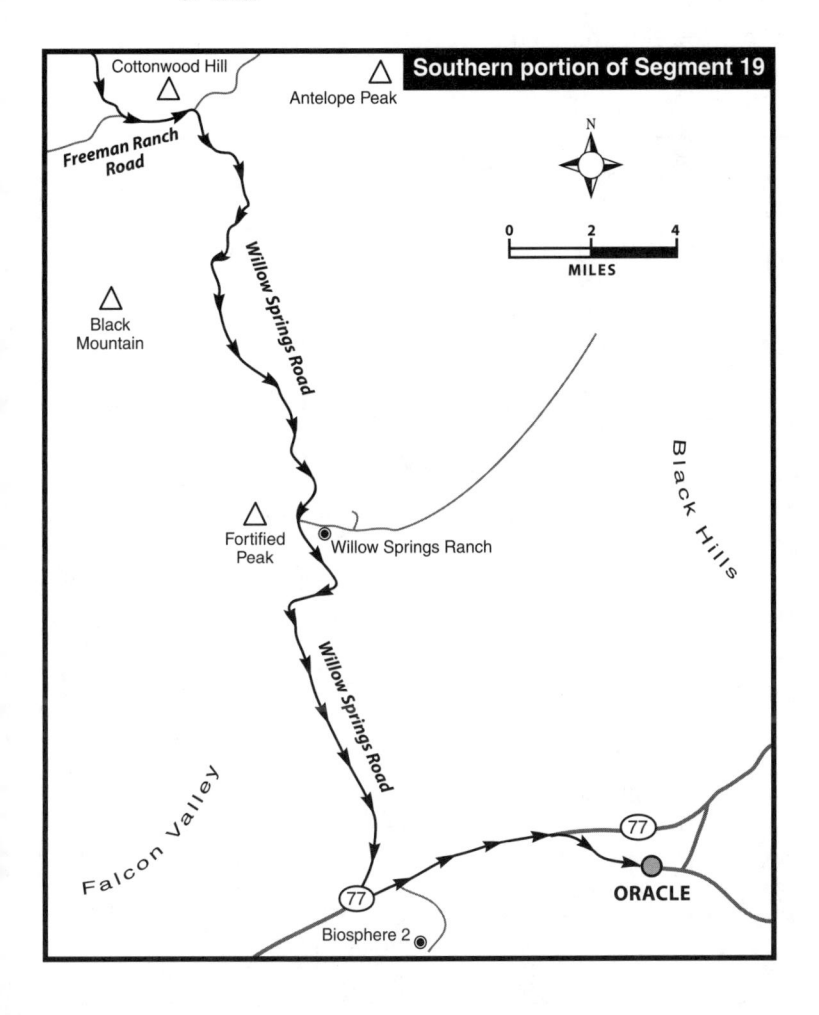

Southbound		Northbound
9.2	Pass a quarry site.	50.0
9.7	At the stop sign, turn left (east) onto the Florence-Kelvin Road. Expansive views open up to the north as the road continues eastbound on a gradual grade. The saguaros give way to mesquite, prickly pear, and the green-barked paloverde.	49.5
15.1	Drop down into a wash. At the bottom, turn right (south) onto Barkerville Road. Cross another cattle guard, then climb out of the wash. Stay on the most improved road as you pass several side roads.	44.1
27.5	There is a windmill to the left (east) and views of Black Mountain to the southwest.	31.7
30.7	At the stop sign, turn left (east) onto Freeman Road.	28.5

The Sonoran Desert

Ocotillo, saguaro, paloverde, teddy bear cholla, prickly pear—the plants of the most species-rich desert of North America sound and look like a scene from a Dr. Seuss story. Chuckwalla, Gila monster, kangaroo rat, collared peccary, horny toad, gilded flicker—the diverse creatures found in the Sonoran Desert enhance the exotic strangeness of the landscape. South of Payson, the route in this book takes you on a journey through miles of Sonoran Desert environments. But there is more than one kind of desert in Arizona. Portions of all four of the deserts found in North America are within the state boundaries. From Utah to the Mogollon Rim, you get to see America's northernmost desert—the Great Basin. Near the Mexican Border, the AZT is teased with flavors of the Chihuahuan Desert grasslands. Only the stark emptiness of the Mohave Desert remains outside the corridor traveled by the AZT. If possible, bikers should take advantage of the trail's proximity to Tucson and squeeze in a side trip to the Arizona-Sonoran Desert Museum. A cross between a zoo, a museum, and an arboretum, this award-winning facility will entertain as well as educate you on all the world's desert environments. The exhibits, which include a hummingbird enclosure, are well worth the trip.

For more information: Arizona-Sonoran Desert Museum, 2021 N. Kinney Road (located 12 miles from Tucson, on the west side of town), (520) 883-2702, www.desertmuseum.org.

Segment 19

Southbound			Northbound
32.4	Turn right (south) onto Willow Springs Road. Begin a series of roller-coaster hills that can be tiring at the end of your day.		26.8
36.5	A cattle-loading chute is on the west side of the road. You can see Mount Lemmon and the Catalina Range to the south.		22.7
41.3	Go under a power line.		17.9
43.0	Willow Springs Ranch can be seen to the east. Mount Lemmon looms bigger and bigger as you continue southward.		16.2
46.0	Go under the ranch sign.		13.2
52.8	Turn left (east) onto AZ 77. Watch for highway traffic as you climb the gradual grade. You will pass the entrance to Biosphere 2 on your right (south). The controversial project put a group of scientists in a self-contained environment for a year and is now open for tours.		6.4
57.2	Turn right (south) onto American Avenue.		2.0
57.6	There is a convenience store here if you need a cold drink.		1.6
58.8	In Oracle, a convenience store, a steakhouse, and a pizza restaurant can satisfy your carbohydrate needs after the long ride. The public library has computers with Internet access for thru-bikers who need to let their families know that they are still in one piece.		0.4
59.2	Mount Lemmon Control Road (Segment 20) is on the right (south) side of American Avenue across from the local market and just west of the post office.		0.0

Segment 20 ▶ ORACLE to MOLINO BASIN CAMPGROUND

Toughest Climb (or best ride to train for the Ironman) and Best Descent

Total Distance: 48.3 miles

Distance from Utah: 510.7 miles

Distance to Mexico: 193.2 miles

Difficulty: Strenuous

Technical Rating: Beginner

Trail Status: Bicycle detour around the Oracle Ridge Trail and the Pusch Ridge Wilderness Area

Season
The road is open all year but can be impassable when it snows.

Maps
USFS: Coronado National Forest, Safford and Catalina Ranger Districts
USGS: Oracle, Campo Bonito, Mount Lemmon, Mount Bigelow, Agua Caliente Hill
Rainbow Expeditions, Inc.: Santa Catalina Mountains, Arizona—A Trail and Recreation Map

Windy Point Vista, Catalina Highway.

Signage
Good: Use FS road signs.

Water Sources
Oracle, Peppersauce Campground, Summerhaven, Spencer Campground, Palisades Ranger Station

Permits and Fees
If you enter the Coronado National Forest by vehicle and plan to recreate (bike), you should pay the $5 recreation use fee. Thru-bikers who enter by bicycle do not have to pay the use fee. The fees are usually paid at self-serve fee stations at various locations in the Santa Catalina District. The developed campgrounds run from $5 to $8 a night.

Trail Access
SOUTHBOUND: Oracle
Oracle is 20 miles north of Tucson on AZ 77. Turn right (south) on American Avenue and drive 2 miles to the intersection with Mount Lemmon Control Road.

NORTHBOUND: Molino Basin Campground
From Tucson, go east on Tanque Verde Road to the Catalina Highway. Molino Basin Campground is 9.7 miles from the start of the Catalina Highway.

Trail Overview
Segment 20 involves a challenging climb to the top of Mount Lemmon from the small town of Oracle. Bicycles are allowed on the Oracle Ridge Trail (AZT) to the top of Mount Lemmon, but the trail is extremely steep and rugged after the first few miles. Day riders in the mood for a short out-and-back should try the American Flag Spur (see p. 149).

For thru-bikers, the Mount Lemmon Control Road provides a biker-friendly option to the top of Mount Lemmon and around the Pusch Wilderness while still giving you the chance to exceed your target heart rate. Southbounders might want to break up the climb by camping underneath the sycamore and walnut trees at Peppersauce Campground. Views of the San Pedro Valley and the Galiuro Range open up to the east as the road switchbacks through grasslands dotted with agave and yucca. This scenic byway on the southeast (downhill) side of Mount Lemmon is very busy on weekends and usually has several areas of ongoing road construction. You will experience the change from alpine forest to Sonoran Desert and expansive panoramas of the city of Tucson as you coast the curves to Molino Basin Campground.

146 Biking the Arizona Trail

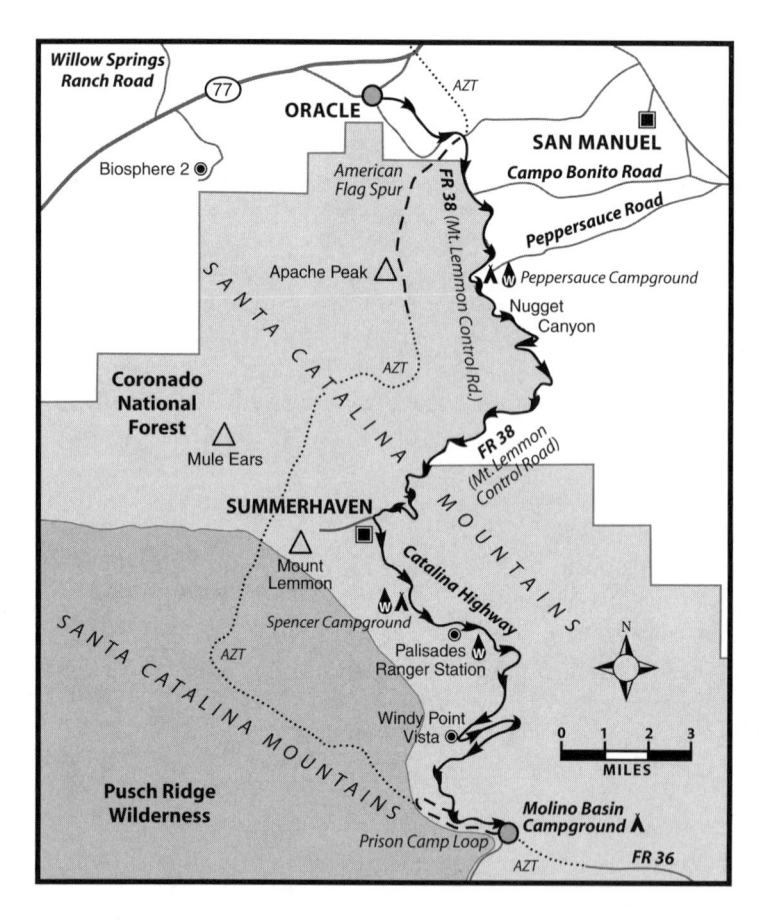

Segment 20 Total Elevation Gain: 4,350 Feet
Total Elevation Loss: 4,350 Feet
Change in Elevation: 3,750 Feet

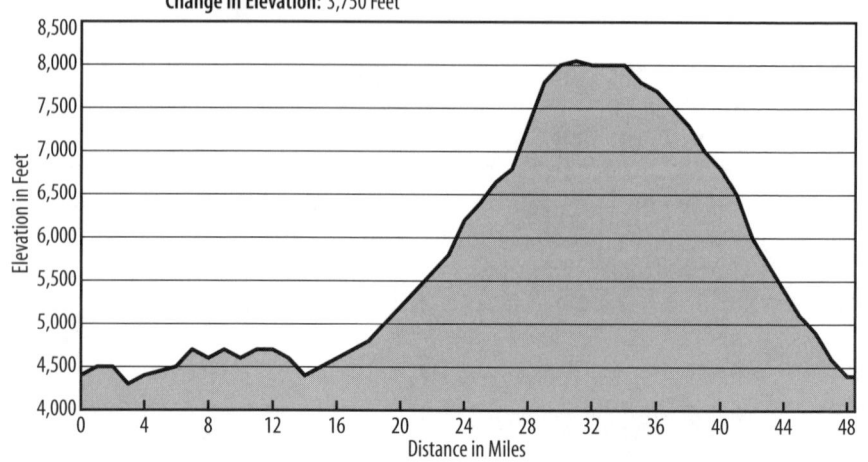

Route Description

Southbound		Northbound
0.0	From the Oracle Post Office, go south a short distance to the Mount Lemmon Control Road. Travel east on the paved road through a residential area.	48.3
1.1	Pass the entrance to Oracle State Park on your left (east).	47.2
1.8	Enter Coronado National Forest.	46.5
2.2	After passing Cody Loop Road, begin a coasting descent.	46.1
3.3	Pavement ends.	45.0
4.3	AZT trailhead is on your right (west). Thru-bikers keep on the Mount Lemmon Control Road. Day-riders may want to ride the short sections of the AZT to the north or the south (such as the American Flag Spur, described in Day Rides).	44.0
7.0	The road gets narrower and steeper as the tough climbing begins.	41.3
8.0	The grade evens out as you travel by a forest of agave plants. Descend along a power line into Peppersauce Wash where there is a Forest Service campground shaded by sycamores. After the campground start climbing again.	40.3
9.7	Traverse the side of a ridge exposed to views of the San Pedro River Valley to the east.	38.6
10.8	Go down and out of Nugget Canyon.	37.5

Summerhaven

The appropriately named community of Summerhaven has historically served as a retreat for Tucson residents to escape the scorching heat of summer. The first inn on the mountain was built in the 1920s. Early visitors traveled up a rougher, narrower version of the road you take today. When traffic jams became a problem, the road was designated as a one-way road with the direction of travel changing during certain hours of the day. This "control" of the traffic flow led to the name the Mount Lemmon Control Road. As expected, a less tedious route was desired. The paved south-side approach was completed in 1950 and became what is now the Catalina Highway. Summerhaven offers limited resupply for thru-bikers and has several restaurant and lodging choices for those who need to recuperate from the climb up Mount Lemmon.

Southbound		Northbound
12.4	Drop down into Catalina Wash and ascend a rocky section of road.	35.9
13.9	Switchback down the south side of the drainage you just climbed. It seems like you are going out of your way as you travel south in and out of the foothills of Mount Lemmon. This is the price you pay for the relatively gradual grade of this road.	34.4
16.2	A USFS sign says you are on FR 38.	32.1
18.9	Go down again before you cross a bridge over Gibb's Wash.	29.4
19.7	Stay on FR 38 and ascend a series of short switchbacks up the ridge.	28.6
20.8	Mine tailings from the Oracle Ridge Mine can be seen on the ridges above.	27.5
22.2	Follow the sign that says "Mt. Lemmon 7 miles." The road to the right (north) leads to the mine.	26.1
24.0	You will begin to see ponderosa pine. These trees grow above 6,000 feet. You are making progress!	24.3
26.0	The grade evens out again as you pass a primitive camping area with views but no water. This is a good spot to camp if you're done climbing for the day.	22.3
27.1	Cross the Crystal Springs Trail.	21.2
28.7	More dry camps can be found on both sides of the road. Expect company. These campsites are popular on weekends.	19.6
29.0	Continue a short distance to the pavement. Turn left onto the Catalina Highway. To the right is the community of Summerhaven.	19.3

Islands in the Sky

Rising 7,000 feet above the desert floor, Mount Lemmon is a prime example of the "sky island" phenomenon. The cooler temperatures and increased precipitation of high elevations allow plants and animals to survive at latitudes far south of their typical range. Surrounded by a sea of harsh desert, these isolated "island" ecosystems are similar to biological communities found in Canada. As you make the grueling climb up the Mount Lemmon Control Road, watch how the vegetation changes from desert scrub to evergreen forests shading lush ferns. In less than thirty miles, you will encounter the same changes in the environment you would see if you rode from Mexico to Canada.

Southbound			Northbound
29.7	After the Loma Linda picnic area, you will begin the long coast to Molino Basin.		18.6
30.6	Stop at Inspiration Point Overlook to see what you just climbed.		17.7
32.0	The entrance to Spencer Canyon Campground (fee) is on the right (west).		16.3
34.0	Palisades Visitor Center has water, restrooms, and information.		14.3
38.0	Take in the views of Tucson and Mount Wrightson.		10.3
39.8	Here's an obligatory photo stop—Windy Point Vista.		8.5
46.4	The Prison Camp Road heads off to the right (southwest). Continue straight and down.		1.9
48.3	Molino Basin Campground—no water!		0.0

Day Rides

American Flag Spur
Total Distance: 2–4 miles
Difficulty: Moderate
Technical Rating: Intermediate

From the American Flag Trailhead at Mile 4.3 of the Southbound route, you can take the AZT/Oracle Ridge Trail west for some interesting mountain biking. Go under the trailhead arch and ride as far as you like. The trail will get increasingly difficult as it climbs Oracle Ridge. When the fun stops, turn around and go down the way you came.

Prison Camp Loop
Total Distance: 4 miles
Difficulty: Moderate
Technical Rating: Intermediate

Four miles of AZT are open to bicycles between Molino Basin and the Pusch Ridge Wilderness boundary. For a short but challenging loop, park at Molino Basin (see Trail Access: Northbound) and ride up the Catalina Highway to the turnoff for Prison Camp Campground. Turn left (southwest) and ride into the campground area. To return to Molino, take the AZT south for a 2-mile, intermediate-level descent back to your car.

Segment 21 ▶ MOLINO BASIN CAMPGROUND to COLOSSAL CAVE

Total Distance: 30.0 miles
Distance from Utah: 559.0 miles
Distance to Mexico: 144.9 miles
Difficulty: Easy
Technical Rating: Beginner
Trail Status: Bike detour around Saguaro National Park and along a proposed urban route for the AZT.

Season
Fall, winter, spring. Summers will be too hot.

Maps
USFS: Coronado National Forest, Safford and Catalina Ranger Districts
USGS: Agua Caliente Hill, Tucson East, Vail
Rainbow Expeditions, Inc.: Santa Catalina Mountains, Arizona—A Trail and Recreation Map

Signage
Good: Use road signs.

Water Sources
Tucson, Saguaro National Park, Rincon Creek General Store, Colossal Cave Mountain Park, Vail

The Colossal Cave entrance is a short distance from the bike route.

Trail Access
SOUTHBOUND: Molino Basin Campground
From Tucson go east on Tanque Verde Road to the Catalina Highway. Molino Basin Campground is 9.7 miles from the start of the Catalina Highway.
NORTHBOUND: Colossal Cave Mountain Park
Take the Old Spanish Trail road south from Tucson to the entrance to Colossal Cave. Segment 21 ends where the road is gated just past the entrance to La Posta Quemada Ranch.

Permits and Fees
In Saguaro National Park (Rincon Mountain District), the NPS charges a $3 entrance fee. Colossal Cave Mountain Park charges a $1 entrance fee.

Trail Overview
The AZT heads southeast from Molino Basin and eventually enters Saguaro National Park. Bicycles are prohibited on the AZT in the park, but it is possible to ride the AZT from Molino Basin to Reddington Road. This ride is listed as a loop ride in the Day Rides section. Reddington Road is a steep Forest Service road, which is used by Tucson residents for weekend target practice and four-wheeling. I recommend that thru-bikers take the "urban" route that skirts the boundary of Saguaro National Park on the way to Colossal Cave Mountain Park. You will have less climbing and a more pleasant experience. You will pass several resupply opportunities and can take a side trip into downtown Tucson if you'd like. The road along the Old Spanish Trail is popular with local bikers. Segment 21 is a perfect choice for winter riding and for beginners. At the end of the day, you can tour Colossal Cave and camp at the quiet campground at El Bosquecito.

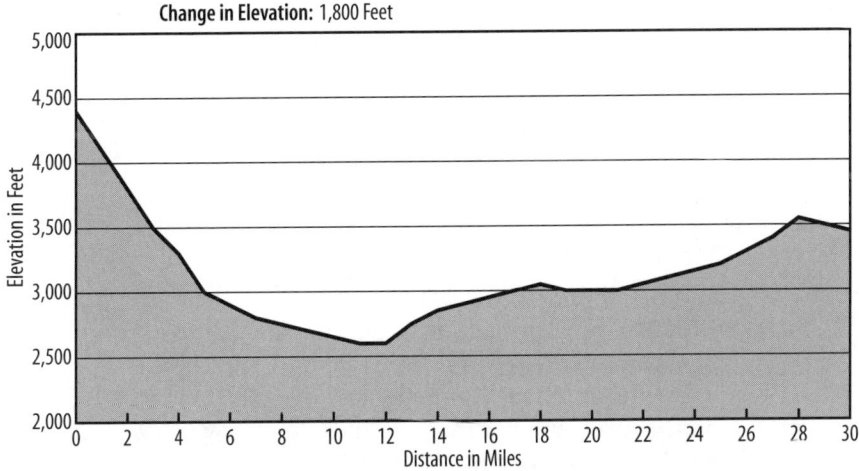

Segment 21 Total Elevation Gain: 1,000 Feet
Total Elevation Loss: 1,950 Feet
Change in Elevation: 1,800 Feet

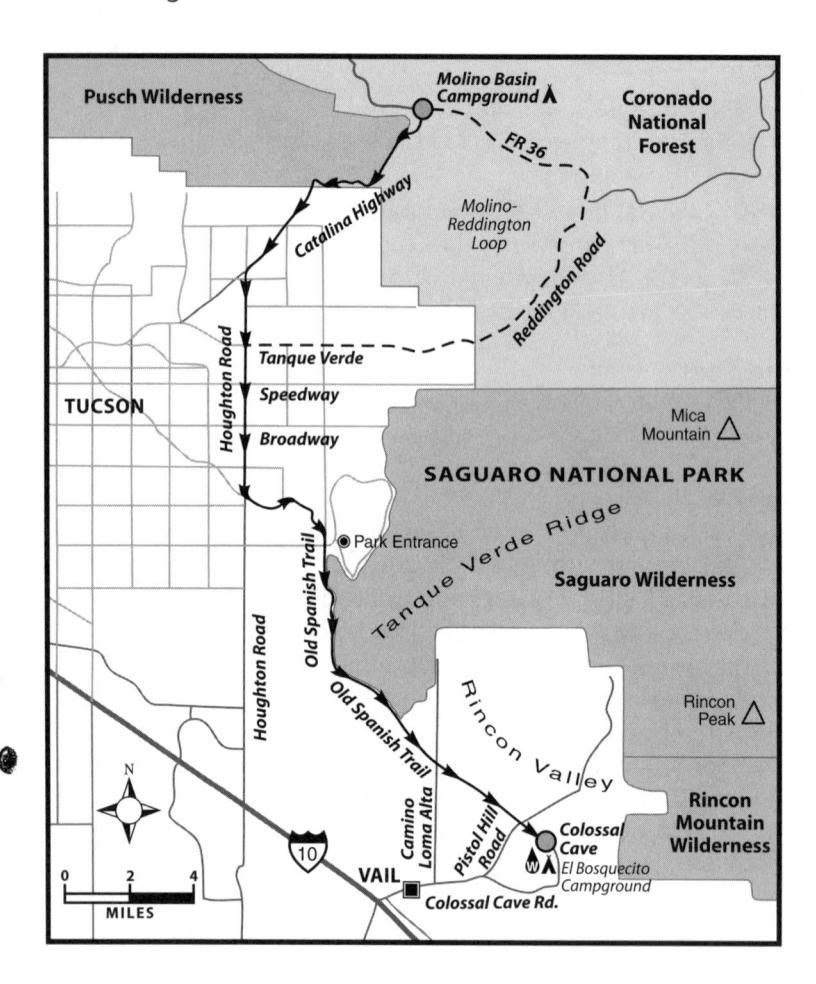

Route Description

Southbound		**Northbound**
0.0	From Molino Basin Trailhead, continue southbound on Catalina Highway toward Tucson.	30.0
8.9	Turn left (south) onto Houghton Road.	21.1
10.8	Cross Tanque Verde Road. Follow the signs to Saguaro Park and Colossal Cave.	19.2
11.6	Cross the bridge over Tanque Verde Creek.	18.4
13.6	There's a grocery store near Broadway St. for resupply.	16.4
14.7	Turn left (east) and get onto the Old Spanish Trail bike path on the north side of the road. If you are in the mood for some urban time, you can go west on the bike path and then west on Broadway for a 9-mile ride into downtown Tucson.	15.3

Southbound		Northbound
17.6	The route travels along the boundary of the Rincon Mountain District of Saguaro National Park. The visitor center (water, restrooms, desert exhibits) is a short distance east of the park entrance. The bike path ends here.	12.4
21.9	Next to the Rincon Creek General Store is a farmer's market open only on Saturdays. Begin the long climb to Colossal Cave. The riding should still be easy unless you have a headwind.	8.1
27.8	If you want to avoid the $1 entrance fee, you can bypass Colossal Cave by turning right (southwest) onto Pistol Hill Road at the sign pointing the way to I-10.	2.2
28.8	Enter Colossal Cave Mountain Park. Just south of the entrance station, you can go left for about a mile to the El Bosquecito Campground.	1.2
30.0	You come to a gate at the turnoff for La Posta Quemada Ranch—a quaint spot worth the short trip to see the museum, café, and butterfly garden. Segment 22 begins at the biker gate.	0.0

Agave, The Tequila Plant

As you travel the AZT, you will pass hillsides dotted with conspicuous plants that have a rosette of thick, daggerlike leaves. These are agave plants. They are pronounced "uh-ga-vay," but I have a friend who calls them ag-ouchies. If the wicked spines on the tip of each leaf get embedded in your skin, the wound can fester for days. An agave plant is not a cactus. However, agaves are also succulents, evident by the thick fleshy leaves that resemble a tougher version of an aloe plant. When an agave matures, the plant sends up a large flowering stalk in a spurt of hyperactive desperation to reproduce. Once the stalk has grown and fruited, the plant dies. But the agave goes out in a blaze of glory and honor. The flowers provide nectar to bats, moths, and birds, and the plant was an important source of food, rope, and medicine for the native people of the Sonoran Desert. You can also thank the agave for the kick in your margarita. The bases of the stalks can be steamed, mashed, and then fermented with liquid to form a liquor called mescal. Tequila is a higher quality mescal that is made from the Agave tequila, a variety of agave found only in Mexico.

Day Rides

Molino Basin–Reddington Road Loop
Total Distance: 30 miles
Difficulty: Strenuous
Technical Rating: Intermediate

From Molino Basin Campground (see Trail Access: Southbound), you can take the Arizona Trail for 8.7 miles to Reddington Road. You will have to climb up a steep section of switchbacks to a saddle and then make a steep descent before the trail follows FR 36 (Bellota Ranch Road) after (south of) West Spring Tank. The trail leaves the dirt road through Agua Caliente Wash, then follows FR 36. After passing a pond called "the Lake," go west down Reddington Road for 10 miles until it becomes Tanque Verde. Then take Houghton Road north to the Catalina Highway, where you can bike northeast back to Molino Basin. You can also use this as an out-of-the-way thru-route from Molino Basin to Houghton Road, but I recommend it for intermediate and advanced riders only.

Saguaro Park to Colossal Cave
Total Distance: 11.2 miles
Difficulty: Easy
Technical Rating: Beginner

This popular ride links two desert parks. See the route description beginning at Southbound mile 17.6. You can get to Saguaro National Park East by taking the Old Spanish Trail east from Tucson. Colossal Cave is 12.4 miles farther south on the same road.

Segment 22 — COLOSSAL CAVE to OAK TREE CANYON

Total Distance:
25.6 miles

Distance from Utah:
589.0 miles

Distance to Mexico:
114.9 miles

Difficulty: Easy

Technical Rating: Beginner

Trail Status:
Thru-route across an area proposed for AZT development.

The sweeping desert grasslands of Las Cienegas lead to the base of the Whetstone Mountains.

Season
Late fall, winter, early spring. Summers will be hot.

Maps
USFS: Coronado National Forest, Nogales and Sierra Vista Ranger Districts
USGS: Rincon Peak, The Narrows, Spring Water Canyon, Empire Ranch

Signage
Good: Use road signs.

Water Sources
Colossal Cave Mountain Park, Vail, Mountain View

Trail Access
SOUTHBOUND: Colossal Cave Mountain Park
Take the Old Spanish Trail road south from Tucson to the entrance to Colossal Cave. Segment 21 ends where the road is gated just south of the entrance to La Posta Quemada Ranch.
NORTHBOUND: AZT Trailhead at AZ 83 and FR 4072
Oak Tree Canyon is near milepost 43 on AZ 83 north of Sonoita. Look for a dirt road (FR 4072) that heads down (west) to a well-used camping area and an AZT Trailhead sign.

Permits and Fees
Colossal Cave Mountain Park charges a $1 entrance fee.

Trail Overview
Between Colossal Cave and Oak Tree Canyon the AZT is still in the planning stage, and it is not likely that a trail though this area will be constructed for several years. Bikers will have to use paved roads to connect a thru-route. There is some climbing to do on AZ 83, but the views of the Santa Rita foothills will provide a nice distraction. Ride with the direction of traffic and wear bright clothing.

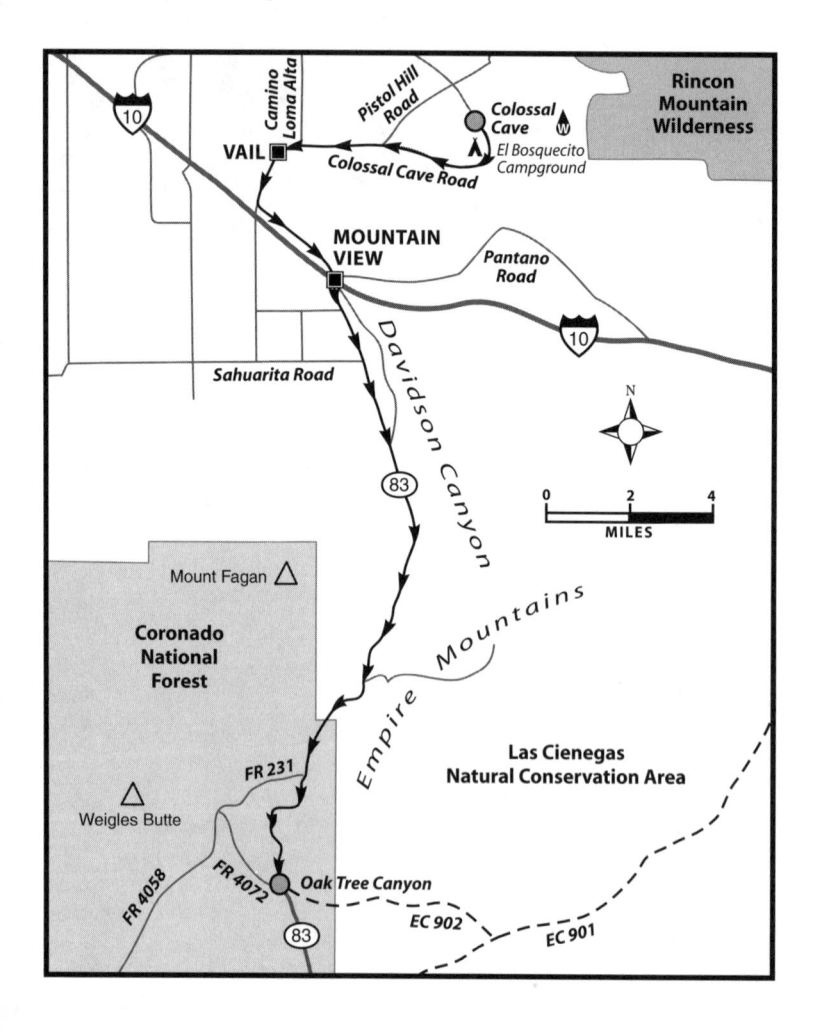

Segment 22 Total Elevation Gain: 2,000 Feet
Total Elevation Loss: 400 Feet
Change in Elevation: 1,850 Feet

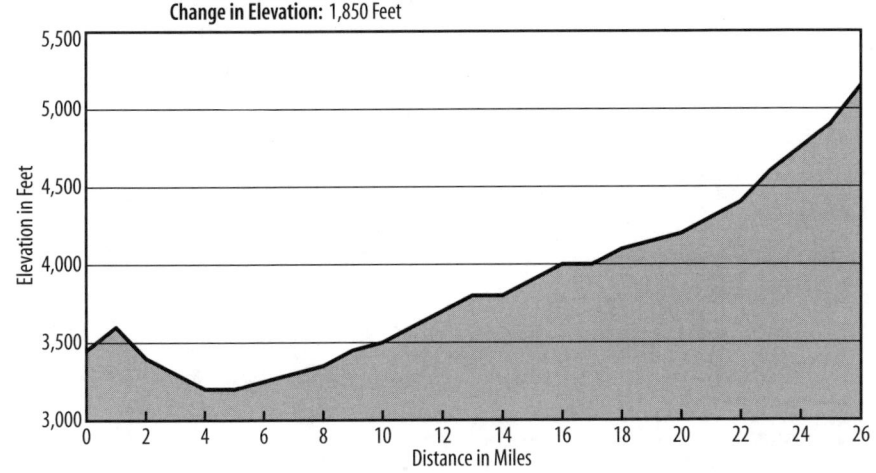

Route Description

Southbound   *Northbound*

0.0	Segment 22 begins at the gate just south of the turnoff for La Posta Quemada Ranch. Go through the bicycle gate and start climbing a lonely paved road between saguaro-studded hillsides.	25.6
1.2	When you get to the top, roll over a series of fun, mogul-like dips.	24.4
2.0	Colossal Cave Road intersects with Pistol Hill Road. Turn south toward Vail.	23.6
	Northbounders: *when coming from Vail, turn right (east) onto Colossal Cave Road. Ignore the sign that says there is no access to Colossal Cave. This message is intended for motor vehicles only.*	N
4.4	Cross Pantano Wash.	21.2
4.6	Enter Vail city limits. Don't expect much in the way of resupply. Continue south on Colossal Cave Road through the town of Vail toward I-10.	21.0
6.1	Just before I-10 Exit 279, go left (east) onto Frontage-Pantano Road.	19.5
8.7	Turn right (south) onto AZ 83 toward Sonoita. You will have several long climbs and a narrow shoulder.	16.9

Southbound   *Northbound*

25.6   On the west side of AZ 83 near milepost 43, look for   0.0
FR 4072. You might see other campers here on the
weekends. Segment 23 starts at the trailhead signs.

Day Rides

Oak Tree Canyon
Total Distance: 3–15 miles
Difficulty: Easy
Technical Rating: Beginner

While researching for "unofficial" thru-routes in this area, I discovered the mountain biking potential of the Las Cienegas Natural Conservation Area. Although the conservation area might not be chosen as the final destination of the AZT, I couldn't resist sharing this ride with day riders interested in exploring. Several primitive campsites that are shaded by large oaks make the route attractive for a bike-packing trip.

From the AZT Trailhead on AZ 83 (see Trail Access: Northbound), go east on the path that goes through the culvert under the highway. For the next few miles, this trail might still be signed with AZT posts. The area was once considered for AZT development but at this printing this trail is not official AZT. Continue east as the trail eventually turns into EC 902 when you enter lands managed by the BLM. In 6 miles, EC 902 will intersect with EC 901. You can go north here for a longer ride or go south on EC 901 then back to AZ 83 where you can return to your starting point.

Segment 23 — OAK TREE CANYON to PATAGONIA

Most Novel Accommodations:
The Kentucky Camp Bed but not Breakfast

Total Distance: 37.5 miles
Distance from Utah: 614.6 miles
Distance to Mexico: 89.3 miles
Difficulty: Moderate
Technical Rating: Intermediate
Trail Status:
Official AZT route and detour around Mount Wrightson Wilderness Area.

Season
All year, but summers can be hot.

Maps
USFS: Coronado National Forest, Nogales and Sierra Vista Ranger Districts
USGS: Empire Ranch, Helvetia, Sonoita, Mount Wrightson, Mount Hughes
Rainbow Expeditions, Inc.: Santa Catalina Mountains, Arizona—A Trail and Recreation Map

Signage
Good: AZT stickers on Carsonite posts.

Water Sources
Kentucky Camp, Tunnel Springs Tank, Sonoita, Patagonia

Adobe foundations backdrop the ride into Kentucky Camp.

Trail Access
SOUTHBOUND: AZT Trailhead at AZ 83 and FR 4072
Oak Tree Canyon is near milepost 43 on AZ 83 north of Sonoita. Look for a dirt road that heads west. This dirt road is marked as FR 4072 and leads down to the AZT Trailhead sign.
NORTHBOUND: Patagonia
Patagonia is on AZ 82 south of Sonoita. The Patagonia Post Office is on the east side of AZ 82 across from the historic rail depot.

Trail Overview
From Oak Tree Canyon at AZ 83, the AZT rolls southwest into the oak-studded, grassy foothills of the Santa Ritas. Between Kentucky Camp and Gardner Canyon Road, the trail is easy and fun, but expect short and challenging climbs south and west of FR 4072. Riders will be treated to spectacular views of the mountain ranges of southeastern Arizona as they pedal through historic mining areas and weave through yucca, agave, and bear grass. About five miles south of Gardner Canyon, the AZT enters the Mount Wrightson Wilderness Area for 5.3 miles then drops down Temporal Gulch. For day riders, a description of the Temporal Gulch section of the AZT is described in the Day Rides section. Thru-bikers can take this route to Patagonia via State Highways 82 and 83. Several loop rides can be designed by taking advantage of the many Forest Service roads in the area, and the lodging at Kentucky Camp makes a novel base camp for all riders. Or you can plan on pampering yourself for a night by staying at one of Patagonia's many reasonably priced bed-and-breakfasts. You'll also find a coffee shop, art galleries, cowboy diners, and a pizza place called Velvet Elvis in this charming town that is often described as "eclectic."

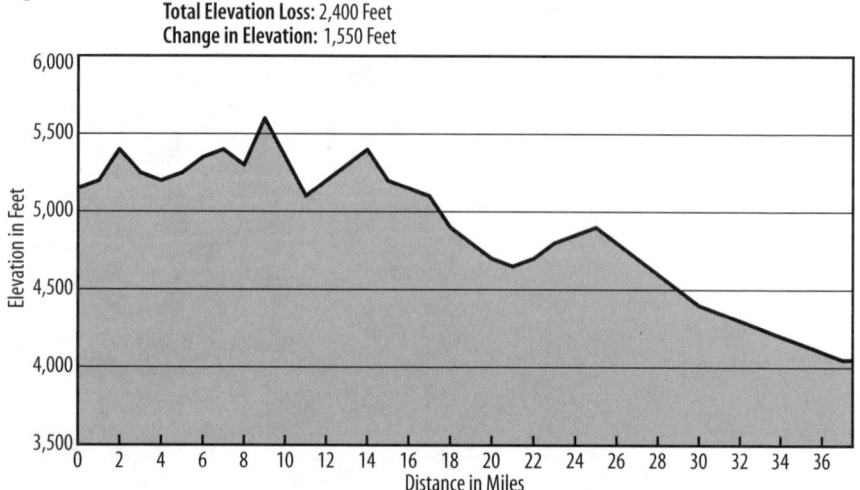

Segment 23   Total Elevation Gain: 1,300 Feet
Total Elevation Loss: 2,400 Feet
Change in Elevation: 1,550 Feet

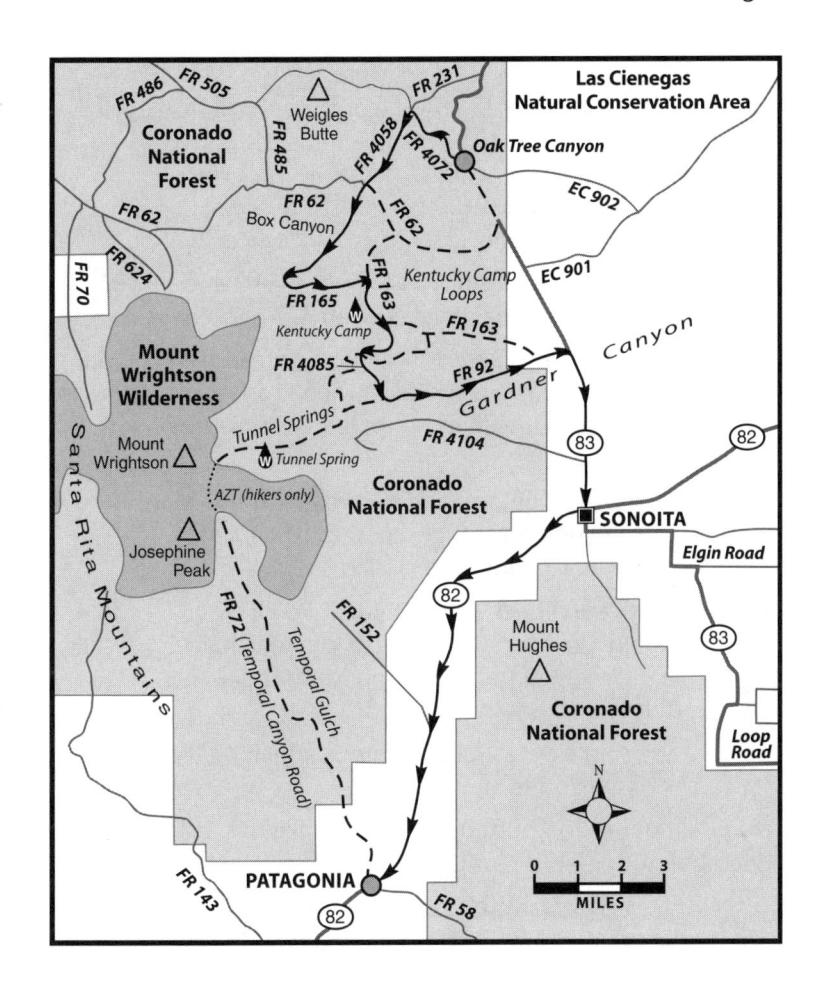

Route Description

Southbound *Northbound*

0.0	From the AZT Trailhead signs on FR 4072, head west on FR 4072 toward Box Canyon. The trail through this area might be realigned in the future, so be sure to follow the AZT signs.	37.5
0.4	Continue on a gradual uphill grade. You will pass a stock tank that might have water.	37.1
0.6	At the first cattle guard, you'll see a hiker gate with AZT stickers. Continue on the road.	36.9

Southbound			*Northbound*
1.2	Cross another cattle guard and then climb up and to the south, staying on FR 4072. Turn left (south) at the "T" intersection. On top, you can catch views of the Santa Rita foothills along with your breath. You will be rolling up and down these foothills for a while.		36.3
1.4	At the top of a short, steep hill, bear right (west) and go through a gap in a fence marked with AZT stickers.		36.1
1.7	Take the trail on the right (west) side of the steep hill. Be alert! There was only a cairn here when I rode it. A fun, although exposed, section of single track traverses the ridge.		35.8
1.9	The trail merges with an old road before going down to the west. After going through another fence, you bear left (south) onto another dirt road.		35.6
2.1	Go right (southwest) back onto FR 4072. You'll cross another cattle guard, and then start to climb a challenging hill. Before you get to the top look for a single-track trail that goes to the right (west).		35.4
2.4	At end of the single track, follow a dirt road, FR 4058, as it curves down and to the west.		35.1
2.7	Before you get to the bottom of the hill, take the signed trail to the right (southwest).		34.8
2.9	Go through a gate and follow along a fence line. Look for panoramic views of Mount Wrightson to the southwest.		34.6
3.6	There are more gates as you cross FR 62.		33.9
4.2	Be alert. The trail goes southwest under a telephone line as it leaves the dirt road for a single-track path. Go up another hill and the trail turns into a road again.		33.3
4.7	After a gate, the trail follows along a fence then goes through another gate at the top of a lung-busting climb.		32.8
5.5	Look for signs directing you left (east) onto another dirt road. Cross a wash and then begin a steep climb/push up several switchbacks.		32.0
6.2	Whew!		31.3
7.1	Go through a gate as the trail continues to weave through grassy areas dotted with yucca and agave plants, as well as oak trees.		30.4

Southbound			Northbound
7.3	Begin your descent now.		30.2
7.7	Keep descending down a primitive road. You'll see a stock pond below that might have water.		29.8
8.0	The trail hits FR 165 at the trailhead sign. Go left (east) and down through the area posted as the Big Nugget mining claim.		29.5
8.7	At the intersection of FR 165 and FR 163, go right (south) onto FR 163. Immediately start a steep climb. You will be following FR 163 all the way to the turnoff for Kentucky Camp.		28.8
9.0	Bear right (west). You will pass by some stock tanks that might have water.		28.5
9.2	You're at the top. Now comes the fun part. Head left (east) and down.		28.3
10.0	After an easy climb, pause to take in the view.		27.5
10.3	Veer right (south) as you leave FR 163 and go through the gate to Kentucky Camp.		27.2
10.6	Peruse the adobe buildings of Kentucky Camp. Refill your water bottles and visit the museum before heading southeast onto a single-track trail through grassy valleys.		26.9
12.0	After going through a gate, you'll cross a road.		25.5

Kentucky Camp

When you roll into the ghost town of adobe buildings at Kentucky Camp, don't be surprised if you feel like you just pedaled onto the set of an old Western. The setting was used in the television series "The Rough Riders." The Friends of Kentucky Camp and the U.S. Forest Service are in the process of restoring the historic mining camp. Late in the 19th century, the eastern slope of the Santa Ritas bustled with mining activity after the area proved to be the richest placer deposit in southern Arizona. As it turned out, water was nearly as precious. In 1902, a mining engineer named James Stetson designed a system to channel water from the mountains so that it could be used for hydraulic mining. The AZT now follows along some of the old channels. But the grand plan was not destined to be. After Stetson's untimely death, Kentucky Camp became a cattle ranch. Now the camp is part of the Forest Service "Rooms with a View" program. Call the Nogales Ranger District at (520) 281-2296 to make reservations for the "bed but not breakfast" that sits right on the Arizona Trail. The house offers bunk space for four, a kitchen with a microwave, and an outdoor toilet and sink.

Southbound			Northbound
12.9	At the top of a long climb, go right (west) onto an old road. Pause for the 360-degree view with the Rincon Mountains to the northeast, the Whetstones to the east, the Huachucas to the southeast, the Patagonia Mountains to the south, and Mount Wrightson and the Santa Ritas to the west. Follow a fence line and just before you crest a hill, turn left (south) onto some fine looking single track. You're going to enjoy this section as it follows an old water diversion route used by the Santa Rita Water and Mining Company.		24.6
14.4	There are interpretive signs here that tell some of the mining history of the area. Make a short technical maneuver in and out of a wash. Just south of the wash look for the exposed flume pipe. Across the trail from the pipe, you can see the evidence of what might have been hydraulic mining activity on the gray rocks.		23.1
14.5	The trail hits FR 4085, turns left (east), and then immediately turns right (south) to where an AZT sign directs you off the edge of the hill. You will be able to see the trailhead parking below. Start down a portion of the trail known as the "descent o' death." Let's not give this name any literal meaning, so be sure to walk your bike down any sections that are above your skill level.		23.0
14.8	Gardner Canyon Road (FR 92) Trailhead. After the trailhead, thru-bikers turn left (east) onto FR 92.		22.7
15.0	Thru-bikers heading east will pass the beautiful Apache Springs Ranch.		22.5
16.0	Continue east through the road intersection following signs to AZ 83.		21.5
19.2	Leave the National Forest after crossing the cattle guard.		18.3
19.8	FR 163 comes in from the north. Day riders can take this road back to Kentucky Camp.		17.7
20.6	Gardner Canyon Road reaches AZ 83. Go right (south) onto the paved highway and begin a 3-mile climb to Sonoita.		16.9

Southbound *Northbound*

24.8	At Sonoita, go right (southwest) onto AZ 82 following signs to Patagonia. The Sonoita Mercantile sells some of the best brownies I've ever tasted. The Sonoita Inn is a biker-friendly bed-and-breakfast next to the mercantile. For reservations, call (520) 455-5935 (www.sonoitainn.com).	12.7
27.8	After the historical marker, the road to Patagonia becomes a downhill coast.	9.7
37.5	Cross Sonoita Creek then turn left into the center of Patagonia. (The post office is the start of Segment 24.) Next to the Stage Stop Inn is a tourist information office.	0.0

Day Rides

Kentucky Camp Loops
Total Distance: 1–20+ miles
Difficulty: Easy–Moderate
Technical Rating: Beginner–Intermediate

From the Gardner Canyon Road Trailhead on FR 92 (see Southbound mile 14.8), go up (north) on the AZT to FR 4085. Instead of taking the AZT, stay left (west) on the dirt road. Follow this road to FR 163, then go east on FR 163 to where the AZT crosses the road. Ride the AZT back to the trailhead. For a longer ride, take the AZT north from FR 92 all the way to Kentucky Camp. From Kentucky Camp, go east on FR 163 to FR 92. Then ride west back to the trailhead.

To reach the Gardner Canyon Trailhead, take AZ 83 south of I-10 for about 21 miles to FR 92 (Gardner Canyon Road). Go west on FR 92 for about 4 miles. The large parking area at the trailhead is hard to miss.

Tunnel Springs
Total Distance: 10+ miles
Difficulty: Moderate
Technical Rating: Intermediate

From the Gardner Canyon Road Trailhead on FR 92 (see Southbound mile 14.8), day riders can go west onto the single track behind the trailhead sign. The AZT goes another 5 miles to Tunnel Springs and can be ridden a little further to the Wilderness Area boundary. Follow the trail until it enters FR 92. Go right (west) for approximately 200 yards. Follow the AZT sign and bear left down the trail and then cross the creek. The trail will go uphill to a gate before it climbs gradually through a meadow. Cross FR 785 and continue uphill on the single track. Just past the top of the hill is the "Penstock," where water was pooled to generate enough pressure for the uphill flow to Kentucky Camp. You are now in the "Flume" section of the trail. Follow this flat section of trail until you cross Gardner Creek. A short, steep ascent out of the creek will put you back on FR 785. Turn right (west) and follow the road for 1.1 miles to Tunnel Springs. The trail travels left (south) from the parking area as you go through a gate. You can ride from here to the Wilderness boundary, and then come back the way you came. Thru-bikers with vehicle support can bike the AZT to Tunnel Springs then have their bikes shuttled to the north end of the Temporal Gulch Trail while they hike the 5.3 miles of AZT that cross the Wilderness Area.

Temporal Gulch
Total Distance: 11.7 miles
Difficulty: Moderate
Technical Rating: Beginner

From Patagonia, bike or drive Forest Road 72 (Gringo Gulch) for 6.1 miles to the AZT Trailhead. From the trailhead, the AZT follows FR 72 to the junction with FR 4090 then to the Wilderness boundary at Upper Walker Tank. Expect views, interesting canyon scenery, and a mostly uphill grade from Patagonia to where the AZT heads into the Mount Wrightson Wilderness. Shady campsites can be found near the trailhead as the trail follows Temporal Gulch.

    The trail will leave the gulch 2 miles before the end near Upper Walker Tank. At the tank, the AZT follows the Walker Basin Trail into the Wilderness. If you have vehicle support, consider hiking the 5.3 miles through the Wilderness while someone shuttles your bike to where the AZT exits the Wilderness boundary near Tunnel Springs on FR 785. Water can be found in Temporal Gulch during rainy seasons and you might find water in the rock potholes above the concrete dam in Walker Basin.

Segment 24 — *PATAGONIA to PARKER CANYON LAKE*

Total Distance: 36.2 miles
Distance from Utah: 652.1 miles
Distance to Mexico: 51.8 miles
Difficulty: Moderate
Technical Rating: Beginner
Trail Status: Bicycle route near AZT hiker route.

Season
All year, but summers can be hot.

Maps
USFS: Coronado National Forest, Nogales and Sierra Vista Ranger Districts
USGS: Mt. Hughes, Canelo Pass, O'Donnel Canyon, Pyeatt Ranch

Signage
Good: FS roads marked with numbered posts.

Sunset over Parker Canyon Lake.

Water Sources
Patagonia, Canelo, Parker Canyon Lake

Trail Access
SOUTHBOUND: Patagonia
Patagonia is on AZ 82 south of Sonoita. The Patagonia Post Office is on the east side of AZ 82. Turn left (north) onto the road just east of and behind the post office and you will be on Harshaw Road.
NORTHBOUND: Parker Canyon Lake
From Sonoita, take AZ 83 south for 30 miles to the signed entrance to Parker Canyon Lake.

Permits and Fees
It costs $10 to camp at Parker Canyon Lake.

Trail Overview

Mountain bikes are permitted on the Arizona Trail between the Harshaw Road Trailhead and Parker Canyon Lake. However, I found the segments to require a lot of pushing. The official AZT is described and shown on the map if you want to try it. The recommended thru-route is more enjoyable and just as scenic.

Between Patagonia and Canelo Pass, the major mountain ranges of southeastern Arizona can be seen rising above the sweeping plains of the San Rafael Valley. The largest remnant of shortgrass prairie in Arizona impressed Hollywood filmmakers so much that they decided to film *Oklahoma!* in Arizona. (I guess that makes up for their putting saguaro cactus in films supposedly set in Texas.) You will cross the Santa Cruz River as it makes its course south for 35 miles into Mexico before curving back into Arizona at Nogales. Eventually, the Santa Cruz flows into the Gila River. You will have to climb up to Canelo Pass, but the road is well graded. From the tiny community of Canelo, this route goes south on AZ 83 to Parker Canyon Lake. The lake was built in 1966 with funds from fishing licenses. At the marina store, you can rent boats, pick up a few supplies, or take the quiet path around the shimmering lake. Prepare to feast your eyes. The vistas on this route are hard to beat.

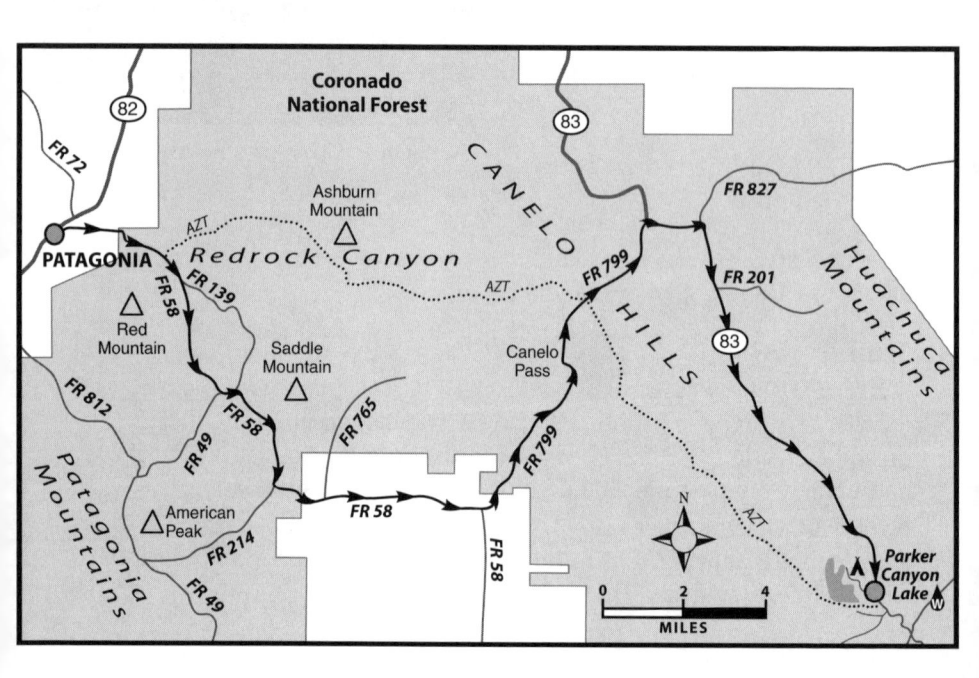

Segment 24 Total Elevation Gain: 2,550 Feet
Total Elevation Loss: 1,070 Feet
Change in Elevation: 1,700 Feet

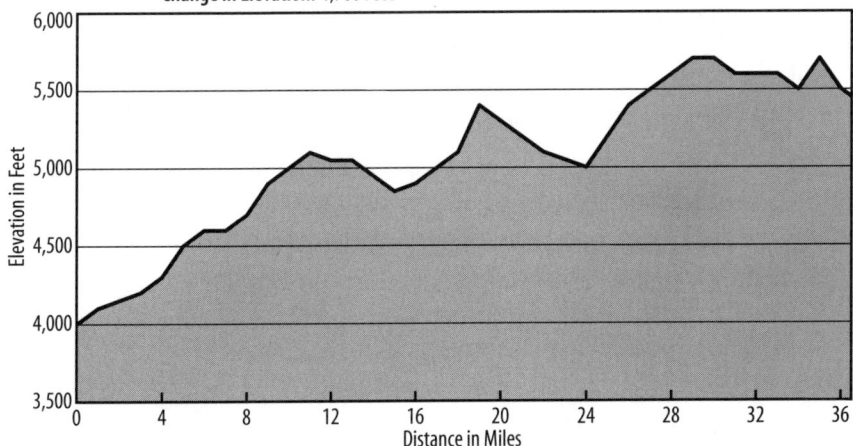

Route Description

Southbound / *Northbound*

Southbound			Northbound
0.0	From the town center, take the paved road to the east behind the post office and head up on Harshaw Road through a residential area. Harshaw Road will eventually lead to FR 58.		36.2
0.7	Go past the Patagonia RV Park.		35.5
1.3	Pass Red Rock Road.		34.9
2.9	The AZT starts here. To check the condition of the trail, head north through the grass. If you are still having fun after traveling 0.5 mile, you can take this trail for 16.2 miles to Canelo Pass. On the AZT, you will climb and descend several ridges with scenic views for 3.7 miles before traveling through Redrock Canyon along a primitive road. You will have to climb out of Meadow Valley to the Canelo Pass Trailhead. Portions of this route can be painfully overgrown with whitethorn. Some have reported enjoying the ride. They must have picked a time when the whitethorn wasn't thriving. The route recommended for thru-bikers is just as scenic and much easier. Stay on the road and enter Coronado National Forest just east of the trailhead.		33.3

Southbound **Northbound**

6.2	At the bend in the road, leave the pavement by taking the dirt road to the left (east). Follow the sign that says "San Rafael Valley 4 miles." You are now on FR 58.	30.0
6.6	Stay on FR 58 as it follows a scenic wash with a view of Saddle Mountain to the north.	29.6
10.7	After a climb, you pass an intersection with FR 765; the scenery opens up to a view of Meadow Valley.	25.5
12.9	The cattle tank at the windmill might have water.	23.3
14.5	Go straight (east), as you leave FR 58 and get on FR 799. Follow signs that direct you to Canelo Pass.	21.7
14.7	Cross the Santa Cruz River. This section of the river is normally dry.	21.5
18.0	Begin a steady climb.	18.2
19.5	A USFS sign indicates that this is Canelo Pass.	16.7
20.4	Make one more climb before you reach the point where the AZT crosses the road. To the left (west) is the Canelo Pass Trailhead. From here, the AZT goes south for 16 miles to Parker Canyon Lake. I really hated the steep climb (push) south from Canelo Pass. I recommend taking the road, so stay on FR 799 and begin descending to AZ 83.	15.8
23.5	At the row of mailboxes, turn right (south) onto paved AZ 83. The slow speeds and limited traffic make the narrow shoulders tolerable.	12.7

Coatimundi, The Scorpion Hunter

If you see a creature that looks like a cross between a monkey and a raccoon, you aren't imagining things. You have just spotted a coatimundi (koh-ti-mun-dee). Coatis have long snouts and ringed tails that are held erect like flag posts. Look for them as you travel through areas near water between Colossal Cave and the Mexican Border. Southeastern Arizona is the only region in the United States where the coatimundi lives in abundance. These relatives of the raccoon also go by the name "chulo" (Spanish for cute), but I doubt that tarantulas and scorpions (significant sources of protein in the coati diet) would use the word "cute" to describe this strange mammal with a voracious appetite.

Southbound		*Northbound*
24.5	Ride past the road that leads to the Forest Service fire station, then cross a low area that can be flooded. Climb up onto a narrow mesa with views on both sides. The tallest mountain to the west is Mount Wrightson. The Whetstones and Mustangs are the austere brown mountains to the northeast. Look above the Huachucas to the east to see if the government "spy" blimp is hovering above the peaks.	11.7
31.7	Soon after you drop off the mesa, the pavement ends. Notice the Chihuahua pines by the road. Can you tell them apart from ponderosa pines? Hint: Look at the cones.	4.5
33.7	I saw a coatimundi cross the road here at Parker Canyon.	2.5
34.6	Parker Canyon Lake can be seen to the west.	1.6
35.7	At the road intersection, go west toward Parker Canyon Lake.	0.5
36.0	The Coronado National Forest sign tells the history of Parker Canyon Lake.	0.2
36.2	After entering the park, go left to the marina parking for the start of Segment 25. Or go right for 0.8 mile to the campground where, for $10, you get a campsite with water, a picnic table, and a view of the lake.	0.0

Oink-Oink

If you hear a strange snorting and grunting coming from the Sonoran Desert brush, don't fear. A pack of javelina (have-ah-lee-na) is the most likely source. Smaller than domestic pigs, javelina have dark brown, bristly coats with white collars of fur around their sturdy necks. Also known as the collared peccary, these tough little porkers eat prickly pear cactus and have two-inch tusks. The razor-sharp tusks earned these animals the name javelina, which comes from the Spanish word for spear. Normally, javelina are harmless, but they might attack if provoked. So, if you see javelina, watch them quietly, and then let them go on their way. A musk gland located on their rumps is to blame for the strong odor, often the first indication that a javelina is nearby.

Segment 25: PARKER CANYON LAKE to MEXICO BORDER

Total Distance:
15.6 miles

Distance from Utah:
688.3 miles

Distance to Mexico:
15.6 miles

Difficulty: Moderate

Technical Rating:
Beginner

Trail Status:
Bicycle detour around Miller Peak Wilderness Area and Coronado National Memorial.

Journey's end at the Mexico border, Coronado National Forest. Photo by Dan Overton.

Season
All year, although summers can be hot.

Maps
USFS: Coronado National Forest, Nogales and Sierra Vista Ranger Districts
USGS: Huachuca Peak, Miller Peak, Montezuma Pass

Signage
Fair: Use FS road signs. Copper Canyon Road to the Mexico border is not well marked.

Water Sources
Parker Canyon Lake

Trail Access
SOUTHBOUND: Parker Canyon Lake
From Sonoita, take AZ 83 south for 30 miles to the signed entrance to Parker Canyon Lake.
NORTHBOUND: Mexico Border or Copper Canyon Road and FR 61
From Parker Canyon Lake, take the route described below. Copper Canyon Road will require a high-clearance vehicle. Vehicle support might want to drop off/pick up bikers at the intersection of FR 61 and FR 4781.

Trail Overview

In Segment 25, the AZT and the bike detour travel through the exciting area where the Sonoran and Chihuahuan Deserts meet. The Chihuahuan Desert is the largest North American desert, but 75% of it is found in Mexico. South of Parker Canyon Lake, the Arizona Trail heads up into the Miller Peak Wilderness Area. (Miller Peak, at 9,466 feet, is the highest southernmost peak in the United States.) Bikers can take a dirt road along the base of the Huachuca Mountains. The route includes some roller-coaster hills that eventually flatten into a long gradual descent with expansive views. Unfortunately, the official end of the Arizona Trail at the Mexico border is also closed to bicycles. No worries; you can take Copper Canyon Road down to the international boundary.

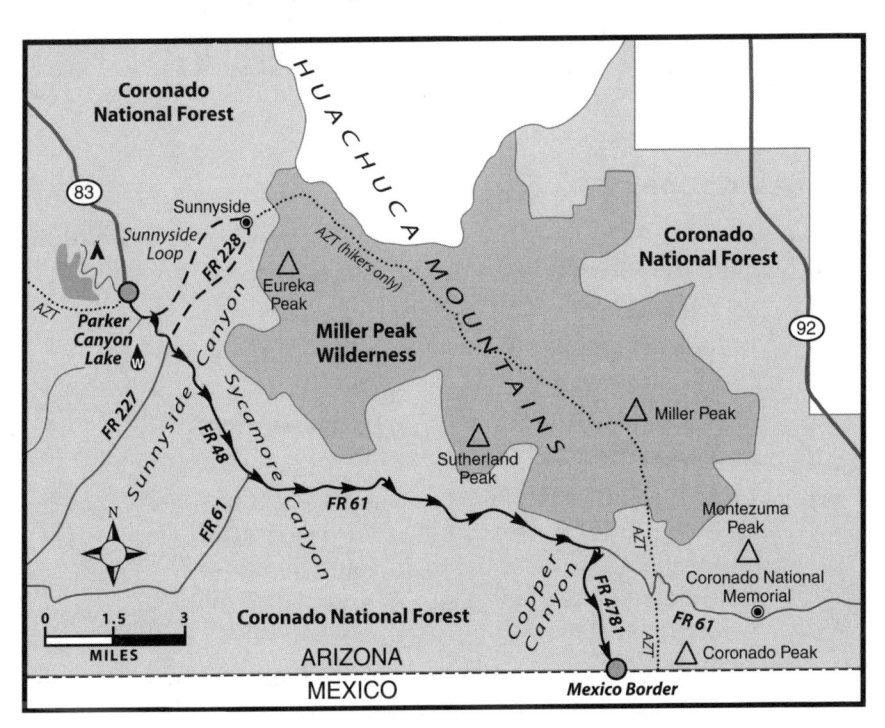

Segment 25 Total Elevation Gain: 1,000 Feet
Total Elevation Loss: 920 Feet
Change in Elevation: 600 Feet

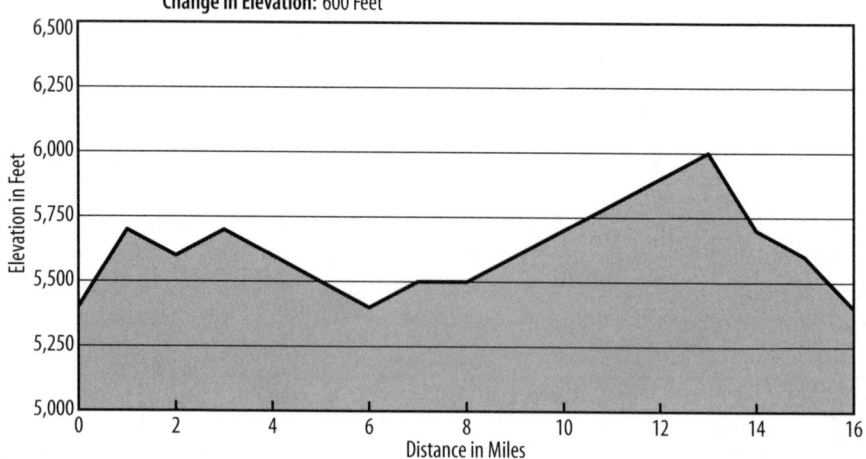

Route Description

Southbound *Northbound*

0.0	From the Parker Canyon Lake marina parking lot, go up the hill to the park entrance.	15.6
0.5	At the park entrance is the intersection of AZ 83 and FR 48. Go south on FR 48.	15.1
1.2	After ascending for nearly 0.5 mile, go over the one-lane bridge and ascend another hill.	14.4
1.5	Cross Scotia Canyon. Primitive campsites can be found on both sides of the road. Within 0.1 mile, you will see where the AZT crosses the road. Southbound (east) from here you can ride the AZT for about 3 miles before the trail enters the Wilderness Area.	14.1
2.2	At the top of the climb, pass the intersection with FR 228 (the start of the Sunnyside Loop, opposite). Stay on FR 48.	13.4
2.9	Cross the sycamore-lined Sunnyside Canyon.	12.7
3.7	The road levels out and begins a gradual descent. Views of chaparral slopes and the Huachuca Mountains will entertain you on your way down.	11.9
5.5	Continue south following the signs to Coronado National Memorial as FR 48 ends and FR 61 begins.	10.1
6.3	The creek sometimes floods the road here.	9.3

Segment 25   175

Southbound		Northbound
7.8	Cross several drainages as you get closer to the pass. The cut into the hill ahead (south) is Montezuma Pass. You will turn off FR 61 before the pass.	7.8
8.3	This is Bear Canyon.	7.3
13.2	Notice the sign for Copper Canyon. Just south of the sign, FR 4782 crosses the road. Turn right (west) and down on FR 4781/Copper Canyon Road. Vehicle support might want to meet riders here instead of at the border.	2.4
13.3	Cross a cattle guard.	2.3
13.5	After passing a metal stock tank, descend along a fence line. Bear left (south) at the old corral. Notice how the corral is made. The descent gets more gradual as you roll through grassy fields dotted with oak.	2.1
15.6	Here it is! The barbed-wire fence is the Mexico border. Cows might be here to celebrate your arrival. Otherwise, the border will be a lonely place. Anticlimactic, isn't it?	0.0

Day Rides

Sunnyside Loop
Total Distance: 5 miles
Difficulty: Moderate
Technical Rating: Beginner

For a short loop and a chance to visit a ghost town cemetery, drive south from Parker Canyon Lake to the intersection of AZ 83 and FR 48. Take FR 48 for 1 mile, and go past where the AZT crosses FR 48. Park where FR 228 meets FR 48 and ride northeast on FR 228 for 0.9 mile to a fork. The right (south) fork leads 1.2 miles to the Sunnyside Cemetery. Go left (north) staying on FR 228. At the next fork, stay right (northeast) on FR 228 toward Fort Gate #7. The AZT will cross the road shortly. Take the AZT to the west as it follows Scotia Canyon down to FR 48. This loop will be about 5 miles long if you don't take the side trip to the cemetery.

Appendix A: 28 DAY RIDES on the ARIZONA TRAIL

The following 28 routes are perfect for day riders. They are fairly easy to access and offer a wide variety of landscapes, distances, and levels of difficulty. However, you can design a day ride on any part of the 700-plus miles of trail described in this book, so don't limit yourself to the rides listed below. Round-trip mileage is given for out-and-backs unless a shuttle is recommended. All the rides include a portion of the official and completed AZT unless noted with an asterisk (*). Refer to the page numbers below for individual ride descriptions.

Segment 1: *Stateline Loop*
Difficulty/Technical Rating: Moderate/Intermediate
Total Distance: 20 miles   **Page:** 38

Segment 2: *East Rim View to Crane Lake*
Difficulty/Technical Rating: Easy/Beginner
Total Distance: 22 miles   **Page:** 45

Segment 3A: *Fall Color Loops*
Difficulty/Technical Rating: Easy/Beginner
Total Distance: 15–22 miles   **Page:** 52

Segment 3B: *Multi-Use Trail*
Difficulty/Technical Rating: Easy/Beginner
Total Distance: 10.1 miles   **Page:** 52

Segment 5: *Tusayan Bike Trails (Loops)**
Difficulty/Technical Rating: Easy/Beginner
Total Distance: 3–9 miles   **Page:** 62

Segment 6: *Coconino Rim Loops*
Difficulty/Technical Rating: Easy/Beginner
Total Distance: 17–21 miles   **Page:** 67

Segment 6: *Russell Tank to Moqui Stage Stop*
Difficulty/Technical Rating: Easy/Beginner
Total Distance: 12.6 miles   **Page:** 67

Segment 8: *Schultz Tank to Buffalo Park**
Difficulty/Technical Rating: Moderate/Intermediate
Total Distance: 8.6 miles   **Page:** 80

Segment 10: *Flagstaff to Fisher Point*
Difficulty/Technical Rating: Easy/Beginner
Total Distance: 8 miles   **Page:** 92

Segment 10: *Flagstaff to Marshall Lake*
Difficulty/Technical Rating: Strenuous/Intermediate
Total Distance: 21.4 miles   **Page:** 92

Segment 10: *Observatory Trailhead to Horse Lake*
Difficulty/Technical Rating: Easy/Beginner
Total Distance: 13 miles   **Page:** 92

Segment 12: *Moqui Lookout–Blue Ridge Loop*
Difficulty/Technical Rating: Moderate/Beginner
Total Distance: 12 miles   **Page:** 104

Segment 12: *Blue Ridge Passage of the AZT*
Difficulty/Technical Rating: Strenuous/Intermediate
Total Distance: 24.4 miles   **Page:** 105

Segment 12: *Mogollon Rim Loop*
Difficulty/Technical Rating: Moderate/Beginner
Total Distance: 25 miles   **Page:** 105

Segment 12: *Battleground Ridge Loop*
Difficulty/Technical Rating: Moderate/Intermediate
Total Distance: 17 miles   **Page:** 106

Segment 13: *Highline–Control Road Loop*
Difficulty/Technical Rating: Strenuous/Intermediate
Total Distance: 28 miles   **Page:** 112

Segment 15: *Mazatzal Divide—Lone Pine Saddle to Sunflower*
Difficulty/Technical Rating: Strenuous/Advanced
Total Distance: 17.5 miles   **Page:** 122

Segment 18: *Reavis Canyon*
Difficulty/Technical Rating: Strenuous/Intermediate
Total Distance: 14.7 miles   **Page:** 136

Segment 18: *Alamo Canyon Loop*
Difficulty/Technical Rating: Strenuous/Advanced
Total Distance: 20 miles   **Page:** 137

Segment 20: *American Flag Spur*
Difficulty/Technical Rating: Moderate/Intermediate
Total Distance: 2–4 miles   **Page:** 149

Segment 20: *Prison Camp Loop*
Difficulty/Technical Rating: Moderate/Intermediate
Total Distance: 4 miles   **Page:** 149

Segment 21: *Molino Basin–Reddington Road Loop*
Difficulty/Technical Rating: Strenuous/Intermediate
Total Distance: 30 miles   **Page:** 154

Segment 21: *Saguaro Park to Colossal Cave**
Difficulty/Technical Rating: Easy/Beginner
Total Distance: 11.2 miles   **Page:** 154

Segment 22: *Oak Tree Canyon**
Difficulty/Technical Rating: Easy/Beginner
Total Distance: 3–15 miles   **Page:** 158

Segment 23: *Kentucky Camp Loops*
Difficulty/Technical Rating: Easy/Beginner to Moderate/Intermediate
Total Distance: 1–20+ miles   **Page:** 165

Segment 23: *Tunnel Springs*
Difficulty/Technical Rating: Moderate/Intermediate
Total Distance: 10+ miles   **Page:** 166

Segment 23: *Temporal Gulch*
Difficulty/Technical Rating: Moderate/Beginner
Total Distance: 11.7 miles   **Page:** 166

Segment 25: *Sunnyside Loop*
Difficulty/Technical Rating: Moderate/Beginner
Total Distance: 5 miles   **Page:** 175

Appendix B ▶ RESUPPLY and LODGING

Segment 1: *Stateline Trailhead*
Distance from Bike Route: 0.0
Water: No **Camping:** Yes **Resupply:** No
Offers: Shaded picnic tables

Segment 2: *Jacob Lake*
Distance from Bike Route: 2.0 miles
Water: Yes **Camping:** Yes **Resupply:** Limited
Offers: ATM, gift shop, restaurant, visitor center

Segment 3: *North Rim Village*
Distance from Bike Route: 1.5 miles
Water: Yes **Camping:** Yes **Resupply:** Limited
Offers: Lodging, restaurant, visitor center

Segment 4: *Phantom Ranch*
Distance from Bike Route: 0.0
Water: Yes **Camping:** Yes **Resupply:** Limited
Offers: Lodging, cantina

Segment 5: *South Rim Village*
Distance from Bike Route: 0.0–3.0 miles
Water: Yes **Camping:** Yes **Resupply:** Yes
Offers: Lodging, restaurants, outfitter, bank, post office, visitor center

Segment 5: *Tusayan*
Distance from Bike Route: 0.0–2.0 miles
Water: Yes **Camping:** Yes **Resupply:** Yes
Offers: Lodging, restaurants, post office

Segment 9: *Flagstaff*
Distance from Bike Route: 0.0–3.0 miles
Water: Yes **Camping:** Yes **Resupply:** Yes
Offers: Bike shops, outfitters, and all conveniences of a big town

Segment 11: *Mormon Lake*
Distance from Bike Route: 0.0
Water: Yes **Camping:** Yes **Resupply:** Limited
Offers: Lodging, saloon, post office

Segment 11: *Happy Jack*
Distance from Bike Route: 9.0 miles
Water: Yes **Camping:** Yes **Resupply:** Limited
Offers: Lodging, restaurant

Segment 12: *Blue Ridge Ranger Station*
Distance from Bike Route: 1.0 mile
Water: Yes **Camping:** Yes **Resupply:** No
Offers: Trail information

Segment 14: *Payson*
Distance from Bike Route: 0.0
Water: Yes **Camping:** Yes **Resupply:** Yes
Offers: Bike shop, restaurants, lodging

Segment 15: *Jake's Corner*
Distance from Bike Route: 0.0
Water: Yes **Camping:** Yes **Resupply:** Limited
Offers: Lodging, laundry, showers

Segment 16: *Tortilla Flat*
Distance from Bike Route: 0.0
Water: Yes **Camping:** Yes **Resupply:** Limited
Offers: Saloon, restaurant

Segment 17: *Apache Junction*
Distance from Bike Route: 0.0–5.0 miles
Water: Yes **Camping:** Yes **Resupply:** Yes
Offers: Restaurants, lodging

Segment 18: *Florence Junction*
Distance from Bike Route: 0.0
Water: Yes **Camping:** No **Resupply:** Limited
Offers: Snacks, phone

Segment 19: *Florence*
Distance from Bike Route: 10.0 miles
Water: Yes **Camping:** No **Resupply:** Limited
Offers: Phone, lodging

Segment 20: *Oracle*
Distance from Bike Route: 0.0
Water: Yes   **Camping:** No   **Resupply:** Yes
Offers: Post office, lodging, library

Segment 20: *Summerhaven*
Distance from Bike Route: 1.5 miles
Water: Yes   **Camping:** Yes   **Resupply:** Limited
Offers: Restaurants, lodging

Segment 21: *Tucson*
Distance from Bike Route: 0.0–10.0 miles
Water: Yes   **Camping:** Yes   **Resupply:** Yes
Offers: Bike shops, outfitters, and all the conveniences of a big town

Segment 22: *Colossal Cave*
Distance from Bike Route: 0.0
Water: Yes   **Camping:** Yes   **Resupply:** No
Offers: Visitor center, cave tours

Segment 22: *Vail*
Distance from Bike Route: 0.0
Water: Yes   **Camping:** Yes   **Resupply:** No

Segment 23: *Sonoita*
Distance from Bike Route: 0.0
Water: Yes   **Camping:** No   **Resupply:** Limited
Offers: Restaurant, deli, lodging

Segment 24: *Patagonia*
Distance from Bike Route: 0.0
Water: Yes   **Camping:** Yes   **Resupply:** Yes
Offers: Lodging, restaurants

Segment 25: *Parker Canyon Lake*
Distance from Bike Route: 0.0
Water: Yes   **Camping:** Yes   **Resupply:** Limited
Offers: Boat rental

Appendix C — AGENCIES and ORGANIZATIONS

Arizona Trail Association
P.O. Box 36736
Phoenix, AZ 85067
(602) 252-4794
www.aztrail.org

Arizona State Parks
1300 W. Washington
Phoenix, AZ 85007
(800) 285-3703
www.pr.state.az.us

Superstition Area Land Trust
P.O. Box 582
Apache Junction, AZ 85217-0582
(480) 983-2345
www.azsalt.org

Bicycling Organizations

Mountain Biking Association of Arizona (MBAA)
P.O. Box 32728
Phoenix, AZ 85064
(602) 351-7430
www.mbaa.net

Adventure Cycling Association
P.O. Box 8308
Missoula, MT 59807
(800) 755-2453
www.adventurecycling.org

International Mountain Bicycling Association (IMBA)
1121 Broadway, Suite 203
P.O. Box 7578
Boulder, CO 80306
(888) 442-4622
www.imba.com

Bureau of Land Management

Arizona Strip Field Office
345 E. Riverside Dr.
St. George, UT 84790
(435) 688-3200

Tucson Field Office
12661 E. Broadway
Tucson, AZ 85748
(520) 722-4289

National Park Service

Grand Canyon National Park
Backcountry Reservation Office
P.O. Box 129
Grand Canyon, AZ 86023
(928) 638-7875
www.nps.gov/grca/backcountry/

Saguaro National Park
Rincon Mountain District
3693 S. Old Spanish Trail
Tucson, AZ 85730
(520) 733-5153
www.nps.gov/sagu/

United States Forest Service

Kaibab National Forest
North Kaibab Ranger District
P.O. Box 248
Fredonia, AZ 86002
(928) 643-7298

Tusayan Ranger District
P.O. Box 3088
Grand Canyon, AZ 86023
(928) 638-2443

Coconino National Forest
Peaks Ranger Station
5075 N. Hwy. 89
Flagstaff, AZ 86004
(928) 526-0866

Happy Jack Information Center
P.O. Box 19664
Happy Jack, AZ 86024
(520) 477-2172

Tonto National Forest
Payson Ranger District
1009 E. Hwy. 260
Payson, AZ 85541
(520) 474-7900

Coronado National Forest
Santa Catalina Ranger District
5700 N. Sabino Canyon Rd.
Tucson, AZ 85715
(520) 749-8700

Nogales Ranger District
303 Old Tucson Rd.
Nogales, AZ 85621
(520) 281-2296

Sierra Vista Ranger District
5990 S. Hwy. 92
Hereford, AZ 85615
(520) 378-0311

Appendix D — BIKE SHOPS, GUIDE SERVICES, and OUTFITTERS

Bicycle Repair Shops near the Arizona Trail

Flagstaff

Absolute Bikes
18 N. San Francisco St. (downtown)
(928) 779-5969

Cosmic Cycles
901 N. Beaver St. (downtown)
(928) 779-1092

Sinagua Cycles
113 S. San Francisco St. (downtown)
(928) 779-9969

Payson

Manzanita Cyclery
321 E. Hwy. 260 (next to Safeway)
(928) 474-0744

Tucson

Arizona Bicycle Experts
2520 E. 6th St.
(520) 881-2279
www.bitchinbike.com

Cycle Spectrum
6171 E. Broadway
(520) 790-9394

Full Cycle
7204 E. Broadway
(520) 327-3232

Bike Touring Gear and Equipment

Arkel Panniers
(888) 592-7535
www.arkel-od.com

Bike Nashbar
(800) 627-4227
www.nashbar.com

Cyclosource Catalog
Adventure Cycling Association
(800) 721-8719
www.adventurecycling.org

Terry Precision Cycling
(800) 289-8379
www.terrybicycles.com

Guide Services

Adventure Bicycle Company
1110 W. Southern Ave.
Mesa, AZ 85205
(480) 649-3394
www.adventurebicycle.com

Arizona White Knuckle Adventures
10527 E. Betony Dr.
Scottsdale, AZ 85269
(866) 342-9669
www.arizona-adventures.com

Arizona Outback Adventures/ Wheels 'n Gear
7607 E. McDowell Rd., Suite 113
Scottsdale, AZ 85257
(480) 945-2881

Outfitters near the Trail

Flagstaff

Aspen Sports
15 N. San Francisco St. (downtown)
(928) 779-1935

Peace Surplus
14 W. Route 66 (downtown)
(928) 779-4521

Babbitt's Backcountry Outfitters
12 E. Aspen Ave. (downtown)
(928) 774-4775

Grand Canyon—South Rim

Babbitt's General Store
(next to the post office)
(928) 638-2854

Tucson

Summit Hut
5045 E. Speedway (at Rosemont)
(800) 488-8696
www.summithut.com

Appendix E — EQUIPMENT CHECKLISTS
(to be used as guidelines only)

Bike Maintenance and Repair Equipment
(Multi-tools incorporate many of the tools listed below.)

Set of Allen wrenches
Small rag
Small Phillips-head and flathead screwdrivers
Bottle of chain lubricant
Chain tool and spare links
Duct and electrical tape
Small, adjustable wrench
Length of multipurpose cord
Plastic tire levers
Spare cleat (if applicable)
Spare inner tube

Patch kit
Spare tire for group (self-sealing or puncture-resistant tubes)
Spoke wrench and spare spokes
Spare bolts (for seat post, rack, shoe cleats, toe clips, etc.)
Spare brake pads
Travel-sized emergency bike-repair manual and/or a good knowledge of how to use all of the above tools

Camping Gear

Water filter and water-purification tablets
Tent or tarp
Sleeping bag (rated at 20 degrees or less; down is more compressible and lightweight, but don't let it get wet!)
Small first-aid kit
Food bag with cord and lightweight carabiner (to hang bag out of the reach of animals)

Small bottle of insect repellent (spray or lotion)
Stove, fuel, and cook set
Insulated sleeping pad
Water bottles/bags (with capacity to carry 1.5 gallons of water per person)
Sunscreen
Lightweight flashlight or headlamp (and an extra set of batteries)
Pack towel

Clothing

Rain jacket and pants
Knit or pile cap
Two pairs of bike shorts
One pair of town shorts and T-shirt
Two wicking shirts or jerseys
Lightweight pile or synthetic sweater
Tights or long-john bottoms
Lightweight camp shoes or sandals

Small toiletry kit
Bandanna
Bike gloves
Helmet
Sunglasses
Plastic garbage bags (to keep everything dry)

Appendix F — REFERENCES and SUGGESTED READING

Arizona Trail and Route Information

Fayhee, M. John. *Along the Arizona Trail.* Englewood, Colo.: Westcliffe Publishers, 1998.

Jimmerson, Michael, and Jim Porter. *Mountain Biking the Old Pueblo: Rides in the Tucson Area.* Tucson, Ariz.: O.F.C. Designs, 1992.

Massey, Peter, and Jeanne Wilson. *Backcountry Adventures: Arizona.* Castle Rock, Colo.: Swagman Publishing Inc., 2001.

Mauer, Stephen, ed. *Kaibab National Forest Visitors Guide: Williams, Chandler, and Tusayan Ranger Districts.* Albuquerque, N.M.: Southwest Natural and Cultural Heritage Association, 1990.

Ray, Cosmic. *Fat Tire Tales and Trails: Arizona Mountain Bike Trail Guide.* Flagstaff, Ariz.: Cosmic Ray, 2000.

Shook, Mike. *The No-Nonsense Mountain Bike Trail Guide for Flagstaff and Sedona.* Flagstaff, Ariz.: Aspen Avenue Publishing, 1998.

Smith, Eric. *The Arizona Trail: Essential Information for Long-Distance Trail Users.* (Pamphlet available from the Arizona Trail Steward, Arizona State Parks, 1300 W. Washington, Phoenix, AZ 85007)

Stevenson, Jeffrey. *Rim Country Mountain Biking: Great Rides Along Arizona's Mogollon Rim.* Boulder, Colo.: Pruett Publishing, 1995.

Tighe, Kelly, and Susan Moran. *On the Arizona Trail: A Guide For Hikers, Cyclists, and Equestrians.* Boulder, Colo.: Pruett Publishing, 1998.

Arizona Natural and Cultural History

Alden, Peter, and Peter Friederici. *National Audubon Society Field Guide to the Southwestern States.* New York, N.Y.: Alfred A. Knopf, 1999.

Dutton, Allen A. *Arizona Then & Now.* Englewood, Colo.: Westcliffe Publishers, 2002.

Hodge, Carle. *All About Saguaros.* Phoenix, Ariz.: Arizona Highways, 1997.

Mangum, Richard, and Sherry Mangum. *Grand Canyon–Flagstaff Stage Coach Line: A History and Exploration Guide.* Flagstaff, Ariz.: Hexagon Press, 1999.

Phillips, Steven J., and Patricia Wentworth Comus, eds. *The Natural History of the Sonoran Desert.* Berkeley, Calif.: University of California Press, 1999.

Schmidt, Jeremy. *Grand Canyon National Park.* New York, N.Y.: Houghton Mifflin Company, 1993.

———. *Cabin Loop Trail.* National Forest Publication, Blue Ridge District, Happy Jack, Ariz.

Camping and Backpacking

Dollar, Tom. *Guide to Arizona's Wilderness Areas.* Englewood, Colo.: Westcliffe Publishers, 1998.

Jardine, Ray. *Beyond Backpacking: Ray Jardine's Guide to Lightweight Hiking.* Arizona City, Ariz.: AdventureLore Press, 1999.

Wilderness Medicine

Forgey, William. *Wilderness Medicine: Beyond First Aid.* Guilford, Conn.: Globe Pequot Press, 1999.

Ghiglieri, Michael, and Tom Myers. *Over the Edge: Death in Grand Canyon.* Flagstaff, Ariz.: Puma Press, 2001.

Tilton, Buck, and Frank Hubbell. *Medicine for the Backcountry.* Guilford, Conn.: Globe Pequot Press, 1999.

Bicycle Maintenance and Touring

Adventure Cyclist Magazine. Missoula, Mont.: Adventure Cycling Association.

Grove, Eric. *Pocket Guide to Emergency Bicycle Repair.* Helena, Mont.: Troutbeck/Greycliff, 1999.

Lovett, Richard A. *The Essential Touring Cyclist: The Complete Source for the Bicycle Traveler.* Camden, Maine: Ragged Mountain Press/McGraw Hill, 1994.

McCoy, Michael. *Cycling the Great Divide.* Seattle, Wash.: The Mountaineers, 2000.

Index

NOTE: Citations followed by the letter "m" denote maps; those followed by the letter "p" denote photos.

agave, 19p, 153, 153p
Alamo Canyon Loop day ride, 137
altitude sickness, 17
American Flag Spur day ride, 149
Arizona Trail
    day rides, 14
    geographic highlights, 12
    history and diversity of, 12
    map of, 6m–7m
    obstacles for mountain bikers, 13
    road/trail surfaces, 13–14
    signage on, 14, 31
    thru-bike routes, 13
aspen, quaking, 39p, 43

Battleground Ridge Loop day ride, 106
bear, black, 18
bikes and bike equipment
    choosing a bike, 25
    finding bike shops, 28
    gloves, 27
    helmets, 28
    making repairs, 28
    odometers, 28
    tires, 27
    using a rear rack and panniers, 26
    using a trailer system, 26p, 27
Blue Ridge–Moqui Lookout Loop day ride, 104
Blue Ridge Passage of the AZT day ride, 105
Blue Ridge Ranger Station
    to General Springs Cabin, 100–106, 102m
    Mormon Lake to, 93–99, 94m
Buffalo Park
    day ride to Schultz Tank, 80
    to Flagstaff Urban Trail, 81–84, 82m
    Forest Road 523 to, 73–80, 75m

cactus, 19, 121, 121p
camping gear and clothing, 28
cinder cones, 72, 78p

climate, 22–23, 30
coatimundi, 170
Coconino Rim Loops day rides, 67
Colossal Cave
    day ride to Saguaro Park, 154
    Molino Basin Campground to, 150–154, 152m
    to Oak Tree Canyon, 155–158, 156m
condor, California, 57
Control Road–Highline Loop day ride, 112
Crane Lake to East Rim View day ride, 45

day riding, 14
dehydration, 17
deserts, 142
difficulty ratings, 29
distances, 29

East Rim View
    day ride to Crane Lake, 45
    to North Kaibab Trailhead, 46–52, 48m
    US 89A to, 39–45, 41m
elevation profiles, 32

Fall Color Loop day ride, 52
Fisher Point to Flagstaff day ride, 92
Flagstaff
    attractions of, 83
    day ride to Fisher Point, 92
    day ride to Marshall Lake, 92
Flagstaff–Grand Canyon Stagecoach, 66
Flagstaff Urban Trail
    Buffalo Park to, 81–84, 82m
    to Mormon Lake, 85–92, 87m
flash floods, 16, 16p
Forest Road 523
    to Buffalo Park, 73–80, 75m
    Moqui Stage Stop to, 68–72, 70m

General Springs Cabin
    Blue Ridge Ranger Station to, 100–106, 102m
    history of, 103, 111p
    to Payson, 107–112, 108m
Gila River
    to Oracle, 138–143, 140m, 141m
    US 60 to, 132–137, 134m
gloves, 27

Grand Canyon, 58, 58p
Grand Staircase, 37
Grandview Lookout
  to Moqui Stage Stop, 63–67, 65m
  Tusayan to, 59–62, 60m

hazards. *See* safety hazards
heat exhaustion and stroke, 17
helmets, 28
high-altitude sickness, 17
Highline–Control Road Loop day ride, 112
highways, traveling on, 20
hiking, combining biking with, 14
Horse Lake to Observatory Trailhead day ride, 92
hunters, 20
hyponatremia, 17
hypothermia, 16

injuries, 20

Jake's Corner
  Payson to, 113–117, 114m
  to Roosevelt Lake Dam, 118–122, 120m
javelina, 171

Kentucky Camp, 159p, 163
Kentucky Camp Loops day rides, 165

lakes, Arizona, 42, 90
Las Cienegas Natural Conservation Area, 155p
Lemmon, Mount, 148
lightning, 18
lost, getting, 19
Lost Dutchman State Park
  Roosevelt Lake Dam to, 123–127, 124m
  to US 60, 128–131, 130m

map symbols, key to, 32
Marshall Lake to Flagstaff day ride, 92
Mazatzal Divide–Lone Pine Saddle to Sunflower day ride, 122
Mazatzal Mountains, 113p
Mexico Border, Parker Canyon Lake to, 172–175, 173m
Mogollon Rim Loop day ride, 105

Molino Basin Campground
  to Colossal Cave, 150–154, 152m
  Oracle to, 144–149, 146m
Molino Basin–Reddington Road Loop day ride, 154
Moqui Lookout–Blue Ridge Loop day ride, 104
Moqui Stage Stop
  day ride to Russell Tank, 67
  to Forest Road 523, 68–72, 70m
  Grandview Lookout to, 63–67, 65m
Mormon Lake
  to Blue Ridge Ranger Station, 93–99, 94m
  Flagstaff Urban Trail to, 85–92, 87m
mountain lions, 18
Multi-Use Trail day ride, 52

North Kaibab Trailhead, East Rim View to, 46–52, 48m
North Rim to South Rim (trekking), 53–58, 55m

Oak Tree Canyon
  Colossal Cave to, 155–158, 156m
  day ride, 158
  to Patagonia, 159–166, 161m
Observatory Trailhead to Horse Lake day ride, 92
odometers, 20
Oracle
  Gila River to, 138–143, 140m, 141m
  to Molino Basin Campground, 144–149, 146m

panniers and racks, 26
Parker Canyon Lake
  to Mexico Border, 172–175, 173m
  Patagonia to, 167–171, 168m
Patagonia
  Oak Tree Canyon to, 159–166, 161m
  to Parker Canyon Lake, 167–171, 168m
Payson
  General Springs Cabin to, 107–112, 108m
  to Jake's Corner, 113–117, 114m
Pinchot Cabin, 103
planning your trip
  Arizona climate, 22–23, 30
  choosing a direction of travel, 22–23
  finding water sources, 24

Index

planning your trip *continued*
  resupplying, 25
  selecting camping gear and clothing, 28
  setting a pace, 23
  traveling flip-flop or leap frog, 23
  ways to bike the trail, 14–15
  See also Arizona Trail; bikes and bike equipment; safety hazards; trail etiquette
Prison Camp Loop day ride, 149

rabbitbrush, 1p, 63p
racks and panniers, 26
rattlesnakes, 18
Reavis Canyon day ride, 136
Reddington Road–Molino Basin Loop day ride, 154
repairing bikes, 28
resupplying, 25
Roosevelt Lake Dam
  Jake's Corner to, 118–122, 120m
  to Lost Dutchman State Park, 123–127, 124m
Russell Tank to Moqui Stage Stop day ride, 67

safety hazards
  being prepared for, 15
  black bears, 18
  cactus and thorns, 19
  dehydration, 17
  flash floods, 16
  getting lost, 19
  heat exhaustion and stroke, 17
  high-altitude sickness, 17
  highway traffic, 20
  hunters, 20
  hyponatremia, 17
  hypothermia, 16
  injuries, 20
  lightning, 18
  mountain lions, 18
  people, 18
  rattlesnakes, 18
  scorpions, 18
saguaro cactus, 121, 121p
Saguaro Park to Colossal Cave day ride, 154
San Francisco Peaks, 73p
Schultz Tank to Buffalo Park day ride, 80

scorpions, 18
Shewalter, Dale, 12
signage, 14, 31
snakes, 18
South Rim, North Rim to (trekking), 53–58, 55m
Stateline Loop day ride, 38
Summerhaven, 147
Sunflower to Mazatzal Divide–Lone Pine Saddle day ride, 122
Sunnyside Loop day ride, 175
Superstition Mountains, 33p, 128p

technical ratings, 29–30
Temporal Gulch day ride, 166
thorns, 19
thru-biking, 15
tires, 27
Tonto National Forest, 3p
tools, 28
trailer systems, 26p, 27
trail etiquette
  dealing with other trail users and landowners, 21
  importance of, 20
  minimizing environmental impact, 21
trip planning. *See* planning your trip
Tunnel Springs day ride, 166
Tusayan Bike Trails (Loops) day rides, 62
Tusayan to Grandview Lookout, 59–62, 60m

US 60
  to Gila River, 132–137, 134m
  Lost Dutchman State Park to, 128–131, 130m
US 89A
  to East Rim View, 39–45, 41m
  Utah State Line to, 34–38, 36m
Utah State Line to US 89A, 34–38, 36m

vehicle supported rides, 14–15

Waltz, Jacob, 131
water, 17, 24
weather, 22–23, 30
wildlife, 18
Windy Point Vista, 144p

About the Author

A former ranger for the National Park Service, **Andrea Lankford** has practiced emergency medicine, law enforcement, and search and rescue in several parks including Zion, Grand Canyon, and Yosemite. After 12 years of service, she retired in 1999. Andrea has traveled more than 6,000 miles by foot, bike, and kayak, including thru-hiking the Appalachian Trail, paddling the length of the Florida Keys from Miami to Key West, and cycling 414 miles to the Arctic Ocean along Alaska's Dalton Highway.

In 2000, she and a fellow adventurer, Beth Overton, became the first to mountain bike the length of the Arizona Trail, an endeavor many people told them couldn't be done. Undaunted, the women took on the motto, "Where there's a girl, there's a way." Andrea believes that women are especially suited to long-distance, self-propelled travel. "Traveling a long-distance route is like being in a relationship with the trail," she says. "Along with the beauty, you must endure the unpleasant parts. In the end, the rewards are always worth it." Stories from her adventures have appeared in *Backpacker, Adventure Cyclist,* and *The Arizona Daily Sun*. She recently moved from Flagstaff to the Los Angeles area.